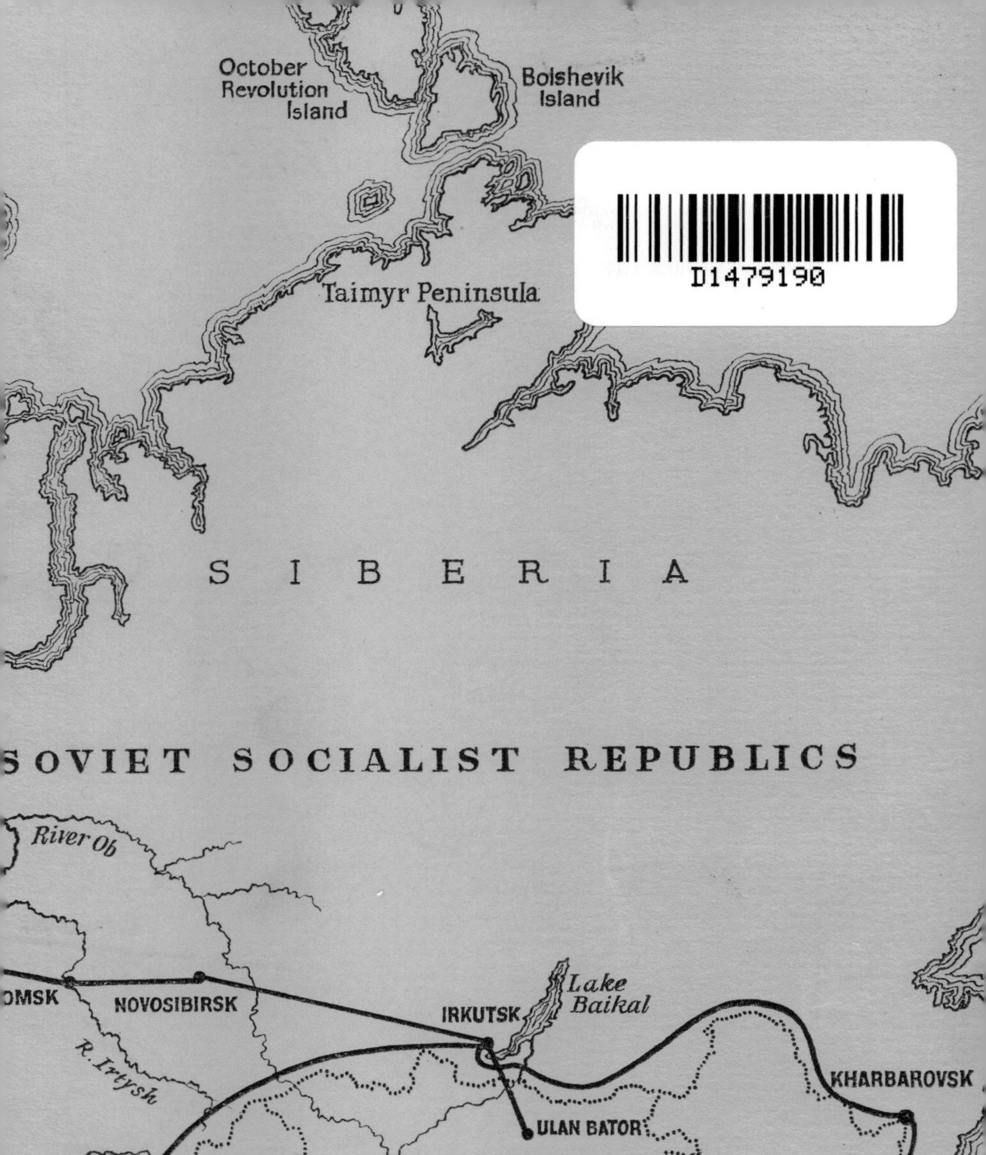
October Revolution Island
Bolshevik Island
Taimyr Peninsula
S I B E R I A
SOVIET SOCIALIST REPUBLICS

River Ob
OMSK
NOVOSIBIRSK
IRKUTSK
Lake Baikal
R. Irtysh
KHARBAROVSK
ULAN BATOR
MONGOLIA
KOKAND
VLADIVOSTOK
NAKHODKA
C H I N A
TIBET
NEPAL
I N D I A
BURMA
Scale of Miles
0 200 400

The Incredible Mile

Books by Harold Elvin

TRAVEL

Ride to Chandigarh
Elvin's Rides
Avenue to the Door of the Dead
The Incredible Mile

FICTION

The Story At Canons
Fandango for a Crown of Thorns
To Heaven with the Devil

MEMOIRS

A Cockney in Moscow

POETRY

When She Cried on Friday

The Incredible Mile

Siberia – Mongolia – Uzbekistan

Harold Elvin

HEINEMANN: LONDON

William Heinemann Ltd
LONDON MELBOURNE TORONTO
JOHANNESBURG AUCKLAND

First published 1970

434 22821 4

The lines from *Hassan* by James Elroy Flecker are quoted by kind permission of A. P. Watt & Son.

Printed in Great Britain by
Morrison and Gibb Ltd, London and Edinburgh

For Surya

List of Illustrations

List of Illustrations

1

My house in St Pancras was being demolished. I was being rehoused one mile away in Euston. My furniture left by road with a removals van. I myself decided to make the journey by train.

'You cannot get from St Pancras to Euston by train,' said the ticket clerk.

'Nonsense,' I said. And made this journey.

2

St Pancras to Newcastle was uneventful. Newcastle to Bergen found the fish getting more to eat than the passengers. Bergen—a five star city beautifully conceived between seven hills—to Oslo was stark mountains, dark torrents, snow in the heights as pure as a nun's heart, fiords below as clear blue as a baby's eyes, a paradise per mile.

Oslo to Stockholm, all flat and affluent. Perhaps no country in history has achieved as high a standard of well-being as has modern Sweden, and there's the feeling there that in at least this one place on earth a government has done all that is possible for its people.

Stockholm to Helsinki, flatter still, pock-marked with lakes and sentinelled by birches. A Surbiton man came down our corridor at night in pyjamas like a ghost in a charade holding a carton of tea in each hand. He was asking if anyone had seen his wife? His wife had awoken, had sat up in her bunk, had asked for tea and sent him out with two marks. As he procured the tea the train was moving so he hurried in. Alas, the train had been broken up, she was bound for Stockholm, via Turku, and we, we told him, for Leningrad. 'Do you mind awfully if I sit down a minute?' he said, sitting on the edge of my bunk. 'I say,' he went on, 'here Alice and I are rushing away from each other at fifty miles an hour in opposite directions, Alice with the passports, visas, money, luggage and tickets and, poor soul, no tea, and I . . . would you think me awfully rude if I tried a cup?' And he sipped at a carton. 'I must say I wish I had taken up that change though, but I saw this train moving you see? Yet it might have helped, mightn't it? But then, if it comes to it, I suppose I could always flog my pyjamas, eh?' And he sipped at Alice's carton as well. 'I say, I bet I'm the first to turn up in Russia like this, eh? Reckon they'll search me? Fun, eh?'

Leningrad, vast, stately, noble and desperately in need of paint, and on, through the flattest of all, to Moscow. Coming up this line a month after the war, I had travelled with my then wife, a Bolshoi Theatre ballerina, and the only other occupant in the carriage had been Shostakovitch. Violetta had played him at chess. Shostakovitch had won. 'I am not really good,' the composer had said, 'but when I am a boy—excuse me I learn the English only up to present tense—I go to a kino in Leningrad too early and I pull a man by his coat-tails and say "Give me a game of chess?" And mister does. He takes very long time indeed over third and fourth move and I think I miss kino. Then he take very very long time over fifth move and I want to leave. And then he win in two moves and I hurry to kino. He comes, pulls me by jacket and says, "You want know why I take so long over moves?" I not want but he tells me. "I, Alekhine, champion of the world, and I never see opening like that." '

Moscow. How many books would it take to describe Moscow? For years I had worked there . . .

But adventure begins in capital letters when territory never before traversed is reached, and this for me would be in my 15,000 miles from Moscow to Odessa.

I left for the Trans-Siberian Express.

3

My friend Zenkovsky, when he was a boy, was asked to write five hundred words on the Trans-Siberian Railway. He wrote: 'If you go to the outskirts of Moscow and stare down the tracks towards Vladivostok the lines get smaller and smaller and smaller . . .' and on for five hundred words.

Zenkovsky was in Kuibyshev now and here was I arrived at the terminus looking for the tracks that would get smaller and smaller.

There were twelve platforms on the Yaroslav Terminal and I asked a seedy looking passer-by from which one the Trans-Siberian Express left. He looked cloak-and-dagger each side of him and mumbled: 'No idea. Do you know Stanley Matthews?'

He behaved as if he were trying to sell me hashish and I moved off but, catching his words, I returned: 'No,' I said, 'but I've seen Stanley Matthews play a dozen times.'

'Bobby Charlton?'

'Oh yes, I've seen him play too. Heaps of times. But I don't know him.'

The little forty-year-old, cheeks so pinched they met inside his mouth, put his hand stealthily on mine: 'I want the truth,' he said. 'Only the truth. Is Gordon Banks better than Yashin?' We were huddled very close now: there could not be an M.I.5 in the world who wouldn't be certain that I was getting my instructions. 'The truth is,' I said, 'that in a life's career possibly your Yashin is greater. But in the World Cup . . .'

'I saw it all on TV! All.'

'In the World Cup Gordon Banks never made one single mistake, so he's our hero for ever.'

And having got that settled the man so thin he'd have to try twice to make a shadow, shuffled transparently away out of the station.

This train was not only not on the station's Departure Board, it was not on any time-table I could find. Yet three others were: three trains left for Vladivostok each day and were all written gorgeously up. Yet the authorities had insisted . . .

I had come one hour before time because I adore railway stations, I adore railway journeys, I adore the build-up, and here was I about to make the world's longest train journey and anxious to have my excitement whipped into a frenzy. I had only just been given my ticket. I had paid for it two months before, begged for it each day for eight days in Moscow, yet Intourist had wanted me to collect this ticket on which 15,000 miles depended 'on my way to the station'. I had protested: 'But something might go wrong!' 'Nothing will go wrong.' 'But something always does go wrong in Russia!' At which they took umbrage. Then something went wrong. Rokosovski died and all the streets were closed and I couldn't get to the office. It had taken me three hours of cajoling to get through. But now I had my ticket so, although I hadn't got a train or a platform, I was on my happy Russian way.

A man with a nose like a banana said he was looking for the Trans-Siberian Express, from which platform did it leave? We decided that it must be platform twelve as that ran alongside an imposing building and looked the only V.I.P.ish platform of them all. We left for there. This station was the least imposing in Moscow and a round tower castellated like a castle bastion, alongside a cathedral-dome over the adjoining Metro, added the feeling that the whole was a Musical Comedy set. And now the most imposing platform proved to serve the least important trains, the locals, so the man with the nose like a banana said we should give the matter a rest. I said it was worrying.

I went out to the high road to glance across at the Kazan Terminal from which I had begun my hitherto longest journey. 15 October 1941: five days on a train and no one knew to where it was going: the Germans belching out their monstrous guns in the suburbs at Khimky and the diplomats ordered to leave and to take their appendages with them. I was an appendage, an Embassy nightwatchman. It had been over there that I had met Zenkovsky for the first time. What was he doing alive in this twentieth century? A dilettante, old-world eighteenth-century professor of a man caught up in a twentieth-century upheaval, and a Party member to boot. 'In the old days,' he droned in his warm butter and soft sugar voice, 'we used to keep one member of the family in the Church to ensure us of a place Up There. Now we keep one in the Party to ensure us of a place Down Here.' God! that night! Dank, chill-death sleet, gloom and tragedies a millionfold, five hundred silk-shirted diplomats stepping over carpets of heartbreak; platforms, waiting halls, corridors chocker-blocked with brown, grey, litters of human anxiety. Cripps was there, Lascelles, Quentin Reynolds, Sir Walter Citrine, the American Ambassador, Lozovski, Prime Ministers, geniuses of art and music, writers Chapiro and Philip Jordan. But it was what we stepped over on our way: those coagulated, conglomerated multitudes of desperate people; concentration-camp fodder all if caught by the Hitler hordes pounding in from the suburbs. Five days to nowhere ending by the Volga: yes, we, the silk-shirted got out. And, praise be, the Germans never got in. While that sphinx, Stalin, had never budged.

Back in the Yaroslav Terminal the man with a banana for a nose stood nettled in front of a wall time-table. The 12.20, 14.40 and 22.50 all went to Vladivostok, but where was the 20.50?

In the precincts and waiting-halls the ever present crowds were indeterminately lulling or queueing or mooching or squatting comatose under their piles of pumpkins, potatoes, melons, tomatoes, loaves, apples, gherkins; women with kerchiefs and shawls and never a hat, men with cloth-peaked caps and clay-pipes and rarely a tie. People didn't seem to wait here for a train for an hour, but for a day, or days, and so they became indefinite amorphisms blending in with the surroundings, masses and walls, multitudes and halls, grew into one another, all became integral, 10,000 people and a station Waiting for Godot.

Only children escaped this canker coma and behaved as if life had been born for living. And now twenty were preoccupied with a red balloon. Dozens had red balloons at the end of long strings but one little boy had lost his hold on his string and lost his balloon: it clung to the hot air by the ceiling and looked desirous to get out beyond that too. A young man, so quiet that I hadn't noticed him at first, was at the centre of the assault group to bring that escapist back. He was so concentrated-quiet that he was camouflaged into absence as deer can be when listening. He had another balloon, this at the end of a string, and by slow movements, then sudden jerks, often brought the prodigal balloon two inches down, but never more. It was so impossible: but long, long since I had learned that

Russians can do the impossible, but never the possible: that's why the country is full of geniuses and no plumbers.

It could have been twenty minutes and I felt I just must leave: then it was down! A miracle. Quietly the young man received it, the only unmoved one present. Twenty sleigh-bell voices soon ran ringing round that red balloon: twenty children released from strife, shouted ecstasy into life.

And the train was there. Platform six. As quiet and innocuous as the young man had been in the hall. Just a small notice, 20.50 to Vladivostok. A few people, a lot of peace, and an attendant to lead me to my carriage.

4

But it was not my right place. Months ago I had asked for the top bunk facing the engine, I had repeated this every day for the last eight days, always I had been assured of it: yet here I was off on a six-day journey with the bottom bunk, back to engine. I appealed. No good.

I felt deflated. Excitement left me. It's like the top front seat of a bus: unless you get that the journey is soured.

After ten minutes feeling dark, a couple came in with a small child called Margarita. They had reserved the opposite bunks, top and bottom, with Margarita sleeping with a parent sometimes up, sometimes down. I said there'd be less danger of the child falling if they took my bunk, and more homey too, all three being at a level. It was mine! We were already friends.

Lighter inside, I went to the corridor. Spartak were

drawing 1–1 with Torpedo over the loudspeaker. People and bags were coming in. But it was all orderly, somehow subnormal. Out on the platform it was also strangely still and only mildly active. No brass bands, red carpets: such a mighty journey, shouldn't the Trans-Siberian Express leave with a ten-gun salute? St Pancras to Flitwick knew twice the action.

I returned and did a little chatting and we were on our way scarcely without my knowing it: a most undramatic departure without even a whistle, without anyone nearly missing the train, without a lover's farewell. Everyone looked at their watches. 20.50 exactly. Spartak had made it 2–1 and there were only five minutes to play. The loudspeaker crackled like a house burning down.

An uninteresting dusk was with us so that except for tall dark buildings like sentinels against a slate sky with a vein of red through it, there was nothing of Moscow to see.

Margarita was the image of Piglet of the Pooh books and was smiling and humming and happy and naughty in a most unobtrusive way. She was two years eight months. The father was an engineer stationed in Vladivostock, having been home in Moscow on summer leave, about forty, and friendly with the whole world instantly. The mother, plumpish, would be friendly with intimates only, but although it was days before she opened out with me, she was never cold. Her dresses were common, there was no taste there, and my stupid Western mind assessed her by her dress, and I was therefore shocked, days later, to discover she was a very important doctor. But the top woman in all Russia could have the most common of dresses, as the top executive could have a shirt without a tie or collar: quality dresses and tailored-handsome suits didn't exist, a commissar's wife was indistinguishable from a washerwoman. (It was the same in Sweden, but there they both looked like commissar's wives, here they both looked like washerwomen.)

Our train was immense and sumptuous. Our compartment was ten feet high inside so, since it was only a four-berth, there was no need to adjust the top bunk in the daytime. The carriage was in a heavy brass, cut-glass, antimacassar, lace curtain, plum colour carpeted, overladen Victorian snuggery style; it had lamps that were works of art in brass, with pleated covers in billiard-table green. The atmosphere was musty and comfy. The roof was arched like the top of grandmama's trunk.

Our window was dirty and curtained. It remained dirty for the entire journey. The engineer and I made efforts to clean it, painstakingly unscrewing the double glazing with kopeck pieces so as to clean the inside, but within hours it filthed up again and it looked as if a sandstorm and Southend mud had attacked it. The carriages and waggons were vacuumed three times a day, but we could get no one interested in cleaning windows.

It was dark but I had a corridor window down and was staring out: a goods train crept along on a distant track like a cat along rafters. A man came, pushed himself in front of me, slammed the window up nearly taking off my nose, said couldn't I see it was letting cold air in and dust and dirt and would I meet his wife? His wife was from Georgia, spoke English; he, from Riga, had heard I was English and it would be a surprise for her. I swallowed my resentment of the window act, and went along. His wife was beautiful, perhaps fifty. He was a smart Alec. Both were dressed as Russians still don't know how to. Latvia had been a Union Republic of the U.S.S.R. for twenty years, but its peoples still retained Western flairs. There was a boy, Andrei, ten years old; smart too: he spoke much English but I never got a word but Russian from the mother.

The boy told me of a mouse who wanted to draw a cat but he was frightened to get too close so he hired some binoculars. I told him the English limerick: 'There was a boy called Andrei from Riga, who went for a ride on a tiger, they came back from the ride, Andrei inside, and a smile on the face of the tiger.' Andrei translated for his parents.

The father wanted strings of facts of comparison between Russian and British standards of living. He was just retired at fifty-five as a machinist on a pension of 120 roubles* a month, how did that compare?

The boy was brilliant and precocious. His was not all baby talk: it was of grown-up mice and men. The parents realized his potential and the father played up to it. The boy clocked-in on this as an American child might, but no Russian child would, or would be allowed to. The boy made startling anti-Soviet remarks and the parents tried to stopper that part of his outbursts, but he only flashed back 'Why?' And what can you do when a bright boy retorts 'Why'?

I left soon, only to meet in the corridor a young lady I had sat opposite at a table in a theatre café the day before. Her name was Valentina. She looked nineteen, but since she was a schoolteacher and married and separated and with a child she must have been more. 'How English your face is,' I said. She could have won a beauty contest in a small English town. But her glory was her hair, unpolished streaks of ebony of an ecstatic quality usually found among the Japanese.

'I don't think much of you English,' she smiled. 'I travelled in a bus from Sherymatyev Airport last week and I was the only one standing, and all the others were English bound for a conference. Not one gave me a seat. And I was so tired and hungry. And I had heard so much about your English politeness.'

We discussed *Anna Karenina* and the latest film version of it we had both just seen. 'I was glad,' I said, 'to see Karenin getting sympathetic treatment at last.'

'That's because of the very brilliant actor who played the part,' she said. 'Why, from what you said earlier, have you never had a child from a woman you weren't married to?'

* Exchange rate: 2 roubles = £1.

'Because,' I told her, 'if I had a child I would feel horrible if I did not play father; and how can you visit a child constantly whose mother you have no love for?'

'When you have a child,' she said, 'you love the child in its own right. Who the other parent is need not matter. Have a child from a moron, a prostitute, or a queen, you will find your love for that child will be tremendous in every case. Anna didn't love Karenin, yet she worshipped his child.'

'But she might have loved Karenin at the moment of conception?'

'No, she never loved Karenin. It was not a love marriage. A marriage for convenience, almost for business. She hated Karenin. But worshipped his child.'

Back in my carriage I tried to be a very polite Englishman and give the mother many chances of undressing with me either absent or not looking. At first they found my actions peculiar, then they laughed.

5

I opened my eyes at a town called Nikola Paloma.

Slowly we pulled through it. Timber, timber everywhere; saw-mills and stacks and yards alive amid a sea of black mud. Cranes were bogged in the mud, trucks and lorries trapped, a bus aslant at 30° viced into it. And the town was as if a war had rushed through it: roofs were off, walls were shattered, sheds battered, warehouses derelict and yet full:

as if nothing progressed in the town except timber. It was 5.30 a.m. Imagine a winter there!

Then out again into the countryside where magpies were up betimes searching out a breakfast.

Past Shariya and past Svecha, the landscape exploding all the time, a one always becoming the whole; thus a field erupted out to the horizon, or a birch forest occupied all space, or a sky was so seeming vast it stoppered up the universe. Thus then did a small thing become so poignant: grasslands one yawn across all space, a stream flowing peacefully through to eternity and a heron rises up and speaks all life to the beholder. Rich black soil from our train to nowhere, and a wooden Uncle Tom's cabin and no fence and no hedge round, six geese and a cow and empty space as neighbour.

A squeak and a squeal may not normally be pleasant sounds—but what is a railway without them?—and our giant nobly squeaked and nobly squealed and nobly rolled on through what a Yorkshireman would call 'nowt but scenery'. We were a blood cell running down an artery, our train down our railway track was the one live contact all these lands had with the outer world.

At Kirov we all got out. Fifteen minutes to stretch our limbs. I could see our train for the first time. Striped in chocolate brown and waffle yellow with a grey roof and called the 'Russia' with Moscow-Vladivostok written across it. The highest train I had ever seen, fifteen feet high standing on a broad gauge. At the moment electricity was our pulling power. The restaurant car had been made in East Germany and I heard all restaurant cars were made there. (Pity the food wasn't.)

Back in the train our next compartment was all laughter. A towering man, with a broken nose but otherwise all elegance, stepped out to the corridor, wrung my hand, and said: '007?' I got back what he left of my hand. He laughed. The train laughed. I had thought everyone must know him, he was on speaking terms—laughing terms—with everyone, but it turned out it was just the way he was made: the world was his family. His name was Yevlarkov.

Yevlarkov had two women with him, I assumed his wife and daughter, and they were infectious too. Suddenly the train glowed with a warmth as if a stove had just been brought in. His carriage was already full with 'friends'. They invited me to join them.

'My card,' Yevlarkov said. He took out a piece of cheap notepaper on which was typed his address. "That's me, I'm the manager of a gold mine. That's my address. Will you send me an English bulldog? I've got a dog already. He's bigger than you. He's got an enormous brain. Bigger than yours. Enormous. But there's nothing in it. What do you want in return? I want an English bulldog, what do you want?'

'A blonde ballerina.'

'In a gilded cage? I can get the gold cheap. Blonde ballerinas are safer in a cage.'

'No,' I said, 'no cage. Just the blonde ballerina.'

'She'll be waiting on your doorstep when you get home. You'll have to give me your address.'

I did so.

'I manage a gold mine. What do you do?'

Authors and artists can be dirty words, and I wanted no one on the train to get the impression I was prying even as a very mild 007, so I said: 'I work for XYZ, a tourist agency. I am a Tour Leader. I bring tourists to Russia.'

'Who employs . . . do you want to be called gaspodin or tvarish?' (Gaspodin was the Tsarist word for Mr but, though it went out for a time, it was back in use again now.)

'Tvarish,' I said.

'Who employs XYZ?'

'No one. He's dead.'

'Then how can he get his profits? Have you got his new address? How can you work for a man who's dead?'

I explained the XYZ establishment. I am not certain

whether he was joking or serious but he appeared unable to grasp capitalism, private ownership. All found it astonishing that no one employed my bosses and also that I didn't really know by name who my exact bosses were.

'Where have you got them now?' he asked.

'Who's "them"?'

'The tourists. I know! You've got them locked up in the guard's van and you are skinning your eyes for a salt mine.'

He laughed with everything he said. His womenfolk laughed with him. He oozed laughter and friendship. His nose was grossly broken: I wonder if he knew how it ruined a manly handsome face?

'Have you heard,' he laughed, 'that very old story of a prim countrywoman of yours who came this way? It was sixty years ago. She was Victorian and proper and going to China as a missionary. She was on the Trans-Siberian Express alone with a raw rough enormous Russian with tolstofka shirt and high boots. Two days went by, then he said as the train drew in at Omsk, "Have you been to Omsk?" "Er, no, my good man," she replied. "I am a maiden lady who has never been out of England before. No I have not been to Omsk." Two days went by and the train was drawing in at Tomsk and the Russian asked: "Have you been to Tomsk?" "No, my good man," she answered. "I am for the first time in these parts and I have not been to Tomsk." Two days went by and the train was pulling in at Kansk and the Russian turned to your sedate English madame and said: "Enough of this courtship. Off with your clothes!"'

Valentina was by the doorway and beckoning to me. I went out. 'They are asking in my compartment,' she said, 'if you'd like a game of chess?'

I said 'Thank them. Say that while it's daylight I prefer to watch the scenery but when it's evening I'll come with pleasure.'

'This Kama river used to be the border between Europe and Asia,' Valentina said. 'It's very beautiful and in parts near the Silva, which it joins, it's very beautiful indeed. There's the Kungur Ice Caves there with scintillating ice grottoes eighty yards long and twenty yards wide, halls of ice chandeliers. You should see them. At Perm, which we come to soon where I live and where I am getting off, it is 800 miles in any direction to the sea and yet we have flourishing shipyards. That's because of all the inland shipping down these rivers. The Kama really was a border between one world and another. They used to say the world was flat. On one side it ended by you, by Ireland, after that you tumbled over the edge at some point out at sea. And at the other side it ended here with the Kama which joins the Volga below. People never knew the other side, and the other side never knew us. There's not a mile of the Kama that hasn't been running with real blood at some time, right from Yermak's time, from the Stroganoffs', right up to Kolchak who held Perm for two years after our Revolution. Funny how they can make war in peaceful places. It seems unnatural, doesn't it, that they can have battles in sweet countryside? Isn't it clean? Isn't countryside clean? Even when it's dirty, it's clean, isn't it? Mud is clean, isn't it?'

'Valentina,' I said, 'shall I confess something? Until two nights ago at that concert I had never heard of Perm.'

Valentina was self-contained: there was a feeling that, like an iceberg, nine-tenths of her was underneath the surface.

'Valentina,' I went on, 'Perm would be in size to Moscow, something like Halifax is to London: and yet that concert and ballet your town put on in the Kremlin Palace of the Soviets, a hundred Halifaxes, all London, even all England couldn't have equalled. Fifty or sixty artists there each one of whom could have gone straight to the top in the English theatre. Those children! They made you drunk with joy! Their performances, their fun . . . surely the Bolshoi doesn't better it? It was heaven, all of it. All this from a far-from-top town in your country. So explain this to me, can you: such taste always from your stages, and none in your worldly life. The standards of your stage skills might be the highest in the world: the taste in dress, furniture, architecture, the lack of colour, the drabness even among these people in this train, all taste in your everyday life must be the lowest in the world.'

Which was one way of tearing up a friendship. It happened now and it happened often, all was well in a relationship until I criticized Russia. They wouldn't accept it; wouldn't see my points, couldn't answer except with blind love and prejudice for all things of their country. Valentina tried to argue that it wasn't so, then a long harangue about priorities: 'You Western people make war on us so we must have guns before dresses.' I said guns before dresses had nothing to do with it. Dresses, buildings and furniture didn't need money; they needed design and taste and proportion and colour: a person had to wear one dress: many Indians and Siamese could afford one dress only but it was a beauty. There was colour and taste on the stage: why not in life? I argued in vain. And to have got us back to our relationship as we had had it I would have needed the whole ride to Vladivostok.

6

Yevlarkov put his hand to his collar and yanked away his tie. I thought it was a party trick and was about to laugh, but realized it wasn't. A splendid phosphorescent green plastic tie (phosphorescent ties were the rage) turned out not to be a tie but just an appendage which pressed into a slit at the collar stud and could be yanked away always retaining its perfect shape. He loosened his collar and put the cards away. He had been playing with his two women. 'I always win,' he said. 'Always.' And he had just won. A grandmother in black came in and Yevlarkov was immediately friendly with her, sat her next to him, put his arm round her and said: 'Once upon a time there were three beautiful sisters and they all lived together in the Siberian taiga*.' 'Their father said he was ailing and that each must set forth immediately to seek her own fortune. The eldest, seventy-seven, had breakfast with a commissar. The middle one, seventy-six, reached the sea of Azov and was shown the rose gardens at the bottom of the waters. The third, seventy-five, the youngest and fairest in the whole of Siberia, met the manager of a gold mine, and here we are together now, aren't we my dearest beloved?' And he kissed the old lady. 'Tell us a story, tvarish 007, about a foreigner in the Soviet Union.'

'A true story?' I asked.

'A true story is a fairy story,' Yevlarkov laughed. When Yevlarkov laughed, his women laughed. When he did not laugh, they had a glow on their faces like smiles at the ready, as if they hummed inside. But they were not ciphers: they were two distinctive individual people, it's just that he affected them like that.

'How is a true story a fairy story?' I asked.

'Ah! A man may live a thousand sorrows or a thousand joys but that's all fairy stories to a listener. Our lives are real for ourselves alone. To our children the last war is already a story book. Tell us a true tale, tvarish.'

'Mr Stevens,' I began, 'was born of British parents in Leningrad, or St Petersburg as it was then. The family moved to Tallinn where Stevens fell in love with a beautiful Estonian. Every day he gave her a red carnation. When your country overran Estonia your government took the red carnation as a sign that they were communist . . .'

* Wild forests.

'A true story?'

'Yes, a true story. Can't you believe that your government can be romantic? They offered her, then Mrs Stevens, the job of Commissar for Shipping for Estonia. After talking it out with her husband, she accepted. When the Germans overran Estonia the two escaped into the Soviet Union with a daughter. Your government alas gave them neither work permits nor food cards. They lived off jewellery for a time but one evening in Astrakhan they had been reduced to such straits that they decided on suicide for all three of them on the next afternoon. Mrs Stevens spent what she thought was her last morning poking the pages of a manuscript into a samovar and burning it. Hitler had requested the Bible to be rewritten with himself as Jesus Christ. A Tallinn man had prepared the script and Mrs Stevens had typed it. The Tallinn man had committed suicide burning his copy. Mrs Stevens had escaped with hers. As she was burning the last pages, Stevens rushed in brandishing a telegram; the British Embassy in Kuibyshev had heard of them and sent for them. They reached Kuibyshev where I met them.' Where Mrs Stevens typed a manuscript for me *A Cockney in Moscow*, saying, 'Heigh-ho! this is my second crazy manuscript I am typing.' Then she told me of the Hitler one. 'Unbeknown to the Stevenses, the British Embassy also half believed the Red Carnation story and didn't like it but, since the Stevenses had British passports, they decided to do the right thing by them and to see that they reached England. The Stevenses sought nothing more, and they reached England happily where they became cook and butler in an ancestral home, later beginning their own Cook and Butler private service which is successful till this day.'

7

I won the chess. I am not very good and I never expect to beat a Russian. I beat three from Leningrad. I have promised to play tomorrow when certainly I'll lose. I have one ploy. There is so much convention in chess that I am wildly unconventional in the opening. The opponent then either thinks I'm a nit or brilliant. If I hold my own for the next six moves he decides I'm brilliant and plays too warily. But my unconventional opening is crazy so that I only get away with it once.

The three were from Leningrad going to work in the railway works near Kharbarovsk. One, Karl, never missed a chance to introduce a proverb. We talked of the Americans in Vietnam 'and as we say where I come from, an elephant cannot swat a mosquito'. We talked of how an idea is born then can spread like a flame throughout half the world, as with Marx 'and as we say, Moscow was burnt by a kopeck candle'. We talked of women 'and as we say, all girls are good, so where do the horrible wives come from?'

8

It was three o'clock at night but I had stayed up to set my feet on Sverdlovsk soil. Such an important city it was ridiculous to go through and see nothing. At least I set my feet down on its station. Sverdlovsk, previously Ekaterina, was 250 years old.

On 16 July 1918, in the pleasant house of Ipatyev, the Tzar and his family were asked to go to the basement. The Tzar carried his sick son in his arms and since some of the household were slow to go, chairs were asked for. Three chairs were brought. Yurovsky read out the announcement that they were all to be shot. The Tzar, astonished, began to speak and was shot point-blank before he had finished one sentence. A volley rang out and most were shot near the floor to which they had instinctively fallen. The sick boy was shot. Anastasia, if the facts are correct that she died there, was bayoneted to death. The family doctor was shot. A maidservant, Demidova, placing cushions around when the volleys began, rushed round trying to parry bullets and bayonets with her cushions. A spaniel, Jimmy, had his head smashed in. A princess, dead in her own blood on the floor, had collected 4 million roubles for bread and clothing for Poles two years previously and it is said that such was her popularity that 3¾ million were given because it was her idea. The bodies were heaped on to a lorry, which had been kept revving up all the time to drown the noise, taken to a mine at Koptyaki, destroyed by vitriol, thrown down a mineshaft. One of the assassins, Voikov, said: 'The world will never know what we did with them.' On 25 July the Czech Army, followed by the White Army of Kolchak, captured the city. They discovered the remains of Jimmy by the mineshaft. Then, many buttons sewn up with gems inside that no fires had been able to destroy. Although Yurovsky claimed his instructions came from the Bolsheviks, twenty-eight Socialist Revolutionaries were arrested in September 1919 for the murders and five were shot. One absent member of the royal family was the Grand-Duke Michael. He and his English secretary, Mr Johnson, were approached by two armed men in their hotel in Perm with a suggestion that they should escape, left, and were never seen again.

Yevlarkov was up to his pranks. The train was about to leave but he was still waving to us from the platform, smiling away, pretending he was going to stay. His two women were at the window.

'He'll miss the train,' I said.

'He's staying here.'

'We can't go on without you!' I shouted. 'Are you really stopping?'

He wouldn't answer seriously.

'He has no luggage!' I said to the women.

'Never takes luggage. He's come for a gold conference.'

He came forward and wrung my hand. But in words he never said goodbye to anyone.

Boxer's nose, green tie flashing, calling out absurdity after absurdity: such an open man that all on the train *knew* Yevlarkov though it had been hours only that we had had his company: tall as a tree and a spreading oak tree at that, a shelter in a time of storm, a razor-sharp mind, an insatiable inborn joy . . . the last man to be left behind on that cold desert of a station as slowly we pulled out and away.

Stunned by the loss, I joined Yevlarkov's women in their carriage. The old one, Babushka, was with them and we all now became introduced. The old lady in black was the mother of the elder of the two. The two women were not related to Yevlarkov. He did, it was true, manage a gold mine, and they were on his staff. He had gone to a conference and they, with Babushka, were on their way for a holiday.

So Yevlarkov went out of my life but Babushka came into it. She was indeed seventy-five and of a sweetness that I had thought had died out with my Aunt Amy, dead thirty years since. A type where all is pure and pleasant, but not weak, because the sweetness is of a strength. And Babushka was from the Archangel district, a district I had visited . . . but there were voices being raised in my own compartment so I went there.

The engineer Stepanov and his wife and I had been happy alone. Now another was forcing himself on to the spare top bunk. The two women guards were disputing his rights: the Stepanovs were receiving him icily, one guard was disputing his ticket. The man, about twenty-five, was grumbling and growling, and swore he was staying right there. He put a ruck-sack, a guitar and a fibre case covered by sacking on the top bunk opposite me and was barring the guards' way to remove them. It was now three-thirty in the night, and saying they'd sort it out on the morrow, the guards left the newcomer with us. He was treated as an intruder and there was nothing to charm us in his character: no one helped him, or made him the slightest bit welcome.

9

Next day we were in Siberia. What had happened to the Urals? We were back to the flat.

Our newcomer was above on his bunk, out on his stomach, reading. We had scarcely exchanged words with him. He had made no gesture towards us.

'Siberia is everywhere,' said the engineer. 'It's a quarter of Asia and 60 per cent of the Soviet Union. And it all began with a small town Siber in the Arctic Circle in the extreme north-east.'

'Are you English?'

The voice came from above. Eyes had been raised from the book and, catching some light, awaited my answer.

'Yes.'

He was up like a shot, rummaging in his ruck-sack. 'Look this!' And he threw a book at me. *Hiawatha* by Longfellow. 'And this!' Gerald Durrell's *The Overloaded Ark*. 'And this!' Jack London's *A Daughter of the Snows*. 'And this and this!' A book by Cronin and a book in English on forestry. The young man had grown highly excited.

'So you speak English?' I asked.

'Not a word. But I carry these everywhere, how you see? They are my companions, how you see? I have just been mountaineering in Bulgaria. I look at them sometimes. And I read a little.'

His legs came dangling over the side of the bunk. He

held out his hand. We shook hands. He introduced himself, Afanasi. He shook hands with the Stepanovs. He offered us apples: enormous maggots in small apples: but if you by-passed the maggots the apples were the sweetest. A maggot fell to the ground. Afanasi was down on the ground. He gathered the maggot carefully on to a paper, went to the corridor and shook it gently out of the window. Stepanov said, 'Even maggots want to live. Shall we have tea?' And we got tea from the guard. Each waggon had two women guards, who cleaned, kept all tickets, and kept a samovar going for tea. Tomatoes and eggs were produced: I got out my English sweets: Afanasi of all things produced a bottle of champagne. A party was on. Stepanov, Afanasi and I were in a huddle talking. Mrs Stepanov remained outside on the fringe, she was both in and out of the conversation, as it were. Little Margarita found a new hum, 'Pigletted' about and purred by the newcomer. No one made any attempt to shift Afanasi.

'How you see, I am an Alpinist,' said Afanasi, alive with eyes bright, unrecognizable from the dead moron of an hour before, 'and, how you see, my very favourite man in the whole whole world is Sir John Hunt.' And he had jumped up to his bunk like a monkey and was scrabbling in his ruck-sack again. This time he came down with photos. One, with himself in sunglasses and a snow-capped mountain reflected identically into each lens, he immediately gave me. The others, 'How you see, there was that earthquake in south-east Russia, you heard? And I did rescue, how you see here, in helicopter. That's me on side of house and gorge that came at its very very edge. I love do rescue work. I in mountain air-rescue team. I, forester, I degree in forestry at Leningrad University. I go to work now in the Bureya region, I as forester. I, how you see, have all my holidays climbing. I come from now Poland, now Rumania. Now Bulgaria.'

He knew much more of Hunt than I did. Then he pressed me to tell of others' exploits so I told about Chichester.

The tea was without milk and always in glasses. Biscuits always went with it. We had a glass of champagne each and each proposed a toast: Afanasi proposed Hunt, I proposed Chelyuskin, Mrs Stepanov Gagarin, and Stepanov Chichester.

The sun came out.

The landscape got vaster and vaster and vaster. I explained what a hedge was. How can you describe England and not think of hedges? And how can you think of Russia with them? Never! Russian landscape knows no ending: it is infinite, boundless. It is grassland and forest, flood-sized rivers, birch, pine, larch, maple, aspen, always a thousandfold . . . yet it would almost be right to say that Russian landscape is sky. Think of Russia and think of never-ending sky.

10

Babushka said: 'I only get 25 roubles a month pension. What did your mother get?'

A chorus prevented my answer. They could not believe Babushka got so little. Vera, her daughter, verified it and began telling the fights they had had to improve it, but she also was interrupted by a chorus of nodding heads or discussing the scandal of it.

I broke in: 'What should you be getting, Babushka?'

'100 roubles.'

'More, more,' some said.

Babushka's daughter got 120 a month as pension.

The man with the nose like a banana was with us, Konstantin Konstantinovitch Rudenkin, a textile worker: we had re-met in the restaurant car: he had taken it upon himself that I should always get very honest answers, that he would carefully correct the flights and fancies of his fellow countrymen and that I should go out with a true picture, be it good or bad. 'About 80,' he said. This brought some abuse but Konstantin Konstantinovitch scarcely answered the others, letting me know by his expression that I could trust in him, he was the purveyor of dry information and no embellishments.

Facts and figures got thrown at me, always seeking comparisons with England:

'Pensions are half our salary if we hold our job for twenty years . . . Men retire at sixty, or fifty-five if the work has been hard. Women retire at fifty-five.'

'Our salaries vary from 80 to 200 roubles a month . . .'

'The lowest salary is . . .' There was hot disputing. The banana man confided softly, '40 roubles. Though I have no personal knowledge of anyone getting less than 60 . . .'

'The highest salary is . . .' More storms of differences from 400 to 3,000. The banana nose confided, 'We don't know.'

Anna, a young schoolmistress from the island in the Pacific of Sakhalin which was half Russian and half Japanese, said her salary was 240 per month, Dr Mrs Stepanov said hers was 400. Karl, the chess player said his, as an engineer, was low at 250 but, winking and clapping his hand down on my knee added: 'Best live and scratch: when we are dead we won't itch any more.' All said they got more for working east of Sverdlovsk—the government's incentive for their people to spread out.

Babushka had them all laughing away in a corner. She had signed an instalment agreement for a TV set that would be hers in thirty-seven years' time: 'When I'm a hundred and twelve! But I'm getting it for my son who'll never have to pay anything.'

'What do you pay for your flat in London?'

And the whole now Black-Hole-of-Calcutta-crowded carriage collapsed in horror. A few said: 'Eh? . . . no one pays that amount!' 'You mean kopecks or roubles?' 'That's not possible!' But Konstantin Konstantinovitch Rudenkin said, no, he had heard strange stories of rents in America so it might be it was true what I was saying.

I said mine was low for London.

Babushka said: 'I pay 6 roubles a month rent.'

Most paid 10 roubles—£5 a month including gas and electricity.

'My rent doesn't include gas and electricity,' I said.

'Oh, but that's impossible!'

I told them what rents could be in London, Barbados, Copenhagen, Paris . . . and the reaction was enough to make any non-believers rush out and join the Party.

Konstantin Konstantinovitch had asked someone to make way so that he could sit at my side and in a dry voice just loud enough for me to hear above the others he said: 'You can work rents out for yourself. It's 13 kopecks* per square metre and 18 kopecks in Moscow. Kitchens and bathrooms are not included in the metreage: only the living quarters. I have three rooms, kitchen, bathroom, a balcony for which I pay nothing, lighting and telephone and pay 15 roubles a month.'

'Gas and electricity are always included?'

'No. My gas is set at 15 kopecks a month, my electricity varies according to useage. My television is 20 kopecks a month and my radio is 15 kopecks. The total is as I said.'

'Your telephone is included?'

'No. That is 4 roubles per month extra. Water is included. And the whole comes to 10 per cent of my salary, which is right.'

'Few people have telephones,' said Karl who was overhearing. 'Little boys should be seen and not overheard,' he winked at me.

* 100 kopecks = 1 rouble.

Another of the chess players said that he had bought some land from the government at 10 roubles a year and that anyone could do this. 'I can grow on it anything I like and that's all mine, but if I build on it I am not allowed to build more than three rooms.'

'And rates for all your houses?'

'What do you mean?'

They had never heard of rates!

A station! We all got out.

II

So here was another station. Barabinsk this time. Seventeen, so far. Nothing yet to distinguish one station from another. A preoccupation with brown. Brown stalls, brown waiting rooms, brown platform seats . . . a soul of brown.

Here brown stalls stood about like shooting-galleries at an English fair: large peasant women stood behind offering produce from farms or allotments. Tomatoes the size of tennis balls, pumpkins the size of footballs, gherkins gut green, apples slugged with maggots, mushrooms asleep in water, potatoes boiled, broken into conglomerated mush, steaming like mildew steaming: produce laid out on wet *Pravdas* and *Izvestias*, or in pudding basins, tin bowls or saucers. The great train rolled in, the women uncovered their wares waiting for the great rush, sometimes no one approached and—it was so sad—as our express prepared to leave the women would, biting their lips, put back the mashed potatoes into a jar, wrap up the carrots in an apron, pour back the milk into tureens—if only someone had bought up someone's entire stock to have sent one dear away smiling inside. Sales were made, much was bought: but most goods went a-begging.

Once in a while we could buy ice-cream. Once in a rare while, a postcard. There was always a bookstall with tiers of tedium and no one near it. A newspaper might be bought; nothing else. Who does buy those grey tracts, statistics and maxims, problems or novels of the Collective Farms, figures for industry? Who reads them? And who, if reading them, keeps awake for three pages?

Every station had its sculpture of Lenin. But they all appeared to have come from one mould, from one factory. Lenin as it is in Siberia, as it is in Minsk, as it is in Vladivostok. Couldn't they have let every locality loose to have its own variant?

It has seemed the ambition of every station to be like the one before it, which has meant no design, no inspiration, no individual touch, and no changes wrought by distance.

Nothing, even if new, looked new. Even the red flags were draining of red.

There was always a slogan in large dreary lettering. Some daring station might have 'For solidarity, peace and friendship' or 'Workers of the world unite' but the best bet was 'Hail to the Communist Party!'

Early films of these stations had shown the locals coming in to greet the great train with ponies and elk, bringing furs and hats and swords and cloth. Where is all that now? Where are the Siberians? Where is the childish delight in our great train's visit?

Conformity had reduced Barabinsk to anonymity. A bigger town might have bigger station buildings, perhaps some columns, some stucco, but even they would be neither baroque nor modern, just nondescript. Even the flowers were geraniums and phlox and daisies, as if there were a law against roses and lilies. Inside the brown buildings the lavatories were unusable, the food unobtainable, luxuries unthinkable.

Not one station on this journey had one article a man could take home to his wife with pride.

They were all uniform in Nothingness.

The trains alone had dignity. They came from all directions and stations were wonderfully active. And the trains were never ugly, never sordid, never poor. I only wish Spike Milligan or Picasso could have been let loose on them to have painted them in the colours of his choice. They could have been beacons of colour gloriously lighting their way through Siberia.

There's a joy in travelling and a joy in stopping.

I had expected more from the stopping than from the travelling. Because of the old films.

Let's continue in hope.

And leave Barabinsk asleep in sunlight and brown gravy.

12

The U.S.S.R. is a field exploded out to make a continent then overspilling to make two.

Malcolm Muggeridge said he was going to live in Ireland where he could escape pressures. Here he would have to escape back into the cities, for the pressure of the landscape is utter. A man here is indivisible from the earth. He is not a man completed by a suit of clothes as in the city, he is a man completed by a suit of birches, grassland, wheat, stream, sky.

We pass a farm which is three shacks. In the mud yard are fifty turkeys, fifty geese. There are no fences, no gates.

In three throngs a hundred and two hundred yards away are clusters of cows. When the man leaves his door the horizon is his hedge and infinity his boundary. The land is as his mother's womb and he remains in it for ever. Our train runs inside his umbilical cord.

In the city the man is master. In the country the land is master.

Eternity in Siberia is a living thing.

13

Babushka dressed in black as the Victorian old people did.

I showed her a £1 note. 'What a beautiful woman. Is that your queen?' She passed it to her daughter.

Looking in Babushka's face it was written that she spoke ill of no one. She had a warm nature, a sufficiency of strong character to protect her, but most of her was unadulterated pleasantness. I felt contentment when she was with us. She had that sort of a presence.

Our queen was popular: the admiration for her portrait shook me, so I asked to see the note myself. In all these years I had never looked at the queen's portrait on our notes. Someone asked permission to show it in other carriages and the queen started on a tour of the train.

I showed my passport. Afanasi asked if it was my internal passport as well.

'We have no internal passports,' I said.

'How you see, how can you exist without documents?'

'We carry no means of identification.'

'But supposing you want to book a hotel?'

'We give our name. Or someone else's name. If Mrs Stepanov and I decided to have a night together we'd give two other names and poor Stepanov would never know.'

'Supposing you wanted to, how you see, travel, to leave London?'

'We'd go. But look, this is a beautiful document,' I said, and asked for my passport back. 'You see this "Valid for all Foreign Countries". You know how I got this? I went to the Passport Office, filled in the most simple form imaginable, just date and place of birth and things like that, and paid £2. Now I have this document giving me the right to go absolutely anywhere. My government doesn't care a damn where I go, why I go, how I go, or if I never come back.'

'But you have to get permission to come here?'

'Only from your government, not from mine. "Do what you like and don't tell us," is their attitude. I have heard, have you? that Russia invented passports? And that until 1914 anyone could go round the world without any papers except through Russia? Your idea has caught on.'

There were fourteen people now crowded into our carriage. As a bizarre sunset painted the outside world in copper lustre, passport arguments filled the little carriage. Some tried to explain how it was possible to exist without internal passports: others couldn't grasp it: some shouted: all talked: all shook their hands to emphasize their points. Copper railway lines, copper goods trains passing us, copper flashes from telephone wires, copper fields, even a copper moon! and copper patches on sheep on a copper field—for there had been hills after Krasnoyarsk. Without his means of identification on him the Russian has lost his identity. It had happened to me twice in the war: I had been arrested in Moscow: my passport had been taken from me: for very many hours I had had no proof that I was myself: I was Mr No One. And that was scareifying.

I said: 'Can I tell you another thing that makes me proud of England?'

And I told them of Conscientious Objection.

The argument grew fierce. They said their government would never call upon them to fight a wrong war. Conscientious Objection was not necessary.

'Then the other side must be wrong,' I said. 'So if they have Conscientious Objection there'd be no war. Both sides can't be right. And war is murder and someone, the aggressor, must have the right to say "No".'

Two women saw a point saying to their men: 'Could you go into the next carriage and kill a man just because you were told to?' but most could see no further than the patriotic 'My country right or wrong'.

We had strayed into opposing waters and the way back to friendship was the Great Train Robbers.

I said: 'An author, Laurens van der Post, advised a traveller through Russia to take along with him books which should add up to all that was opposite to existence in the Soviet Union. So I brought thrillers with me. Yet now I find you know more about the Great Train Robbers than I do.'

'We all followed every move about the Great Train Robbers!' they laughed. 'And we all read thrillers!'

Did the authorities admit there were murderers and thieves and criminals in the land?

'Who are your criminals in the books?' I asked.

'Spies!'

Afanasi rushed up to his ruck-sack and threw down a book in front of me. 'The spy is a Dutchman,' he said, 'working through, how you see, the British Embassy.'

Omsk.

We all got out.

14

We were into the third game of chess when Konstantin Konstantinovitch's nose came through the carriage door and he, following it, said 'They are asking if you can give a little talk on London?'

Karl, to my surprise, answered for me: 'He can't now.' And he looked at his watch. 'Tomorrow.' I got the impression that something had been arranged.

'I am honoured. But could it be tomorrow?' I reiterated. There was some mystery, and Konstantin Konstantinovitch also got the impression that there was something preventing it and left.

Then the mystery came in. I had won my first two games and was winning the third when everything stopped as a bumptious little Napoleon, a Red Army colonel, small as a tit, perky as a sparrow, came in. He had an entourage of one. He came in talking, was introduced to me still talking, shook my hand, and continued talking to his entourage. He seemed to be talking to everyone except me.

The board was cleared—though I had nearly won—Napoleon accepted the place opposite me, though he never faced me, sitting sideways, the pieces were placed in position and it seemed we were to play.

He turned his arm, though not his body, moved a pawn and went on with the conversation. He looked out of the window, at a magazine, at a map, discussed the Yenesei, told of his experiences on the Ob, and, when necessary, moved his pieces. If I paused two minutes, he looked back from time to time, and seeing I hadn't moved, drummed his fingers. I bit my lips and swore, 'I'll beat this bastard!' but the clack clack, the drumming, the rising to see if he could see the landscape, the laughter and reminiscences with the entourage . . . it became nagging.

He won in twenty minutes and rose to go. The others pressed for a second, wouldn't I like it? I said I would. The Little French Corporal (now a Russian colonel) sighed and, as a great honour, agreed to be martyr to waste time for one more game.

I began calling on a God I had disowned for decades and silently swore I would never move till I was ready, even if the game went on for the night. I was wondering what ploy Stephen Potter would have answered with.

Napoleon yawned, said he was sleepy what was the time, asked his entourage if they shouldn't be up in five hours to buy stores at Marinsk, looked at Karl, raised his eyebrows, knit his forehead, never looked at the board except for the few seconds necessary to move, yawned again, got up to stare out of the window—it was as black outside as his gamesmanship inside—stood sideways above the board, moved his jaw about, cracked his fingers, sat down, moved, and was damn well winning.

I kept him half an hour for the next move: that was the only contribution I could make. He looked at his watch, then, under my nose, shook it to see if it was still going, took it off, wound it, put it back under my nose pretending that the light was better there, shook it again and yawned. In the end I smiled. There are many sorts of games and this was one. I'd have done a year in a labour camp to have beaten him.

'Marvellous!' I said. 'Are you a champion at all?'

He shrugged his shoulders. Champion? what was that? Oh, did I mean at chess? Yes he had played a game or two before. It was charming to have met me and he started to leave. My friends begged him to stay for a drink. He couldn't possibly. But it was very kind of them. And Napoleon left. Perkier than a sparrow and half as lovable. Yet . . . I liked him.

Quietly, as our giant train chugged gloriously into the night, snugly and calmly I began beating Karl again. He let a fart. 'That might sound unpleasant to you,' he said, 'but that's music to me. I've been constipated since Moscow.'

'Why, Karl,' asked one of the others, 'does what is music to you have to smell so foul for others?'

For the benefit of the deaf.'

15

I returned down the corridor.

All I had seen of Omsk was the name 'Omsk' lit up by a dying carmine sun—never seen such a coloured sun before—on a high parapet. We would pass Novosibirsk in the night. We lost one and sometimes two hours a day as we travelled east—round the world in twelve days if we could keep going—we slept: so almost half of our short day was spent in not seeing things.

I found my compartment number and went in. But it was the right compartment number in the wrong waggon! Four young ladies. And Afanasi serenading them! I apologized. Afanasi invited me to stay. He played his guitar and sang. Just as a person never expects to win a game of chess in Russia, so one never expects to hear bad singing but

Afanasi . . . our Afanasi was very below standard. His guitar playing had neither skill nor sensitivity, just a dull monotone. And it was uphill work for him too. One girl on a top bunk half shrimp-coloured, half wax-coloured, had a cold which ran like a flood, and she insisted on trying to finish a book: on the other top bunk the prettiest lady present, who everyone assured us had a brilliant voice, yielded up not one note to all coaxing ad nauseam; a plump one opposite stared dour and solid and bored in front of me, and an ugly one at my side made efforts to help Afanasi to get the whole compartment going, but her cracked-crockeryware voice never held a tune for six notes and no one else joined in.

After every song Afanasi asked them what else they knew and having been told, tried it, hoping they'd join in. They remained glum. Then he got into songs of the type of 'Ilkley Moor Baht At' that went on for ever and are all right if your spirit's with them and are an unholy suffering otherwise.

The last page was done and the sniffler above closed her book, put out her bed light, turned her back on us and wheezed off. At that the glum one opposite also turned in. Still Afanasi, with less and less support from the ungainly lass beside me, braved on.

Feeling beaten, Afanasi asked me what Russian songs were known in England. I said: 'Song of the Volga Boatmen', 'Stenka Razin' and 'Black Eyes'. But no one had heard of any of these. So he returned to one from their district, Ivanova, and the gallant ugly duckling beside me who had the words pencilled out in an exercise book, made broken-reed efforts during the entire song.

Novosibirsk and midnight. Nothing could be seen but soon I'd be back, staying some days there.

So our train moved forward. Into the vastnesses. Into the tales of heartbreak, of suffering, of injustice, of prisoners, and of the oh so unearthly cold. Our warm, snug, well-fed, singing train . . . into the hell so hopeless that terror and tears made gentle comparisons, for they are human words, and the tales in the everlasting ice-box emptiness of Siberia are too inhuman for our comfortable train-guitar-chess-conversational minds to conjure.

16

The 'Russia' was of seventeen-carriage length. We passed one slow luggage train of fifty-one waggons and another of thirty-nine. This was the greatest railway line in the world yet instead of signals, at hundreds of points down the line, were the frailest little women with sad little flags, yellow for O.K., red for not O.K., looking numbed and half absent like Statues to Pathos by Rodin, yet in fact signalling the enormous giants that all was clear, they could continue on their way.

We finished the last of the toilet paper at Omsk. After that it was each man for himself.

In the middle of our train, in a cubby-hole, was a Captain. He decided on the music for the loudspeakers, was beginning now as we progressed to give pleasant short descriptions of the towns we passed through, was in charge of the staff of the train—two attendants per carriage—and the train was *his*: his was the law: if he decided to run us into a siding for twelve hours while he took a walk there was nothing anyone could do about it.

He had sought me out and pressed his friendship on me. He had taken me to his cubby-hole, offered me literature, wished me a happy journey. He was small, bald, with flashing eyes, he was tough, bustling; that he liked his power was obvious, though he probably would not abuse it. A selected man, certainly: and, from the State's point of view, a fine selection. He looked a man of resourcefulness, a man to have with you if lost in the Arctic: a man for decisions if the train was trapped in an avalanche. He bubbled and would be happier if his talents were called upon and bored if all went well.

I had picked it up on the grape-vine that he was disappointed so few people had taken literature off him, so I sought him out and asked for more. He yanked out from under his bunk a large brown fibre case and told me to help myself. Why must they offer only propaganda? I took some of the women's magazines, I even took a novel in English (but I couldn't face it): it all made me want to fall on my knees and thank God for James Joyce and John Cleland. But I took a shoal back and I think the Captain was pleased. Mrs Stepanov looked through everything. Afanasi looked through nothing and stuck to his Dutch spies and British Embassies.

We had passed Irkutsk and were approaching Baikal, the most remarkable lake in the world. In Irkutsk waiting-hall had been a bookstall with a long row of postcards of film stars and People's artists. I had said to myself: 'I am twenty years old, I live in a small Siberian village, I have one minute to select my pin-up for my wall.' I bought two copies of the one of my choice and dashed off for the train. On the train I looked at the cards. Underneath the photos it was written ВИВЬЕН ЛИ—Vivien Leigh. All wanted to have my spare copy and I gave it to Mrs Stepanov. All had seen *Lady Hamilton*. Afanasi had seen it three times.

Everyone stood by the corridor windows in anticipation for Baikal. I had my camera ready. The Captain passed. 'You must put that away,' he said.

'Yes, yes,' I answered, anxious not to pursue the point.

He passed me, but as I made no move to put the camera away he returned: 'Let me take it for you,' he said. 'When you need it back you can ask me for it from my compartment.'

I acted quickly and buried my camera deep in my own luggage.

'No photographs from the train,' he said.

I walked away with him, hoping to take him away from the thought of confiscating my camera.

'I have got permission,' I said.

'I don't care what permission you have, I am the Chief of this train and I say no photographs.'

'Yes, I know, but you see I asked higher authorities in Moscow. They told me what I could take and what I could not. It's all right, you need not worry.'

'I say no photographs!' And he looked at me squarely and fiercely.

I went back to his cubby-hole and argued with him. He didn't seem to hear what I was saying. He, in a strange way, was friendly: he turned a stone-wall ear to appeals and wanted to talk of other matters.

It was true that there was a rule that no photographs should be taken from trains; but I had specially asked in higher circles in Moscow and got the O.K. Unfortunately the permission had been verbal. The only good it was doing me now was I felt that if it came to a show-down I would be cleared. How to impress this man that my photographs were vital for me?

'When I return,' I said, 'I have to lecture about your country. I can't lecture without photographs. I want to photograph the countryside only: never a factory, never a bridge, never an airfield.'

'This is a developing area. Plants are going up, installations erected. I have told you, no photographs from the train. You can photograph in the stations and nowhere else. You can tell the people you lecture to, and your higher authorities, that the reason you have no photographs is my fault.' Opening sentence at a London lecture: 'The Chief of the Trans-Siberian Express would like me to assure you that the reason I have no photographs to show you is due to him.'

I left determined to ignore the matter. Within ten minutes I had taken one picture through the lavatory window and two through my dirty compartment window. Feeling better, I put the camera away and went into dark thought while awaiting Baikal. Van der Post hadn't been allowed this far by train a few years ago. I'd be seeing a dozen places he was not allowed to see. That's progress. Where was my gratitude? I hadn't any.

Stepanov joined me by the window. I said: 'How smooth this railway is.'

He said: 'It should be, and it should be better. This is such an easy run and so much terrain to select from. But the Swedes are making longer sections and we should do so. A train jolts because of each join in the line. The Swedes now make lines three times longer than any other country. This automatically cuts out two-thirds of the jolting.'

We were among hills, closely cropped and rolling, yellow at earth level but green just above, as if a yellow scalped land had carelessly dyed its hair green; or as if the Sussex Downs had topaz underneath the grass instead of chalk.

17

'Baikal!'

The cry ran down the corridors like a flame down a fuse.

The hills had crowded in, pressing against our windows: a split, a rift, we gushed out and twenty million dancing diamonds naked as light flashed up and blinded us from below. Then scimitars were slashing at tiny mirrors, then spikes and lances were being flung, then the sun appeared taking its morning bath in the King of Lakes.

Here was such brilliant phantasmagoria it skinned the mind.

Baikal: older than man, deeper than sound, purer than air, as mysterious as death: eight hundred species of flora and fauna here unknown elsewhere on earth. More water here than in the Baltic Sea, than in all the American Great Lakes put together; the length of England, Snowdon could be buried 1,500 feet down. Fed by three hundred and thirty-three rivers and emptied by one, the raging Angara, encased by the Maritime range, the Baikalsky range, the Khamar-Daban range, by forest and by field, the home of the wolverene, the bear, the stag, the boar, the sable, the eagle and the swan. Baikal's extreme majesty held its silence still. For centuries men had fished here, cut timber and hunted here, but in such minute numbers as hardly to register. Hotels and restaurants as yet did not shoal its shores, cafés and camps remained unborn, it still was itself untouched by the festers that men create by beauty spots.

Our giant train gracefully and gently slid down mile by mile to meet the lake at its level. There was a shack or two, one boat heaved up; yet all mostly gloriously deserted.

And as we levelled down to greet it, the knives and prongs of white gave way to darting sapphires, till blue blooded the scene.

The Captain kept his Baikal People's Songs going on the speakers: it contributed: but it needed a Shostakovitch or a Beethoven to have done the scene any true mote of justice.

My camera screamed at me from its hiding place.

This was probably the greatest single wonder in the Soviet Union. I passed it lightly only because I knew I would return to have many days beside it. At 200 feet down iron railway lines could be twisted out of recognition by the pressures, yet at 1,000 feet down the little twelve-inch golomanya fish could resist all pressures in spite if its no-bone structure. Ducks flew in daily 200 kilometres to feed at Baikal then flew 200 kilometres to return to sleep. Seals, 2,000 kilometres from the open sea, bred on the northern shore. The Ice Age finished here, then receded so quickly that the seals were trapped and bred on, and by allowing 7,000 to be harpooned every year the government did not decrease the population. Seals see for two kilometres so the hunters have to do some clever hiding. A mother takes eleven months to produce its young, and young seals taken in their embryo at ten months fetch the best price. When a storm breaks Baikal does not play with a ship, it can splinter it and toss the wreck inland on to a rock. When a volcano erupts beneath its surface it can smash out ten miles of land and give it to the lake.

Now we were level with the lake. A quarter of a mile of green between us and the water, but we began to curl with the curve of the shore and wind slowly around to its utter edge. Baikal is 20 million years old. Sturgeons, four feet long, live 100 years there. One was taken out recently, all its caviare was extracted, it was placed back into the lake and lived on, breeding more caviare. This can be continued for twenty years, the length of the female's fertile period.

There is a rock, the Sharman Rock, where the Angara leaves the Baikal, to which doubtful criminals were chained with their hands behind their backs. If they drowned it meant they were innocent and would reach Paradise; if they reached the shore they were guilty and must have their throats cut.

Sometimes it's not what a thing looks but what it is, and it is what Baikal is that overawes. The Ice Age was yesterday here, the dinosaur just around the corner, the pterodactyl scarcely out of sight, silence was here before death. Worship and admiration and songs of praise are too puny offerings; this unbelievable sheet of nature in the middle of the world's largest land mass is from another dimension; it is outside us. Just go and stare and wonder and be increased by seeing it. And be silent. Let all adjectives retreat before it.

And let silence continue to be the only conversation at Baikal.

18

For four hours our giant of the twentieth century rounded that colossus, oldest in all time, and then quietly moved off east, skirting Mongolia.

The social commitments on the Trans-Siberian Express were getting harder to fit in. Tonight there was to be dinner with one—with the schoolteacher, Anna from Sakhalin—chess with three, serenading with four, and questions and answers on London with a capacity compartment.

Anna, of Sakhalin, had a sunny nature. Her smile was mainly underneath, basic to her, so that although she might be smiling she might be actually disturbed in a surface problem. It was as if her smile had got switched on, and the switch had got stuck, so that the smile never went off. She spoke fine English and taught it.

'Where are the Siberians?' I asked.

'Siberians?' she smiled.

'Yes, the locals, the indigenous peoples, the Siberian races.'

'The indigenous people are in the interior,' she said. 'But there are very few of them; less than 1 million out of 18 million. There never were many. They are in pockets, by the big rivers, the Yenesei and the Lena. Would you like a little history of Siberia?' she smiled. 'I am a school-teacher, you know?' and she smiled broadly. 'Which accent would you like it in?' And she mimicked the Archers, the cockneys, the aristocrats. Uncanny that she, a Russian, could so distinguish our accents.

'You listen much to the B.B.C.?'

'So. All the time. But sure it is as an Irish lass yiz 'id like me to be giving yiz the history in?'

And with her Irish she was laughing her head off.

'I'll have it in Sakhalin English,' I said.

'Sae ye dinnae want me tae speak in ma aen Scots tongue?' And she was Scotch!

The borsch came and the beef Stroganoff came. And as was always on this journey the soups and the borsches were the best, the second dishes were asleep in chilled fat, the service gruff but friendly. Nothing spick and span; a seeming ban on hard liquor, the Captain or the government having decided that restaurant cars should not become abodes for drunks. Beer and champagne and wines were sometimes available: ice-cream never, and fruit rarely. The waiters were one man and one woman who worked fourteen hours a day for the fifteen-day round trip and then had two weeks off.

And after the borsch and the beef Stroganoff came the coffee and the little history of Siberia . . . 'So. In the best Sakhalin English,' she laughed.

19

'As it was in the beginning—isn't that an English phrase? As it was in the beginning there were no Siberians. Siberians, like Americans, are not indigenous. The indigenous in America are the Red Indians, here they are Buriats, Bashkirs—tribes and races like that. A Siberian is a Russian who has come to live in Siberia, as a Canadian is someone who has come to reside in Canada. There are Old Inhabitants and Young Inhabitants—as they have in Boston haven't they?—Early Settlers. Well you see, as it was in the beginning,' she smiled away, 'those first natives lived by hunting. It was peace, sweet, lonesome, classless, trouble-free and freedom-full in this the world's biggest—or should I say largest, which is best?—ice-box—oh, that's an American word isn't it? Now it came to pass—isn't that another English phrase?—now, you see it came to pass that one Yermak did a little too much pirating on the Volga to please the Tzar so he became hounded. It was in 1581 and he fought, conquered, his intrepid—is that a right word?—intrepid way from the Volga to the Pacific then offered the Tzar the whole territory as a pardon and the great, kind, good, generous-hearted Tzar thought, well, maybe, for 13 million square kilometres he might grant it. Yermak had Cossacks with him and instituted tribute from the unfortunate locals, in your modern London jargon "protection money", but see you know,' she smiled, 'when the government decrees something that the individual would be shot for, it gets a nice name, taxes is the usual word.

'Now, then does Siberia begin to open up its refrigerator doors to let in anyone who fancies a life in cold storage. Cossacks came first: a daring free life. Fur was the trade. Serfs came: there has never been serfdom in Siberia. Serfs came, fleeing from their masters. Intellectuals came, fleeing from intolerance. The religious came, fleeing from dogmatism. Then to add to it all the government banished their own unwanted, first the petty crook, then the politicals, then the criminals. The Mongols came, and mixed, and left us the Tartars. Men escaping military service came—and military service for the Tzar could be thirty years. Tell yourself, you see, and tell the world, from me, Siberia has kissed as many as it has hurt. Prisoners have come, camps have been, an ice-cold, soulless horror has been lived here, but to many many more than prisoners, tell the world, Siberia has blessed, played refuge, opened up as a sanctuary, and granted in return a hard life but a free one. No classes, no slavery, no intolerable civil services and, after the Cossacks, little taxes: tough, lonely and free. When your Englishman, Price, came this way in 1912 and saw each Siberian with his own plot of land he said: "This is Socialism in a way the British worker seems going away from rather than towards." You see, well, serfdom existed for two centuries in Russia proper, then finished by decree in 1861. It was not here in Siberia because no landed gentry wished to live here. In 1860, another English traveller, Mitchie, found only two serf-owners, brothers, Rodinkoff by name, in Siberia: one, vice-governor of the Yeneseish province, whose grandfather had been granted lands there by Catherine the Great, never tried to exercise his serf rights; his brother did and was promptly murdered. In 1861, when the serfs gained their freedom in Russia they still flocked here to Siberia because here was real and plentiful land for them. Laws were passed forbidding it, peasant labour being needed in Russia. Thus the law forbade emigration and yet sent thousands of prisoners to emigrate. The railway was built and then there was no check. Streams came. Often encouraged, often breaking the law, which, as you say in England, was an ass. In 1700 there were 200,000 people in Siberia. Before the railway, migrants came at 2,000 a year. After the railway, at 100,000 a year. Before the railway it took two years to cross Siberia. After the railway it took seven days.

'The secret of Siberia is that it offered agricultural individualism and even Stalin, who it is now said, lost 8 million souls trying to force collectivism, here in Siberia had to leave the peasant with a little plot extra for himself and his own plough.

'As Russia went east, America went west until our borders met and there are great parallels even in our buildings. Also stage coaches and mail routes. There was the fact, though, that the Russian migrant had more to escape from than the American. One tit-bit. During our revolution there were once four Russians whom an Englishman, Colonel Ward, decided were not going to have a fair trial. Colonel Ward had a hundred British soldiers with him. They commandeered a train, put the four on it and brought it down this line hundreds and hundreds of miles till they found a place where a trial was possible, flying the Union Jack like billy-o—good phrase?—the whole way.

'Another thing, Mr Englishman, you come from an island: the sea is outside your front door. Try to understand the largest nation in the world with no decent access to the sea: we had an urge to get to the sea as compulsive as the lemmings of Norway. Russian history has been an obsession about borders. I know it's difficult to see the other chap's —very English word isn't it?—the other chap's point of view: but know that and you will understand a little. We have a pathological kink about borders, ports, decent access, which you must find it hard to imagine. We are not a bad people, but we are growing. Now a repeat: always tell your people, don't forget Siberia has been a white hell to many but a white Raven to many many more.'

With a little enlarging of her never-ending smile she laid her hand on top of mine and squeezed it lightly: 'Here endeth the first lesson.'

The serenading did not go well. Afanasi was a wrong wooer serenading wrong people. Afanasi was well meaning and earnest but I believe he lacked the magic that women like. His performance also lacked craft. Even so, with four better disposed students than the four from Ivanova, an air of warmth and romance could have crept in.

Before questions began crowding in on London Konstantin Konstantinovitch asked:

'Tell us, comrade, what do you find the greatest single achievement in our country?'

'It is not political,' I said, 'and I am certain it is an achievement you are unaware of. Yet the politicians deserve this much praise: they have allowed this achievement to flourish. It is the family. Sex is right here. Of course there are variations and deviations but from what a stranger can judge the average family consists of children who speak their minds but respect the reasoned authority of their parents, of a wife who speaks her mind but in finality stands by the reasoned decision of her husband, of a husband-father who listens to all but then makes the decision. The husband leads by about as much as a man leads in dancing and for the same reason too, that someone has to lead. There are no rules, no conventions as to what is one person's work or another's, a man might wash up, sew buttons on, a woman might do any of a thousand tough jobs: there's no thought about who should do which: each does what he or she can or feels like doing. The whole family is closely knit. The parents wallop their children, and shout at each other: but they have murder in their hearts against any outsider who speaks against their kin. So Dad leads, Mum is a close second, and the children full of themselves, yet following their elders. All respect one another. I generalize: but I have seen more wholly satisfactory families in Russia than in any other land.'

'We have 25 per cent divorce,' said the banana man.

'But divorce is simple and humane,' I said; 'by mutual consent. It is after all logical that some couples must make a mistaken choice at the outset. You have a tremendous percentage of the remainder that are very contented families. And your politicians deserve some praise in this. Most revolutions end up by interfering in matters outside politics. China now is having a go at changing family relationships. Franco, with his Catholicism, refuses divorce and contraception. Your politicians have kept out of it. Your women have complete equality, the State assures that the children get cared for in the case of divorce: and beyond that, that's where the State should stop interfering and that's where your authorities have stopped. Your government in the Kremlin is probably totally unaware that the greatest single strength in this country, and therefore their strength too, is that your domestic lives are possibly as perfect as human nature can attain.'

Vera asked: 'We hear something about unmarried mothers in England. Can you tell us more?'

And I told them.

'But who supports them, and the children?'

'The State.'

'But don't the mothers work?'

'How can they with young children?'

'Here if a woman is to have a child she gets fifty days off before and fifty after: this is soon to be increased to seventy: then she returns to work and the child goes in a crèche.'

Vera cried out: 'I want to be an unmarried woman and live in England! Anybody give me a baby? I'm going down the corridors explaining and seeking a Don Juan!'

The whole idea tickled her, she could scarcely believe it, and she left to tell the next compartment all about it.

Konstantin Konstantinovitch, still fishing I felt for a compliment for their regime, asked: 'And what on this train journey is one single thing that has pleasantly surprised you?'

'Seeing so many televison aerials,' I said. 'I had no idea your television went so far. To live in the small places of Russia and Siberia, for centuries there must have been nothing but scandal to talk about. And unending boredom. Now in the heart of Siberia you can see the World Cup, the Red Square parades, Rokosovski's funeral, the Olympic Games. Those people are in the world now for the first time ever. I have met such lonely people in Lapland and found what radio has meant to them. They had become a part of things for the first time, they had got a sense of belonging, of brotherhood.'

Then it was the turn of London. Afanasi, happier back with us than he had been with his ladies, began it: 'How you see, does Sherlock Holmes's house in Baker Street still exist?'

Our train thrust forward drilling its seventeen-carriage bore into the jowls of the night. Siberia, graveyard quiet, deserted as death, trees stark-still, standing with their dark cloaks pulled round, our wheels so frightened at their own click-clack that their echoes scurried back to rejoin us and we heard our own carriage wheels following us to Chita. Past Ulan Udz and Petrovski Zavod, past Zaigraevo and Bada. At Kharagun some shawl shadow shacks and a pond drinking a thousand stars; little Margarita asleep on

Stepanov's lap slugged by a capsule of eternity; Karl, opening a window to throw out a cigarette and the wind rising to stage whisper escape stories to the stars stilettoed up in the sky; and London, alive, bolt upright in front of our imaginations, as our Trans-Siberian Express writhed on into the void, an anaconda into the black.

21

Anna of Sakhalin, the Captain and I were talking on a platform and were joined by a needling hawk of a woman, who almost immediately threw out to Anna: 'You're not Russian! You're no more Russian than he is!'

'She is Russian,' I replied. 'And so am I. We're all Russian.'

The Captain joined in: 'They're all Russian. What are you Madame?'

The needling woman was needled herself, almost shouting at the Captain: 'They're not! You are, but I don't know from where. She isn't, and he certainly isn't.'

We all insisted on our common origin, and she left like a frustrated hen. The Captain laughed.

'You look like Kruschev,' I said. 'Smaller: a pocket edition.'

He said: 'I've lived seven years in China and I get letters from my friends: "How's Kruschev's double? how's Nikita's deputy?" '

'But Anna,' I said, 'have you really an accent?'

She didn't like the question. She went on smiling because

her smile was as much a part of her as her hair, but she hadn't liked the fussy woman's remarks and I dropped the matter instantly.

Stepanov had an accent. He was from the Ukraine. But in the 7,000 miles of the country accents vary less than from Whitechapel to Kensington.

We passed a bend in a river and there were forty to fifty youths there in bathing shorts and some playing football. I pulled down the corridor window, took my camera from its hiding place, went six inches out of my compartment to the corridor to get a better view, snapped; and immediately felt hollow inside. The corridor had been empty except for the little hawk. Certainly it must have been her.

In minutes the Captain was with me.

'You've been taking photographs.'

'Oh dear, I'm sorry. It was such a pleasant sight, some bathers and some footballers at the side of the river.'

'I told you not to!'

'It seemed so innocent. O.K. I'm sorry. No more photographs, I promise.'

He fumed. He wanted my camera. He wanted my film. He wanted to put me into prison.

Dear heaven, yes, I had done wrong: but where does sense start? What earthly harm was in my action? In the present state of the world when a man visits another country he must obey the rules of that country and if he finds them too imbecilic he should stay away. If a Frenchman is riled by not being able to get a drink in England at three o'clock in the afternoon to such an extent that he breaks the law to do so, he should stay in France. If a man cannot control his camera-happy fingers in the trains of the Soviet Union, he must stay away—or leave his camera behind. What had conquered me was the knowledge that I had higher permission and also that anything I took, if developed, would show my innocence of purpose: but I also knew the Captain controlled everyone in this set-up, and I had been a fool.

Yet there comes a time when a man must ask, where is sense? What right have they with their restrictions? I am a world citizen as well as an Englishman. It's as much my world as theirs, Siberia belongs to me as much as to the Kremlin: more so, because I have not diminished myself by squatting there as a conqueror: what wrong is there in a photograph of bathers by a river?

Yet in accepting a visa for Russia, I should accept their conditions, so I had been at fault.

The situation was hot. The Captain was livid. I apologized and I promised: apologized and promised.

I was going to be let off.

I even kept the camera.

It was desperately, desperately near.

And it killed the rest of that day.

At the next station I was again with Anna of Sakhalin. The Captain breezed up: 'You tell your friend,' he said to Anna hotly, 'that the next time he takes photographs from this train, he goes straight to prison! On the stations, and nowhere else.' Then he turned to me: 'You see that entrance!' He pointed through the waiting-halls of the station. 'A hundred yards down there on the left is a prison. Can you see it? Next time, you're off the train and straight inside. No argument!'

He left.

Anna was puzzled. Smiling, of course, and I don't think my crime sank in: she never pursued the point: she couldn't understand the tirade and left it alone. But later, over tea in the restaurant, she said, looking out of the window:

'Look, kilometre signs down all the 9,297 kilometres of the railway from Moscow to Vladivostok and every kilometre divided into ten, so if a person wanted to know anything, he could note that at 5,422·6 kilometres a bridge begins, at 5,422·8 it finishes.'

I think she tried to tell me that authorities had no imagination; that there were a hundred legitimate ways if a person was a spy of achieving sounder results than by taking pictures from corridor windows. She went on immediately to tell of a district near Zoya where she had been as a child, where there were Mongol bears with enormous heads although only four feet high. They had eyes like hard buttons.

'Do you know Pooh bear? Do you give your children such books as Winnie the Pooh to read?'

'So! They are grown-up books!' she laughed. 'I keep Pooh bear for myself!'

22

Little Piglet Margarita was frail and pasty looking but Mrs Stepanov said she was healthy and always humming. Her greatest joy was telling secrets. Now she was telling me one. We were having tea and biscuits and she had hidden her father's biscuits and he was pretending to be bewildered. Margarita thought I should know they were behind Mamma's back only I mustn't tell. She said it was all right as she would let her Dadda have them in the end.

Babushka was with us and she was allowed to know the secret only she mustn't tell either.

Margarita was the quietest yet happiest child. For all that, her parents were very much in control. If she interfered, perhaps to annoyance, with another passenger, if she spoke while the others were speaking, if she failed to offer others an apple or cake, she was unfailingly rebuffed: the rebuff was accepted, there was never a tantrum, and relationships were warmly normal in an instant.

'A child must not be a social nuisance but only a social joy,' said Mrs Stepanov. And all children on this train, though noisy and robust, held all grown-ups in respect, and showed contentment that that was the way the ball bounced.

Poor Piglet grew so frightened her Dadda would never find his biscuits that she showed him.

'Do you know,' I said to the mother, 'that we think you're very old-fashioned in your medicine? Even backward. Is it true a child is not allowed to write or draw with his left hand?'

'It's against the law.'

'But we think it's dangerous. That these things are a matter of which side of the brain each hand links up with, and that it can be harmful to force a left-handed person to use his right.'

'We know you think that, but it is our law.'

'And I've heard that a doctor can only give a patient a certificate to stay away from work if he has a temperature.'

'Yes, that's so.'

'But in some things the temperature goes down not up?'

'Yes, I know.'

'Then what does the doctor do?'

'We find our way round it.'

'I went,' I said, 'to the best dentistry clinic in Moscow with a tourist and they removed pus from her abscess with cotton wool on the end of an ordinary pin.'

'The pin was cauterized?'

'I suppose so.'

'These things don't worry us.'

Piglet was rubbing noses with Babushka.

'I get twenty-eight days holiday,' said Stepanov. 'But my holiday only starts when I arrive at my destination, and as I have come by train I get forty-two days. I had wanted to go by air but there were no tickets. My holiday time commences at my time of arrival at my place of holiday.'

Piglet wanted to try her father's nose now.

If we passed a village it was a line of one-storey shacks. No village had a centre. If a village wanted a meeting, and they have loved meetings for centuries, they held it at any point they fancied at that moment.

Babushka said she had had twelve children, four killed in the war and one now with the Embassy in Alexandria. She asked if I had been to her birthplace Kola, in the Kola Isthmus and had I heard of the Pretension of Malmis?

Piglet was on my knee testing out my nose. 'No,' I said.

'Well, one freezing February day in 1650, three strange sledges were seen drawing near our tiny town of Kola. Well, our deputy went out to meet them at the edge of the town. It was Niels Knag, bailiff from Malmis in Lapland in Sweden. He had come he said at the command of King Gustav to collect his taxes. Well, our deputy bade him most welcome but sorry said he, he had received no instructions yet from the Tzar, would the good bailiff make merry. So, made merry he did, and merry he left. Well, the next February the procession of strange sledges was seen again approaching our tiny town of Kola from the distance. Out our deputy goes and commands to know their business. This same Niels Knag said he had had instructions from his King Gustav of Sweden to come and collect his taxes and 200 long miles he had come through the long nights—for it is all night in winter up there. Well, our deputy bade him most welcome but sorry said he, he had received no instructions yet from his Tzar, would the good bailiff make merry. So, two weeks he stayed, two weeks he dined and wined and wenched, then off again he set with his followers across the 200 miles of the frozen and dark wastes. Well, for 160 years in the terrible cold and dark of each February this deputation came. There was always the halt at the frozen river outside our tiny town of Kola, always the Russian command to know the business, always the Swedish demand for the taxes, always the Russian apology that sorry said they, they had had no instructions as yet from their Tzar, and then the wining and the wenching and the sporting and then the return across the inhospitable wastes. Well, in 1813 the King of Sweden met the Tzar of all the Russias and they mutually agreed on the borders between the countries and, well, the Pretension of Malmis was no more.'

23

It was eleven next morning when we pulled in at the station Ushumun for a ten-minute stop.

The steps lowered for us to dismount. This was an action of the door: as the door opened it transformed a part of the iron floor into steps and they dropped, and as the door was closed the steps pulled up too: so that hobos, for instance, or late passengers, had nothing on which to gain a foothold.

I had been to Ushumun before! As I dismounted I recognized everything and felt instant foreboding. Something, what was it, had happened there? A nightmare. I remembered it had been hopeless, if not loss of life then something that, had it really happened, was so complete that it would have been impossible for me to have been there now. That was what decided me to go forward, as my first instinct had been to return to my carriage and not stir.

I remembered it was not a straight disaster, like an

assassination, or a train wreck, it was something less big yet more hollow, more hopeless, more helpless.

It was uncanny that everything on the station was recognizable. In a mixture of smile and disturbance, I went forward. I would watch my every step. Let's start off with two pictures of Lenin, that should start me off right.

It was there in the centre of the station by Lenin that it should have happened. Nothing happened. Stepanov and Piglet were queueing for ice-cream. I saw Afanasi and thought I'd photograph him; he was near the wizened hawk of a wench who I am certain had told on me to the Captain—must get a picture of her; but at another station. I walked instead up to see our engine. Nothing harmful in that. It was Diesel now. Beyond our train were some gigantic museum piece steam engines. A glorious monster engine was approaching us from a down line. What a wonderful sight.

I moved out twenty yards to an open plot of ground and waited for it to come in to fill my view finder.

And was crashed into as if a brick wall had hit me.

'No you don't! Foreign pigs! Go and photograph in your own country! No you don't! No you don't!'

A man, much larger than me, was fighting to wrench my camera from me.

He had come into me like a truck. My very first thought? My absolutely instant thought was: 'Nobby Stiles would never get away with this one.'

I stumbled half a dozen paces and he with me. My strap round my neck kept my camera in my possession. (I also thought: 'He might have let me have my click first. As it is, I haven't even got a picture for my pains.')

He struggled: and I hardly knew what I was at beyond trying to free myself. He giraffe-strode back to the train and joined a possible group of sixty, all watching. He gesticulated, called me everything, explained it to them, pointed at me, the villain, what should they do? He raged.

He was tall. He was fifty. He was in plain clothes. If he was an official he was not dressed that way.

I went into the group: 'What the hell do you think you're up to?' I said.

He raged still: practically inarticulately. If the others were not against me, there certainly was not one who was for me.

He must not get away with this. He was blurting away out of reason: I knew that in his state he could magnify: he could declare that I had not been after the engine but after installations, the signalling system, a factory, who knows, perhaps even a bridge, and the fifty-nine odd others would have backed him up.

I said: 'I was photographing an old steam engine. I had every right to do that. And you were god damn rude.'

And I walked away. He, bellowing that I had no rights, something about capitalist spying pigs.

I walked the eight or nine coaches back to my own, climbed the steps, and went to the toilet to be sick. But it was not that sort of sickness: the nausea that filled me was in my soul, not in my stomach.

What did that man think he was up to? Dear God, what did he think he was up to? I was another human being and a stranger in his country.

It was much more than that. I had seen the other fifty-nine. It was too clear: I had not a friend on the train. Stepanovs, Afanasi, chess players, Konstantin Konstantinovitch, all were suddenly shadows as by a click of the fingers. Friends? They dared not be.

Solzenitsyn mentions a naval man who had got ten years for receiving a wedding anniversary photograph of a British captain he had helped—had had to help—during the war.* Times have improved since then, but memories remain, and memories tell people that, who knows, things can change again?

If British people under no pressures would not support me in some such matter, how could I hope that Russians

* *One Day in the Life of Ivan Denisovitch*, Pall Mall, 1963.

with unearthly pressures would? I had been travelling on a train from London on my way to Dublin: in my carriage were three Englishwomen: we were friends instantly, swopping magazines and stories and cameraderie. After Crewe a thin character in a Burberry appeared at our door and, pointing a revolver at me, asked if I would go quietly? I laughed and said what for. I turned to the women: but they were not laughing. He said I was wanted for murder, I was an Australian on the run who had killed in Liverpool: it would be best if I would go quietly as he had four other men on the train and I would not get away. For ten minutes we confronted each other, I demanding to see his papers, he demanding to see mine. At last I gave in and showed him mine. After very minute inspection he declared I was not his man and left. I turned to the women, expecting sympathy at least. They had frozen. The man returned, sat in a corner seat, and said softly: 'I am sorry. You can report me if you like. I have no right to have this gun on me. The man we are after has sworn to shoot anyone who tries to arrest him. I am scared, I've had some whisky and I got this gun. You must report me if you feel you ought to.'

'I will not report you,' I said.

'You should know better than try and make an arrest in front of women!' was all the women said.

Soon the pathetic Burberry-ed man left us, with a last apology, saying that the police at Crewe had noted me on the platform and agreed that I, with my hang-dog yet underlying defiant manner, was certainly his man.

I spoke with the women. But in the train and on the boat and still at Dun Laoghaire, and at Dublin, they were frozen ice towards me and not one syllable spoken.

I had been accused in their midst, proved innocent in their midst, there was not one single thing, social or otherwise, would have happened if they had defrosted towards me; yet they didn't.

And here at Ushumun, irrespective of whether I was innocent or not, if one Russian stood up for me against other Russians or the authorities, it would be night for him.

The only one who just might have spoken up, Babushka, had left the train with her daughter and friend in the night. Babushka, weakest on the train, was also the strongest, her simplicity was transparent: even the hardest Russian authorities could recognize a Babushka and would lead her gently away from her misguided desire to speak up for a foreigner.

I felt sick all day. Everything was shadows. We all continued at playing at friendship.

I did not know who the man was who had attacked me but the Trans-Siberian Express had a faster grapevine than the smallest village and before the man himself, or someone else, could inform the Captain (in Russian, the 'Chief') I went along.

He was sitting arranging some tapes. I sat beside him. 'Tell me simply with a yes or no,' I said, 'can I, or can I not, take photographs in the stations?'

'Yes.'

'There was an argument at Ushumun. Someone thought I shouldn't.'

'You can take photographs at any station, but not out of the train, while it is in movement.'

Little 'Kruschev' could be bloody-minded, but he was very direct, very firm, very reliable, very fair within his own limits . . . such a man is an excellent man.

We talked a little of other things and I left.

I would phone Moscow at my first chance to speak with my contacts and, until then, the camera had better sleep.

And who had given me that camera? The Russians! They had heard I had won a Winston Churchill Fellowship to travel through their country and within two weeks had offered me that camera.

This is my first journey I had ever wanted to end. I wanted to be off that train. Let's get on with the next stage of this travel: all I had felt for this train had been killed. Normally if the train had kept going round the world for a year I would have loved every day.

Piglet stood in front of me. Look, ice-cream. She had asked her Dadda to get one for me only it had been a secret.

When the friendship between Stepanov and myself can be stronger than the fears or commands of our own governments, mankind will have made one step forward.

24

The scenery had become the grandest of the journey. It was like the Tyrol only strained out, elasticated out, and squashed down, less high. The beautiful Shilka River kept us company. Rail and river ran together, blue doves in hundreds and sunny weather, yellow wheat waving, a Collective farm reaping, Manchuria sighted and my camera sleeping.

The chess went on. With another brief visit from Napoleon, who flayed me alive. What happened to him during the rest of the time? I never saw him once.

The Stepanovs had almost adopted Afanasi as their own son. They played cards together, chess together and gossiped together non-stop.

As I returned from my own chess and entered the carriage there was little Margarita playing her nose game with Konstantin Konstantinovitch and he, revelling in it. The sight of them was partly delicious, partly grotesque. But how happy they were. It was the first time I had seen

Konstantin Konstantinovitch unbend into joy. Perhaps it was the first time his nose had been accepted at its true worth.

I had returned to my carriage because a concourse were going to collect that had asked me to talk about my bicycle. Paper-thin friends now, I felt everything had become a shallow mockery between us: I hope it did not show: I tried to present them well with the wanderings of my push-bike: because after all, they were not paper-thin friends, they were not shallow people: governments could ram down curtains coated with leprosy between us but under the curtain and above the curtain there was a contact deeper and higher than governments could disturb.

25

Vladivostok was closed to foreigners. It had become a naval port. Travellers to Japan were diverted to the Pacific, to Nakhodka, a port sixty miles E.S.E. of Vladivostok. The station of change was Kharbarovsk, twelve hours from Nakhodka. I would not go to Japan but had asked permission to visit Nakhodka and had got the permission. Usually permission was only granted to those in transit.

I arrived in Kharbarovsk at five-thirty in the morning.

Karl was up to see me.

He came down on to the platform. 'As they say in the parts I come from,' he said, 'friendship between nations begins with a single handshake.' And he offered me his hand.

The nearly fifty-year-old waitress from the restaurant car was coming towards me. 'See how many friends you have!' she said. There were some faces at the windows.

Kharbarovsk station was one of the finest.

I met two South Americans going home via Japan. We walked around the town together. It was ugly, depressing, sordid. And at least four groups of civilians wanted to get us into trouble for taking photographs.

We breakfasted back at the station, then were taken by Intourist to a hotel in town. Two days in Kharbarovsk and all the time it grew more pleasing. We had seen its worst first.

I had phoned Moscow. And been reassured that I could take innocent photographs from trains. I asked them to tell Intourist or the train authorities: they said they would but they never did, yet I felt easier for the reassurance.

26

'I want my cat back!'

A tap on my shoulder and I turned round. 'Olga!'

'I thought it was you!' she said. 'Where's my cat?'

'More than twenty years dead,' I said.

Twenty-six years and yet we recognized each other! Olga had been a young assistant manageress of the Grand Hotel in Kuibyshev in the war. We had not met since.

'What a nice birthday gift. I'm fifty today,' she said.

Fifty, yet still recognizable from age-long ago: a line or

two under the eyes: still slim, still in grey: still with a croaky voice as if a frog with a cold lodged in her throat.

This was in the main avenue of Kharbarovsk. Instinct took us to a side turning sharply. We were Stalin's children and foreign men did not meet Russian women in daylight in broad avenues.

'I must give you a present,' I said. 'But I have nothing with me except a bottle of French brandy, will you accept that?'

'Yes.'

'Will you come to the hotel?'

Of course she wouldn't. Stalin's children didn't do such things. It has been said that the difference in life for a Soviet citizen between then and now was that under the Stalin regime anyone at any moment could fall foul: now, if you made the desperate effort to keep your nose clean you could walk though your days without fear. Olga was government employed, loyal to the backbone, she'd always keep her nose clean: had she been under thirty she would have come to the hotel to collect her present, but old habits and memories die hard. I left her and re-met her ten minutes later, not even in a side street, but in an alley. I handed her my present in the shadows then we continued in the side street. I offered her tea in a café and she accepted. This was something: she dared not have done that earlier.

'So my darling cat died?' she said.

'You did not know?' I said. 'It is not a pleasant story.'

'Tell me.'

John Evans, *Daily Herald* correspondent, had been about to leave Kuibyshev for Moscow. He was living in the Grand Hotel, Kuibyshev. I asked him if I could have his cat. The cat was Siberian, an outsize, and never, never a more beautiful animal. John Evans said I could, but the hotel claimed him as theirs, so I would have to smuggle him out. I took an immense suitcase along, put some fish in it, the cat half stepped in, I pushed him the rest, slammed the lid and left. In the corridors were plain-clothes men stationed at ten paces distance. I walked the cordon with a sad mee-ow at every pace. The plain-clothes men looked at one another, made a move, drew back, seemed bemused, but they had nothing in their books for such behaviour and I made the street.

Within twenty-four hours this most wonderful animal decided that home was round my neck and, two paws down each side, he was a fur collar of paradise. We lived that way whenever I was at home.

Olga had been sent to interview me to get the hotel cat back. I had stuck to my guns: and the hotel always remained bitter.

'We had a sadist on the Embassy staff,' I said. 'You never heard the story, Olga?'

'No.'

'He poisoned my cat, boasting that he had enough poison for ten thousand cats. He poisoned four Embassy cats. It was said that he couldn't bear to see the friendship this beauty and I had for each other. The cat would never accept food after that poisoning. Once, after two weeks, he went to a tap and caught two or three drops of water. My heart leapt up. He would not touch the actual tap with his lips. I did everything, everything. I got him forcibly fed by injection, but he sicked up everything. He took a month to reduce himself from his fabulous size to the skeleton of a rat. Then he died from starvation.'

'He was so beautiful!' Olga cried.

'Where do you live now?'

'In Kuibyshev. I'm here on holiday. I'm going back this afternoon.'

'Is Zenkovsky still there?'

'Oh yes. And with his wife a lot too.'

Zenkovsky had been forty-five and had had a passion for eighteen-year-olds. He went regularly to concerts, music being his food, but always with one of his students. He became interested while they were seventeen, doted on them while they were eighteen, abandoned them at nineteen.

'Eighteen is a year of marvel, the bud has become a flower, the girl a maid, the heaven of the still growing child has joined with the earth of the now grown woman and is as yet unspoiled, all is in the last stage before bursting, after which there is no development of growth, only of being. It's anatomy's greatest master stroke. It's elixir, it's champagne.' Zenkovsky's wife was a long-suffering mouse who did however adore her husband.

'And now they are together very much?'

'Very much. He is retired but lectures still. He likes her about and she is so happy in her funny little way. He is really rather nice with her.'

'Did you hear of Zenkovsky and Sir Stafford Cripps?'

'No.'

'Zenkovsky, on a whim one day, wandered into the British Embassy and asked for the Ambassador. It is possible he would never have seen him but Sir Stafford Cripps happened to come to the hall desk just at that moment. They had a long session. Rumour is that it worried some of the Embassy staff, a Party member being locked up like that with the Ambassador. Zenkovsky said to Cripps that one saying of Oscar Wilde had deeply affected him: 'Give me the luxuries of life and I will dispense with the necessities.' He told Sir Stafford that the war had almost obliterated luxuries: could he exchange Russian cigarettes for cigars from Britain? Sir Stafford said he didn't smoke but he had a right to a ration and he would arrange this and did. And then they talked British eighteenth-century literature for an hour and parted. Cripps was furious with some of his staff who wished to put him on his guard, saying of course he knew that Zenkovsky would report the meeting, he'd have to, just as he himself would have to report it to the Foreign Office who employed him. They remained friends. Henry Fielding was their common meeting ground. I never heard either Cripps or Zenkovsky confirm this story, nor did I ask them either: but I did see Zenkovsky surprisingly often in the Embassy and always friendly with Cripps and always happy with his visits: so I like to believe it is true.'

'Well it could be,' said Olga. 'He smokes endless cheroots now, is becoming very forgetful but seems even to enjoy his forgetfulness.'

'It's not every Russian who could flit in and out of a foreign Embassy nonchalantly as he did in the war.'

'Ah but Zenkovsky has a shield of protection. He wrote a remarkable thesis which Lenin highly praised and ordered to be published. Lenin's praise probably keened him up to enter the Party, while it has also always acted as a magic for him.'

A young woman nodded at Olga and for one brief moment was with us. Natalia was her name.

27

Natalia was twenty-eight. She had a figure which would have satisfied Zenkovsky but a look close up at her face showed a wear that had lived through more than eighteen years.

Natalia and I saw each other in the street next afternoon.

And were still together at midnight.

We decided to get a taxi to see a museum.

Her dress, tight about her throat, was sleeveless, displaying slim arms of burning bronze. It had circles on it like a Pierrot costume, circles of hot brown and claret red. Her hair was curls of gold with the wind playing them about like coils. Her eyes were water with a dip of green.

She covered her eyes often with abnormally large sunglasses. Her face was beautifully and sharply cut with sunken cheeks—Dietrich cheeks—sculptors would have revelled refashioning those bones and hollows.

She had a walk which made grandfathers throw away their crutches. Her legs were saplings lacquered in copper.

In the hot taxi we had all windows open and a watering cart brushed by burying us under a fountain of water. The driver and I laughed outrageously.

'You syphilitic dog, what d'you think you're doing?' shrieked Natalia. 'Son of a pig, where's your sense? Snuttering snivel-nosed snout, tell me your number. I'll report you!'

'I didn't know it would shoot through the window,' said the driver.

'Can't you look, you cliff-side product! You should have told us to close our windows! Your name! Give it to me! And your number!'

She raved and raged. And she swore enough to make a sailor blush.

I loved the water. The heat was scorching. I would have liked a bath in it.

But the sculptors now would be passing Natalia on to the cartoonists. For her hair was now neither gold nor coiled. Its dye was running out and it hung like corded matting stringing from its roots. Her complexion, no longer marshmallow, was soddened oatmeal. Her creamy cottony dress was now a saddened rag on a hag. It took an hour before the first touch of tranquillity returned to her. At every half chance she was off to a woman's room to work at herself. She had had dignity. She was now a rat half drowned. She had been chic. She was now a mess of mash.

We drove through Lenin Square full of expensive buildings which looked splendid in photographs and doldrum dull in fact. It was a square filled with gardens and flowers. There's something mysterious about public gardens and flowers: some have soul and love in them, and some are frigidly formal and the flowers don't speak. The gardens of the Moscow Kremlin have feeling and beauty: but most gardens in most squares in most modern cities in the Soviet Union have none. And since the guide-books are so often emphatic about the love showered on them by the populace and the authorities, that's a pointer that it is not so, because it is a law that what an individual or a public asserts for itself can usually be taken as the opposite. Whoever heard of a generous man saying he was generous, or a brave man acclaiming his bravery: yet the mean and the coward do nothing else. (Beware of the country that talks of its love of peace.) Whoever heard of Kew Gardens or the Kremlin Gardens rubbing it into the viewer that they were planted with love?

'This square used to be a cemetery,' said Natalia as we drove through it. 'And the old still come and stand on this spot or that spot and weep over the ground of their ancestors. They swear they know the place to an inch. Many feel the gardens should not have been built here.'

We went to the heights above the river to give Natalia a chance to dry out.

The Amur was sumptuous below us, grandiloquent. "Everything", said Gogol, "from steppes to human feet is huge in Russia." Nothing seemed puny in the whole land: rivers, steppes, human feet, woods, squares, streets, theatres, stadiums and human hearts all were of overwhelming dimension.

We could see a mile away where the elegant Amur joined the eloquent Ussuri. The rivers wound graciously like aristocratic giants. And beyond the green on the opposite bank was China! The blue hills of China.

'This boundary,' said Natalia, 'was agreed on by conference and the Amur is the boundary for hundreds of miles.'

'Can we go to the other side?' I asked.

'Yes. After the museum.'

In the museum was the skeleton of a sea cow twelve feet in length. Six sea cows were found in the Pacific Ocean three hundred years ago. They fed their young with milk like cows. They had a large front fin three feet long which looked like a leg. Sea cows are now extinct.

There were photographs of American troops occupying Kharbarovsk in 1917.

'Americans here?' I asked.

'You were all against us! The whole world was against us!'

'I know. But I had thought somehow American strength was a new thing in the world. I'm surprised they were concerned with these parts fifty years ago.'

'We have your Churchill tanks in Archangel. We had your American forces fighting our brave revolutionaries here!'

She had turned very dark towards me.

'Did you know,' I asked, 'that Ernest Bevin organized a dockers' strike in England preventing arms being sent against "their Russian brothers"?'

'You sent arms! Why couldn't you mind your own business? We were starving and fighting for our lives and liberty, for our great cause.'

Natalia had gone black and didn't want to excuse my ignorance of the American participation.

We went to the shore to cross the river. The boat stations were like reproductions of old Mississippi boats. We crossed the Amur. On the opposite bank was a grey sand beach mixed in with grassy shrubs like creekland in Essex.

She took her shoes off and off we set walking.

'Somerset Maugham is the easiest writer to read,' she said, 'such direct English. But Galsworthy is my favourite. Burns too, Robert Burns.'

She stopped and turned in towards me: 'I wish you English would become famous again. We all liked your fame. A third power is necessary. You should keep your

Commonwealth as a unity, build it to real strength, and be a real third power. But you must be independent of America. A power. Not a subservient. Why don't you do it?'

Then she set off walking, swinging her shoes.

Then she turned on me again. 'The last war finished you. Finished an era. Exit England. Enter the U.S.S.R. and the U.S.A. It was a fine way to end. You gave your all, but played the game of Power-Chess with a lack of cunning. When an Empire you were a tyrant: but, strangely, we sigh for that tyrant now. Come back, be great: your greatness was different from ours, different from America's. If it will help you, we'll lend you Kruschev and Molotov to help you bulldoze your way back.'

Pasternak's name came up. I said he was famous outside Russia. 'What a way to become famous!' she cried. 'How can you say "famous". It was betrayal. He was a traitor.'

'A man has a right to try and get his books published.'

'Not like that. And not that book.'

'If an English author has a book refused in England, England wouldn't worry if Russia or anywhere else published it. And *Dr Zhivago* isn't anti-Russian. It isn't even anti your regime. It merely doesn't acclaim it, and that's how your own critics have spoken of it. In London alone we have more than 400 publishing houses and an author can offer his book to any. Here, one refusal, and that's your lot.'

'It isn't; we have lots of publishing houses!'

'You have lots of publishing houses with only one mind.'

Natalia was black again. She got storms inside her and no argument got through.

But she went to the water and paddled. Her dress had got its creamy surface back, her hair was regaining its curls and the breezes were coiling it again. Her figure was strong, athletic, and calling to all fires in all men.

'Aren't you married?' I asked.

'I'll never find a husband,' she said. 'I was a teacher. How I hate teachers. There's something so grey-serious, watery-earnest about them. Their humour . . . shall I give you an example: "Boys," they say, "I will tell you a humorous story: there was a Paris count who said to his friends he would go to Kharbarovsk and come home with pictures of bears in the streets." And the boys are supposed to laugh because we have advanced so much that we don't have bears in our streets any more. And I hate teaching myself. I've turned against children. I teach in night schools to grown-ups because they only come in if they are keen to learn and that's right. But I'll never find a husband. Something about Russian men: no grooming, no suavity, no polish, they don't click, no style, I can't . . . not with me. I used to meet English. I was born in Kazan but was at the University in Moscow. What is this coldness? I never yet have been able to get inside an Englishman. Can you explain it to me? I met them: I loved them: they were wonderfully courteous, considerate . . . but there's something, I don't know what it is, can you explain it to me?'

'Perhaps there are some of us can't let ourselves go. I feel I'd give anything to commit one rape, to scream at someone, to hit someone, to panic, to be overcome . . . it never happens, I remain locked up in my Anglo-Saxon armour and I am worried that I will never come out into a life.'

Natalia said: 'I like everything I know about the English and their history except that. You remain closed books. Lawrence of Arabia . . . you breed the most fascinating introverts. You know Rupert in Aldridge's last book? Explain that to me. He had his English wife, he preferred the Russian Nina, he stuck to his English wife. I love the first half of the book, but cannot understand or like the second part: Aldridge talks of emotions like dead wood, he doesn't explain. I don't feel he's inside his characters. I feel he stays at intellectual level, never gets in the soul. James Aldridge is my favourite modern author, but can you explain his last book better to me?'

Natalia had become animated. She herself had come out

of a shell and was shining excitedly. Her eyes caught light. Her hair sported in the wind. Her handsome head had come out of the cold mould the sculptors would have loved to have encased it in and gathered a dancing brilliance.

'I would like to marry Laurence Olivier,' she laughed. 'I'll never find a husband. There's something wrong about men.'

'I'll send you a Spaniard,' I said.

'Send me Laurence Olivier!' she laughed again. 'Is James Aldridge married? This is so cold here,' she burst on. 'Do you know for six months of the year it's 25° under zero? And for the other six months it's over 35° hot. But the terrible, terrible things in the winter are the winds. Oh it's not the temperature. It's the ice in the wind which eats at you. Eats at you. And knifes through you too so you feel like a ghost, like a transparent apparition. We get paid more for being here. We used to get 30 per cent more for leaving Kazan, then nought per cent and now 20 per cent. Look at the blue flowers just behind. I get 300 roubles a month for teaching, but my flat is dear, 10 roubles a month. I would like to tell you something, something that I know very certainly.'

I waited.

'The Amur River knows that it is the boundary line between the Soviet Union and China.'

Every minute a new part of her caught to life. She became all animation. And all that was comely in her became champagne.

'I know something else,' she said.

I waited.

'The pleasures of the body are brief, the pleasures of the heart develop into sorrows, but the pleasures of the mind are with us always and go on till the end of our journey. The sun is nearly set. The Amur is nearly gold. And if we don't scamper like two hares we'll miss the last ferry back to Kharbarovsk!'

28

Natalia was at the station to see me off. Dressed in yellow.

I explained to her the sad English phrase 'Ships that pass in the night'.

Then I left her. Taking from Kharbarovsk, a little of Kharbarovsk, everywhere; richer still for knowing, somewhere the wind is blowing, through her hair.

29

The train from Kharbarovsk left at eight o'clock at night and would arrive at the Pacific at Nakhodka at eight o'clock next morning.

It was the grandest train I had been in. Still Victorian in taste but Victoriana at its most refined. Made in Hungary. Most carriages on this line were made in Hungary.

I went to my brass and glass and white and cream compartment and there was a chic woman's jacket on the bunk opposite. It couldn't be Russian. I had seen its owner on the platform. Small, auburn-haired, auburn-eyed and young. No one else seemed arriving and the train was leaving.

The owner in a cerise silk blouse came to the door, looked at me and said, in English: 'I am mad.'

Her mini skirt was of grey gaberdine and was the other half of the costume's jacket on the bunk.

'Mad. Mad. Mad,' she said.

What could I say?

She turned round and paced the corridor.

She returned, opened some rich suitcases, took out the shimmiest of nightdresses, and laid it at the head of her bunk. She started unbuttoning her blouse.

'I'm not mad crazy. I'm mad angry.'

'Oh.'

She rose. Closed the compartment door. Asked, 'Do you mind if I bolt it?' And continued unbuttoning her blouse.

'I paid De Luxe,' she said, 'and look what they've given me.'

She took her blouse off. It seemed a little early. The Englishness in me, no doubt.

'I thought it was a nice carriage,' I said.

'Have you seen the De Luxe? I paid De Luxe!'

She was not at the moment taking her brassière off but put her diaphanous blue nightdress—very mini—over it.

'Then why haven't you De Luxe?'

'It's those Japs! The De Luxe are full with three large parties of Japs. Don't you think one could have given up his place to me?'

Her skirt was coming off.

'I'm French,' she said. 'What are you?'

'English,' I said.

She was getting into bed, but some other juggling was going on: she was taking the bra off.

'Will you have supper with me?' I asked. And can't think when I've ever said anything so idiotic.

'Yes,' she said, and turned over to go to sleep.

She turned back: 'When's that?' she asked.

'Well, it's eight o'clock now. I suppose nine or nine-thirty.'

'I don't know what the time is!' she said. 'I've just flown in from Moscow and they tell me I've lost six hours. Or is it ten? Or is it twelve? But it couldn't be that, could it, or else it would be the same only different, wouldn't it? I don't know where it is, night or day. If you can wake me I'll have supper with you.' And she put her bra on a hook, dangling down.

She turned again for sleep, but again turned back to me. 'I'm not mad at you,' she said.

'That's good.'

'Did you think I was?'

'Just for a moment. I thought you were mad angry because they'd put you with a man instead of another woman: because if so——'

'I'm not.'

Now she was taking out a book to read. If she wasn't really going to sleep . . . it was all this reasoning: why must I reason what I should do? I must do what was right. But why care what was right? And what is right? And isn't wrong right? And who cares?

'*Angélique*,' I said. 'I haven't read it. I've brought some of Simenon's books with me.'

'I wouldn't bring spy stories. I thought they'd take spy stories off me. Would they?'

She was going to sleep.

'Shall I wake you in an hour?'

'Yes. I'm so tired. I don't know when I last slept.'

And she was on the way to Morpheus.

Something else had been getting at me. I would have this night on the train, twelve daylight hours in Nakhodka, then the next night on the train: so I had left almost everything with the station at Kharbarovsk. I thought I'd go bohemian and travel with nothing: a passport, money, a camera: no pyjamas, no clean shirt. When was my last bath? And it had been so sweltering hot. At least I had a bar of soap. I left for the lavatory. A tiny hand basin. No plug. I jammed the basin hole with lavatory paper, filled the basin, stripped, and washed in a mouse-hole of a room, with angry passengers impatient at the door. The boy scout's motto 'Be prepared', never stopped drumming at my ears. I had never been less prepared. Who would have guessed such magnanimity from Intourist? Perhaps the French lass was a spy? Oh to be seduced for my secrets! I knew the secret formula for making vodka . . .

30

At supper she wore a black dress sparkling with neatness as if we kept an iron in our carriage.

'I hate Japan,' she said.

'Where are you going?'

'To Japan. I hate working for the Japanese.'

'What are you going to do in Japan?'

'Work for the Japanese.'

She was French but as Irish as the Russians.

'Then why work for the Japanese in Japan?'

'I want to,' she said. 'Can we have vodka? I've never tried vodka.'

There was no vodka. She had to be content with wine.

The entire restaurant was full of Japanese except for us. I felt an uplift. Such cleanliness and here and there such beauty. At least six twenty-year-olds were like divine orchids. They all wore white and they were all starched and prim. They each had a million strands of unpolished ebony for hair. If the animals ever turn tables on us and hunt the human, the hair of these women will be their prize of all prizes—the mink of the human species.

'Japanese men,' said Colette, 'treat women abominably; with no respect. They are "funny". They behave "funny". After a year in France they are better. They behave at first as if women don't exist.'

Don't exist. There were at least six women with us who gave you the feeling that nothing else existed. They had the white skin of magnolias. Do racialists call them coloured? We are a pasty shrimpy pink in comparison. Socrates said his idea of heaven was to talk neverendingly to beauty. To have Socrates talking to these . . . it would justify bugging.

A Jap was staring down hard at the menu and saying to the Russian waitress beside him, finger on an item: 'You are beautiful.'

'What is beautiful?'

'You are beautiful.'

The waitress sought out the head waiter to ask what was 'beautiful', as a man wanted it.

'I have forty introductions, do you think I'll get work?' asked Colette. 'I have enough money and clothes for six months. If I don't get work I'll go home to mother and father. I can get the work but it's the working permit: do you think I'll get it?'

It was dark now. The short glimpses we had had of the Amur, and China, and the Maritime Province which was the name of this region now out of Siberia we were travelling through, had been the most beautiful scenery since Moscow. And it was to grow finer: in the morning, hills and mountains were with us, waterfalls crawling down slopes like tears down giants, rock faces sheer to the sky so that the train hardly squeezed through . . . it was obviously all planned by the Russians; that to keep my mind off the greatest scenery by their most dangerous border as we ran for most of our twelve hours alongside

China, the sinister cunning Russians had made it night, thrown in an auburn-eyed auburn-haired, Irish-touched French lass in mini-dress, added six glory-orchids in the forms of Japanese, prepared the best food and the best Georgian wines since Moscow, sought out the best carriages on the line . . . it was obviously all done as distraction.

'I have a fiancé,' said Colette. 'At least I think I have. He's gone to Vietnam. He's a correspondent for the Americans. I'm all for all the Americans do in Vietnam aren't you? I thought if I went to Tokyo we could meet in Hong Kong. Don't you think that would be nice? Do you like Russia? I must say I am surprised. They are much nicer than I thought. Do you find them nicer? They seem quite happy in Russia. I must say I didn't expect to find them happy . . . I must say I don't know what I expected, but somehow, I don't know how to say it, it's quite different from what I had expected. Do you find it different?'

31

Don't go to Nakhodka, they told me: there's nothing to see but a few shacks and some water. You can't stay there, they said, there's no hotel. And if you do stay there, they said, if you miss the train after twelve hours and have to stay, you'll have to wait nine days for the next.

Nakhodka proved to be a thriving town, most beautifully situated on many hills, the 'some water' was the

Pacific Ocean. There was a hotel. And there was a train every day.

Were they lying?

I went to the hotel at ten o'clock and asked for coffee. Don't come in here, they told me: we're closed. But the notice outside says you're open till eleven, I said. There's no coffee, they said. Tea will do, I said. And if you do stay, tea will take half an hour, the electricity's broken down. I'd wait. We only take coupons, not money, they said. I had coupons.

I got coffee in five minutes for money and stayed till eleven and they were so friendly and hoped I'd be back for lunch and supper.

Were they lying?

Harriman is supposed to have asked Stalin why he had broken an agreement? I have not broken it, he said, I have changed my mind.

Was Stalin lying?

If an Arab swears it is more than his life's worth to sell us a length of cloth for anything less than twenty piastres, then he sells it to us for ten and is delighted: is he lying? If a salesman says his powder washes whitest, is he lying? If someone cheats over his income tax, is he lying?

I think a Russian, maybe for expediency, or laziness—helping being too much trouble—or love of drama, can tell you other than the truth. Love of drama . . . I couldn't get a theatre ticket in Leningrad. An Intourist girl said she'd help. She phoned the theatre: she burst into tears, called the administrator darling—sweetest, kindest, 'such a nice foreigner, and only one ticket, dearest, but a good one, in the front stalls: you know I've never asked you anything before . . will you sweetest?' End of emotional voice and tears, down with the telephone and, in a matter-of-fact tone: 'They're sending the ticket round.'

It's possible the authorities wanted to discourage tourists in Nakhodka. I soon found that organized excursions, as in every other town, didn't exist and that I was a rare bird to be staying twelve hours. But I felt they had ad libbed the rigmarole to keep me away, which is unimpressive when you find out the true position. I was once with a tourist who begged for an hour in a gramophone shop for an Oistrakh record and was told ceaselessly there was none. Then let's see what you have got, she said. The assistant took any record from the rack. It was an Oistrakh record.

Nakhodka was near China, in the Pacific and near the naval base of Vladivostok . . . but I clung to emphasizing that it was too frustrating to go all that way and not reach the coast and see the ocean. So I came to tread 'where so few foreigners had trod'.

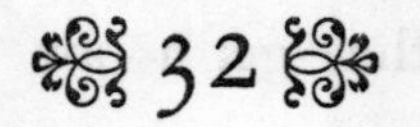

I met an Intourist girl, Gallia, who had some time off and said she'd show me something of Nakhodka. And she managed to persuade a taxi driver, Yuri, to drive us. Gallia was inclining towards fat, was ungainly, had ugly grey metal-rimmed spectacles: but was all heart and kindness. Yuri was lively and inclined to joviality: which was astonishing because, as Gallia whispered to me in the back seat, on the next day he was to be divorced by a wife he loved deeply.

'Will she get the divorce?'

'Oh yes. If divorce is requested by mutual consent or if

there are no children and only one partner wants it, it is automatic. In Yuri's case there are children but Yuri knows it is useless to stand in his wife's way so divorce is being requested by mutual consent and it must be automatic.'

We set off up hill, down dale, to see the town. The sun was hidden: it was pleasantly warm.

'So there are children?'

'Two.'

'Who gets them?'

'The woman always gets the children.'

'Supposing she doesn't want them?'

'She is forced to take them.'

'And if he is a saint and loves all his family deeply: and she is wayward and goes from man to man . . .'

'There is no question. She must take the children.'

'And if she is mean and stops him seeing the children?'

'The children are all hers.' Yuri leaned back pointing to three blocks of flats of sandwich-form construction: 'Only last summer,' he said, 'I picked wild strawberries there.'

'It could be hard on people like Yuri?'

'The men think so. Russian men think they get a raw deal from our government.'

'And must Yuri give maintenance for his children, or does the State?'

'Yuri must.'

'He can't escape from such duties?'

'Never. It's automatic. He gives 25 per cent of his salary if there is one child until that child is sixteen, 40 per cent if two, 50 per cent if three. The wife never gets anything for herself unless it can be proved that she has become ill during the marriage and resulting from that is unable to work.'

Yuri knew the laws for photography and was firm but pleasant about it. He was driving us to his favourite view of the Pacific. 'No photos,' he said. 'Stand with your back to the water and photograph inwards if you like. But never the Ocean, never the harbour and never any of the bays.'

Gallia said: '"Nakhodka" means "finding". It was "found" a hundred years ago. A Russian ship called *America* was so buffeted about in a storm that the sailors gave up hope of survival. Exhausted, they slept. And found themselves becalmed in the morning in the main bay here. It was a small place until Vladivostok became a naval port. Now this is the civil seaport for Japan and America and the world: we have received our status as a town and we grow alarmingly every month, every day even. The very first foreigner set foot here in 1961.'

We had left the town by some high hills where housing estates were mushrooming up and it was becoming scenically more like Scotland every minute. On a rolling landscape, perched high, were two cemeteries, one Russian and one Japanese. I asked if I could photograph them. Gallia said yes, Yuri said yes but why? There is a feeling among many Russians that if a foreigner isn't photographing Lenin or achievements of the State he is suspect or, at least, incomprehensible. I said I wanted to photograph the Japanese cemetery because the gravestones were strange and unique. And that I wanted to photograph the Russian one because for me it was even more strange and more unique: cemeteries have been abnormally rare in my journeys; what happened to all the dead? They said they didn't know and seemed genuine in their answer: yet how can that be? The only graveyard for individual Russians dead in the last war I have seen is in Norway where the Norwegians have honoured prisoners who died in camps. The Russian authorities have built only mass graves with always a flame and never a name, except perhaps of a hero. A well-known poem is of a little man who gave his life for his motherland. Such a little man but there was no space in all the world large enough for his grave. There must have been a lot of little men around in the last war. This graveyard here, though old-fashioned, had flowers on a score of crosses: three calves and a cow grazed round . . . yet there wasn't a house in sight. So the set-up was mysterious.* The Japanese cemetery was for Japs dead in 1939 fighting against Russia. Japan had asked permission to raise it, permission had been granted and Jap tourists never missed it.

We reached the end of the road. It pushed out to sea and died in a track, a path, then the smallest bridge across the smallest inlet. This was the spot where Yuri dreamed Nakhodka would build its resort, its strand, its funfair, its holiday camps and hotels. I turned to see what I could photograph inland . . . the Scots needn't go there! Inlets, hills, mauve greens, clouds, heather: Scotland was on the Pacific.

Nakhodka was a town planner's dream: at every turn and every hill a different, brilliant vista showed. So far the architecture was as dreary as in most other cities: there remained a few fine oldish timber places, grand three-storey structures: 'We'll soon have them down,' cried Yuri and Gallia. 'But they are beautiful!' I cried. 'We don't think so,' they answered. 'Our people have a right to smart new apartment blocks.'

I saw a café placed on a cliff edge and asked for coffee. They kept us so long and dozens of others were served, I was about to remonstrate when Gallia said: 'Aren't they nice? They've never had an Englishman here before and the manageress herself is supervising the snack. None of that stale stuff for Harold Wilson—they call you Harold Wilson. They like Harold Wilson very much. At my school we only spoke English. Have you got schools like that in England, where everything, even mathematics, is taught in Russian? We go to the school at eight, by twelve or fourteen they have sifted the most gifted out, and from fourteen on every subject is taught in, and every conversation is spoken in, English. We "live" English. It's an experiment, but I

* Although until this point I had scarcely seen a cemetery in all my travels, as if to prove me wrong I was to come across half a dozen in the next week.

know at least eight schools like that myself in the Soviet Union and I think the experiment will go on.'

I had told Gallia how I loved the Russian landscape painter Kuindji. She spent the time between the end of our excursion and the time my train left to dash off to her house and dash back with only seconds to spare, to give me a book of Kuindji's work she had had at home. It was her only copy. And it was out of print. But that was the sort of person Gallia was.

33

I saw three miracles!

Some hundreds of yards away from Nakhodka station on the high road were three gypsies looking as if they had just stepped out of an Essex caravan. Two women and a man: the women with dresses to their ankles, the man with trousers as if he had slept in them: the women with little ear-rings and tanned complexions, the man carrying a small female purse. I was alone with Gallia at the time.

'How is it possible that there are free gypsies still?'

'Most,' she said, 'have been rounded up and rounded in and coerced into our way of life. And until the death of Stalin no one realized that there were still those who lived in the old ways. After Stalin they began emerging from the forests: they have never had any cards, any papers, any citizenship. It means that they had survived without ration cards, work or travel permits, without, from our point of view, existing at all. They occasionally appeared at fairs, told fortunes, they occasionally did some tinkering, but they were always off before they could be rounded up. Now some are cunning. They appear before the local Soviet, say they have at last decided to conform, could they have money for a house and to set themselves up while they get on to their feet. The Soviets proudly give them the money, and then they are seen no more. Most of us have never seen free gypsies. This can't be more than the second group I have ever seen in my life. No one knows how or where they exist. Some people think that one or two of the men work in towns, helping others to get by with their earnings.'

'I shouldn't have thought it was possible to survive fifty years in the Soviet Union without papers?'

'Neither would we think it could be possible. It was not until 1957 that any showed their faces at all. Our government find the gypsies are the strangest people: nothing in the world will get most of them to work. Once we handed over to them a complete Collective Farm. You should have seen the chaos! We do have a a few settled gypsy communities where gypsies live and work as we do. These absolutely free ones like this with their old clothes and customs are rare.'

Fifty years!

Dictatorships can't abide the freedom-loving. It is said that Hitler was worse to the gypsies than he ever was to the Jews. The Russians rounded up all gypsies, Lapps, nomads, and forced them to conform—or thought they did.

Almost the whole world secretly admires the freedom-loving, and shouts hosannahs for the democracies that are freer than the dictatorships. There are no people in history with such a record of a lust for freedom as the gypsies: yet there are no people who have less acclaimed their own virtues themselves: and there are few outsiders who salute that incredible race for what they are . . . and then there is the equally incredible fact that gypsies in Finland, Austria, England, Nakhodka or anywhere, look alike, and that they are bonded together without any defined bonds, bound without any prescribed allegiances or by any contrived links . . .

Let every man or woman who has ever cried the watchword freedom take pause now and salute with the absolute highest honour, three *unbelievable* miracles! What an example to the world of man! A kingdom each for their stories! Fifty years!

34

'Forgive a quirk,' I asked, as Yuri and Gallia were leaving me: 'in which direction might I walk so that I might feel that no foreigner has set foot there before?'

'Why?' asked Yuri.

'Why not?' asked Gallia. 'Almost anywhere, off the main road, into the interior.'

I crossed the square where the hotel was standing. There was a kiosk much as a seaside resort might have. It was closed and it displayed mostly clothes. A nylon slip was £5: a handkerchief £1.7.0: a pair of men's shoes £17: a raincoat £22: and all the most ordinary. I saw no clothes in the U.S.S.R. that weren't between four to ten times as expensive as in England: and never, at any price, anything smart. Not one foreigner who didn't stand out as from another planet.

On the far side of the square away from the sea I went up a side street. It rose. Soon it was a mud road. I passed timber one-storey houses almost attacked by giant sunflowers they were so numerous. Women nodded good afternoon. A turn, and the road was a path only. It twisted like a stepped-on snake. There were terriers. They too said good afternoon if giving me the once over and rubbing their noses on my trousers meant that. The path was only a foot wide but it passed another timber house, poor perhaps . . . why have the old and the poor so often got more colour and attraction than the new and the not so poor? . . . I could see signs of grandmama's needlework inside, quilts, cupboard covers, bits of the crafts the modern Soviets frown upon . . . the crafts are dead in the Soviet Union, they are 'individual' which is sinful: such a tragedy! . . . the seat in this garden might have been made by a great-uncle, the fretwork flower-boxes by a neighbour: there'd be cups and saucers in a home like that which told of a family's history . . . officially, possessions are frowned upon and it is considered possessive and bourgeois to want to take heirlooms into a new apartment, so that a new apartment is not only mundane dead outside but is mundane dead inside. It is in the backstreets, in such houses as I peeped into now, that an aspect of the Russian soul still breathes. The shawl of the old lady who greeted me and gasped when I told her I was English, gasped with slight fright and much delight, her shawl was like Joseph's cloak, of mauves, hazel greens and dawn yellows. 'London!' she said. 'London! London!' and went back to her house muttering and, turning at her doorstep: 'London!' and with a shake of her head, went in as if she had been hit with a fairy wand.

I had to climb through rocks, over rocks, through briars, over briars and, it was strange, down on my right was a mud flat badminton court, and at the side was some garden seating under a wooden garden shelter, three men drinking, beyond that a garden of sunflowers, delphiniums and phlox half hiding a house . . . pinch me, that surely was a stage set lifted out of Chekhov.

I did not intrude but kept up my path which was twisting up first across a field, then through allotments, mostly potatoes and turnips, with a blue duck wandering worried and lost with its hands tucked angrily behind, then to wild gardens, phlox again, pansies and tansies and an enormous six-inch black butterfly among an entourage of unimposing white and ungainly brown ones, then to ferns and a green woodpecker on a single ash with its red cap jauntily aslant, then to willows and oaks, through a snip of a wood to a clearing, some so handsome long fork-tailed swallows swooping, then to a road which perhaps would never be a road . . . as if they had begun making it without looking to where it was going. It marched to the top of a hill, gaped down a near-precipice, was cut to continue but surely it was utterly impossible: the incline was tremendous. I stared down it and beyond it at a vast view of the Pacific, of inlets, of fields, and of undulating hills. I fell in love with the scene and sat there for two hours, plumb centre in a road which would probably be for ever a way to nowhere.

Just on the left I could see the edge of the two mountains Gallia had called Brother and Sister. The Whites in 1919 had captured two young communists and flung the brother off one height and the sister off the other in full view of the town.

Two romantics in England had given me a note to bury in any beautiful spot on my travel 'To be collected by Marc and Sandra' etc., etc. 'To be collected by'! How innocent lovers can be! What overtone was in that phrase! I tore that part off and buried the rest for Marc and Sandra to collect at their leisure.

Three people turned up below me, saw me, seemed to have a conference about me, I waved, they seemed to O.K. me, they waved back and walked slowly away. A black Alsatian appeared. I didn't wave. And I wasn't sorry to see him go.

The way the sun played through the clouds: the hills were half of gold, the Pacific was half of bronze, and a rivulet running in from the Pacific and across the only plain was struck alive like a line of alight magnesium and died far far away into the horizon smaller and smaller and smaller and on for five hundred words.

35

'Let's hope your dream doesn't come true,' said Valodia.

'Let's listen in to the ten-o'clock news,' said Nikolai.

It was in my room back at Irkutsk. They had both come early and found me in bed. I had told them of my dream. England had been invaded by Germany. There had been troop movements all night. No one was going to help England. Certainly not America. In case America was likely to, Germany was ready with offers for the sharing of the spoils. The capital of England seemed to be in the centre of the land. I had been on my way to it. Then Russia announced it was coming in. It was for expediency only. Russia had no intention of allowing Germany to rise again and would nip any effort in the bud. Would Russia leave England after the invasion was halted?

'If you had given me another few minutes' dreaming I could have told you,' I said.

Nikolai was from the Leningrad Society of Writers. He and I were friends of some years' standing. He had told me in Leningrad that he would try and join me somewhere on the tour and, if possible, here in Irkutsk. He lived, almost, for fishing and there was no fishing in the world, he said, like that at Lake Baikal.

Valodia was from Intourist. He was very tall, very young, and came from Yakutsk which I had thought was the coldest place on earth but he said there were places near there colder still. 80° below zero meant nothing to him. He lived for hunting.

Nikolai was trying to arrange for me to go with him to a sanatorium for V.I.P.s at the edge of the lake forty miles away.

Valodia had arranged an excursion in Irkutsk for me for that morning.

Nikolai suddenly realized that ten o'clock on the radio from Moscow meant 14.00 o'clock in Irkutsk, so there would be no news for hours.

So Valodia and I left.

Everything for a foreign visitor is done by Intourist. He pays Intourist: begs and argues with Intourist: Intourist is both his master and his servant. I was met at every step by Intourist, taken to one of their hotels, and escorted on a tour of the town if I wanted one; if not, I was left alone. The difference in Intourist personnel is shattering: from the most moronic and boorish, to the fantastically businesslike, charming and intelligent.

Intourist should take Valodia as their model. Icily efficient, transparently understanding, sunnily warm.

On our tour that morning we went to the Church of the Risen Cross. It was one o'clock and it was Monday. There was a service on. It was packed. It was overflowing. I have entered four churches and cathedrals this year in Russia. All were packed. All were colourful. All retained all the old rituals. All were affluent. A tiny choir of six, in a pen like a witness-box in a law court, had sung in Smolensk Cathedral with a beauty that brought tears to the eyes at its lovelinesss. Here in Irkutsk, pencil thin candles, candelabras, ikons filling every inch of each wall, rich voices, shawled old women, tolstofka-clad, peak-capped old men straight out of a Tolstoy book, beggars, a feast of offerings, baked bread, pies, works of culinary art on a table draped in a blue cloth, the priests white-hatted, old ladies attending a library of little notebooks containing family registers and lists of dear departed that prayers could be said for and candles lit for . . . for the irreligious such as me these churches were living theatres at their richest. This morning the priest was talking in a rich clear voice to the gathering. What could he be saying? I listened. 'Christ is everywhere, He's with us now.' What diction! If everyone spoke Russian as he did, the lot of the struggling foreigner would be easier. 'He's the same as in America, Poland, France, He's the same among us now giving us His grace, His presence, His help in our needs as He was in the past and as He is outside our lands. Listen for Him and you will hear His words.'

I asked Valodia about religion. 'It has to be self-supporting,' he said. 'If the people want it they can have it. No church is closed unless two-thirds in the district where it stands elect for it to be closed.'

Inasmuch as a person can guess, religion will soon come back to any point the people want it. After fifty years it is no longer a threat to the authority of the State. Anyone can go to a church, there is always at least one per town open, and thousands go. But a stigma remains and probably always will. There might never come a time when a church-going Russian will hold high office.

'Something strange,' I said to Valodia: 'if you find an old church you build it up. It's admirable. It's so colourful. And lends a touch of the past to the present. There are at least seven close to Red Square in Moscow; just in the last two years you've found the old plans and rebuilt them: they stand like jewels: four there are together in a little row alongside the new Russia Hotel opposite the Kremlin: such care expended on something of the past you are supposed to abominate. Yet no one will point them out to the foreigner when it's just the thing the foreigner would like to know about. It's as if you are so proud on one side, and still ashamed on the other: because if you mention them to an Intourist guide he'll change the subject.'

Valodia smiled. 'It would be propaganda. Did you hear of the rich American tourist who said to her guide: "Now this tour of Moscow should be three hours. But cut out all the propaganda." He brought her back after one and a half hours. She complained of the shortness of the tour. "The rest was propaganda," he said.'

Irkutsk was dreary, soulless. Not a nice café or shop in town. No architecture at all since the revolution: only buildings, monuments to melancholy. Not one item in one shop meriting one glance. Even the bookshops: full of paper and print signifying deadness. When I wandered alone in the back streets, wooden buildings a hundred years old told of a time when elegance was not a forgotten word. The greatest thing in Irkutsk was the Angara River. Wide, grand, nobly flowing. Is there such a thing in the Soviet Union as a narrow, mean river?

The guide-books acclaimed Irkutsk as one of the most beautiful cities in Siberia. Blimey!

We listened to the news.

Russian troops had occupied Czechoslovakia.

It was announced like a father going to the aid of a son.

36

Nikolai had arranged for my stay in the home for V.I.P.s at Baikal. He even talked of camping out for some nights. An unheard of honour this: foreigners might camp at organized places but never freely.

The people of Irkutsk had taken the Czechoslovak announcement in their stride. That their government did right and had things well in hand was the feeling. Many explained it to me:

'After the last war we were able to show the benefits of our democratic socialist system to some countries around us. It is to be expected that there will always be some reactionaries who will want to hang on to the old ways, and there are always those outside anxious to feed such elements with revolt. The Germans have invaded across their borders [some said "had invaded" and some said "are set to invade"] and the peace-loving democratic people of Czechoslovakia have asked our aid in protecting them against such elements within and without. So overnight the forces of our fatherland have occupied the country and sealed the border off against Germany. There has been no fighting, our forces have been welcomed, and when we have sorted the matter out and restored a state of calm, our forces will withdraw.'

A few said they realized they had only heard one side of the story.

All seemed convinced that the communist countries were a bastion of goodness surrounded by a sinister warmongering ferment of degradation against which a constant alert was needed. There had come about a chink in the bastion and it was necessary to seal it up quickly for the sake of the entire bastion and as a gesture towards the majority of the Czechoslovak peoples who were solidly together with their other communist brotherhoods. A family with one erring member, so dad would sort it out in the best loving-dad manner.

37

Nikolai could not stay with me. He had been recalled. Ostensibly he had come to visit Irkutsk writers and to scout out more: actually he had hoped to steal some days fishing at Baikal. The three days he could have been there he had spent trying to take me with him. Now, with all the permits granted, he could see me out there, then after four hours return. Yet if he had not worried about me he might have been out there, uncontactable, and spent the rest of his annual holiday due to him among the fish and waters of Baikal.

He, Valodia, myself, a chauffeur and an influential someone whose name I never knew, set off by car for the lake. The sun shone, the forests shone, and the road undulated slowly like an elongated switchback.

'I'm sorry, Nikolai,' I said, 'that I will not be playing you at chess.'

'I'm not,' he said. 'By the way, do you know, I am a lazy person. I like politics and fishing but nothing else. Only being lazy, I play my son at chess but, do you know, I do not like it. Chess is not a lazy thing. By the way, I like picking mushrooms too. I go out in the woods and I pick the mushrooms and I come home and, do you know, I keep them for ages and then I throw them away. I do not like to eat mushrooms. Occasionally I like to eat some with vodka. By the way I like cooking my own fish, and fish soup, I love cooking fish soup. And I boil milk over my fish. I could eat fish for every meal and for every course in every meal. And I could catch my own fish. Do you know my wife doesn't like fish? But I don't love to do anything else. I could play you at chess. But I would rather be lazy. By the way, talking of politics, do you know that Bertrand Russell yacht that goes everywhere making peace propaganda? They sent me to talk with them near Leningrad. An archaeologist from France was the captain, there was also a Scandinavian. A small crew, all speaking English. They anchored off Leningrad and when we asked them to leave they broke their engine. They tried to swim ashore. We took them back and repaired their engine and gave a store of food and towed them out to sea, but they still stayed three weeks. They wanted to land and take leaflets to Moscow. Do you know they amazed us with their navigation. They went everywhere, they amazed us. By the way, we liked them, but we could not let them land.'

Valodia's heaven was hunting bear at 60° below zero. His wife went with him. I said I would go hunting with him, or fishing with Nikolai, but not to participate as I was one of those hypocrites who eat flesh but cannot take life. Valodia had recently completed his national service of two years: it is one and half years for some, and for others it is included as part of a university curriculum. He complained that he could not get used to Irkutsk's only 45° below in the winter.

'Look,' he said, 'an English ship!'

We stopped the car. Up a small river was a two-funnelled steamer. British! The things I have seen the British leave around! A full-sized billiard table in perfect condition from Burroughs and Watts of Soho Square in a tiny Cambodian hamlet a hundred miles from a town, played on by locals naked to the waist who treated the table with utmost reverence; a 1922 Rolls-Royce without tyres in a Lapp Arctic field, not even a road or path for two hundred yards to show how it got there: and now a 1905 steamer two thousand kilometres from the nearest sea.

Valodia said: 'In 1891 the Trans-Siberian Railway was commenced in Vladivostok and Moscow at the same time. But the lines could not meet as Baikal and other water prevented it. That was the position until 1916. In the winter lines were laid on the frozen waters and the train got across. In the summer rafts were built with lines on them enough for one carriage at a time. The rafts were towed across to link up with lines on the other side. That steamer did the towing. How it got there no one has the slightest idea.'

'And now?'

'It's a holiday hostel. It's anchored. Been used like that for tens of years. By the way, did you know, you left something else behind,' smiled Nikolai. 'Your engineers left us with one of our most common words 'voksal', our word for 'station' from your word 'Vauxhall'. And the French left us with a word too. Napoleon ran out of his favourite sauce on his march on Moscow. A captain concocted what he could with what the field kitchens had to offer. The captain's name was Mayonnaise.'

38

Impossible not to think of 'Uncle', 'The Avengers' and many a fictional spy film. Here was I with four Russians entering a top sanatorium. No one else knew where I was. Place: Siberia. Circumstance: Czechoslovakia had been occupied by Russian forces and England had just denounced the act.

Up goes the schlagbaum.

The best doctors were waiting.

I was taken straight to the surgery. Many particulars were noted. All people were in white smocks.

But there was much yet still to do. Of Nikolai's four precious hours at the place of his dreams, three were taken up with the endless red-tape of getting me installed.

While waiting I was shown the V.I.P. houses. I sat on a bed Eisenhower had slept in, by a table Ulbricht had eaten at, on a lavatory Castro had squatted on: saw a room Mikoyan was expected in any day. All décor was formal, chairs were in rows, spruceness was harsh: I wondered if Germans had been let loose on the place. Beautiful billiard tables everywhere, great vistas of the lake from the windows, TV sets at every turn, neat, neat, neat: a Prussian grandeur, impressive but not homely.

Every moment of Nikolai's precious hours and days were spent trying to add this touch of splendour to my tour: all was completed with just time for lunch and then departure. We all dashed off to a lakeside restaurant and ate a meal for kings—kings who liked fish that is to say: and unique Baikal fish at that. Bottles brought all the way from Leningrad were produced.

For those who like nice touches here are three: first, Armenian cognac followed immediately by a wafer-thin slice of lemon with icing sugar sprayed on top: second, ditto, but add a sprinkle of coffee powder: third, wine as a sauce to ice-cream.

Nikolai is as interesting a person as I know in the Soviet Union: it was a pity to lose him so quickly. He is a communist. I am not. And there ends the difference between us.

39

The rains came. The lake disappeared in a mist. It was pointless to climb the hills behind and behold the famous views. I walked in the woods. Under the spell of Rawicz's masterpiece *The Long Walk* I had to see the sort of terrain he and his companions escaped through. Impossible to be in Siberia and not to think of the unfortunate multitudes who had suffered over the hundreds of years. Guilty or not guilty: right or wrong: who gives a damn for such empty phrases! Men suffered here. Why, near here, Rawicz and his friends disturbed the bushes and discovered the Polish woman hiding who joined them . . . Show me a shrub that has shielded a prisoner for a night and there let me raise my shrine.

They put me at a table with the most famous doctor and his most famous wife. The two of them took the Czecho-slovak question too easily: 'of course our government does right' 'some elements have got out of hand': it was too comfortable a conclusion, too 'obvious'. Nothing is 'obvious'.

Our waitress had an early-Bardot walk. She was seven-teen. Where her top lip joined her lower lip at either side were two wells the breadth of sixpences out of which smiles radiated in ever-increasing circles across her face lighting up anyone's spirit who happened to be noticing. Her smiles' time-table was two per minute. Any suitor must have only one ambition: to keep that time-table up to scratch.

No one will believe the next chapter. Yet it is true. I will try and tell it simply. It is called 'How to get into Outer Mongolia without a visa'.

40

Last year I was in a bus in Minsk with thirty tourists when I saw a beautiful face in a public garden. I stopped the bus, arranged with the Intourist guide to pick me up again at the main hotel in an hour and left.

The beautiful face had disappeared before I reached it.

I wandered. I saw a stationary car with G.B. on it. I approached it. The owners were a young couple, Michael and Jennie Sullivan. They had recently married in Moscow where they had worked in the British Embassy. They were motoring home to London. They had finished their spell in Moscow, had been bitten by a bug of interest in those parts of the world, and had asked for work in Mongolia. We kept up a rare correspondence. They got their work in the Embassy in Mongolia.

When I got my Churchill Award and knew roughly my route I immediately wished to visit Mongolia. There were two approaches: one on my own, one through the Sullivans. In theory Outer Mongolia is independent, in practice some reckon it is 90 per cent under the U.S.S.R. The Soviet Union and many other countries prefer foreign visitors who stay well clear of their Embassies. They are convinced that Embassies are hot-beds for spies, and tourists who have truck with them are the most suspected. So I was tempted to ignore the Sullivans.

It was not possible to ask for a Mongolian visa in London, there were no representatives. Application was to be made in Moscow three months in advance. Mongolia is almost the most difficult country to get into. For long periods of history it has been as closed as, and perhaps even more than, Tibet. From 1922–1952 not one Englishman set foot there. I hummed and ha-ed, then decided after all to make both approaches. The result was that on my own I would not have got anywhere, would not even have begun to get anywhere: that the door slowly became ajar was entirely due to the Sullivans. Which, gentlemen readers, proves this: always chase a beautiful face, you never know to what it might lead.

But even through diplomatic channels some of my letters took six weeks to reach the Sullivans. Then came the charming telegram that my visa had been granted and I could pick it up in Moscow.

In Moscow I got the address of the Mongolian Embassy and set out in a taxi. The taxi driver couldn't find it. I asked the police: they didn't know it. I decided to telephone and ask where they were. How to find the number? There are no telephone directories to look up. A Russian denied this to me, but I have never yet seen a telephone directory anywhere, not even in a post office, Embassy, hotel, tourist agency, or telephone kiosk in any single town: and I have been with Party officials who proudly pull out little notebooks of numbers they happen to know and can help you with, such as a hotel number. The most anyone has is a personal list. In leaving for this famous sanatorium near Baikal I had wanted to leave my number with Intourist at Irkutsk but no one had known it or could think of how to discover it.

Magically the number for the Mongolian Embassy turned up from a woman in an office: I phoned, found out the nearest Metro and set out for it. The stationmaster there, the passengers and the military, did not know the address. I saw a woman I thought was Mongolian and began to follow her. She did much window shopping and when I passed a post office I left her and asked there. An old lady of seventy overheard and left all her duties to take me to it. She adored the books of Cronin. She left me at the door of the Embassy with these words: 'You have given us literature, we have given you music.' As she said it, a woman sidled past. It was she who had been window shopping and had looked Mongolian.

The Mongolian Embassy knew nothing.

I telegraphed again to the Sullivans. Four days later they reiterated that the Embassy in Moscow had been told to grant me my visa.

But the Embassy didn't. They were friendly but had had no instructions. I phoned them twice every day. On the morning I was to leave they said: 'What's the hurry? You are not leaving till this evening, there's plenty of time. We will be in touch with Ulan Bator this afternoon. Come an hour or two before the train leaves.' But that was the same time as when the Russians wanted me to pick up my railway tickets. However, I tried . . . Telephone communications with Ulan Bator, they said, had broken down: the Embassy could not get through. No visa. 'Try in Irkutsk,' they said.

I telegraphed to the Sullivans.

In Irkutsk the Mongolian Consul had gone on his summer vacation. Not a soul could help. The hotels were full of people trying to get into Mongolia and the only person who might have helped them had gone off in the peak period for his holiday. A James Bosson from California had written a text-book for teaching Mongolian to foreigners which was used in Ulan Bator. The Mongolians were delighted with it and him. They told him so. But he never got in. He waited a week in Irkutsk while I was there, expecting to get in at $100 a day: then he returned to California. The Sullivans had warned me that the Mongolians would charge me £15 a day. That was the lowest figure I ever heard. £50 a day was a common price. Three American hunters got in at $800 a day each: all transport and porters and assistants were provided and an agreement included that they could bring out anything they shot. They stayed a week. I met them. They all looked like Hemingway. And they were the only people I did meet who got in.

The Russians all the time had told me I had no chance: I was wasting my every minute trying. And after four days of trying at Irkutsk to get through to the Sullivans by telephone and being told there never was an answer, I felt the Russians were blocking all my efforts. The Russians told me that the Embassy personnel lived in a hotel outside their Embassy where they never seemed to be. It turned out that they lived in an Embassy which was in a hotel they hardly ever left.

Then I sent still another telegram. I went to the sanatorium thinking I would carry on the battle from there, not realizing that I appeared to be 100 per cent cut off.

I lived on the third floor of the sanatorium and my room was near the end of a long corridor. At the very end a telephone was ringing. I paused at my door, thought, well, I might as well tell them there's no one around, and walked towards the ringing. It was in a tiny surgery in the very end room.

There was no one inside. I went in. I picked up the receiver.

'Is that you, Elvin?'

'Eh? Who? . . .'

'Sullivan. Michael Sullivan here.'

'Eh? What? . . .'

'It's about this visa . . .'

'Eh? Where? . . .'

'From Mongolia. I'm speaking from Mongolia.' Not even an operator had introduced us! There were 250 people in forty buildings in this sanatorium: it was in an isolated spot and forty miles from the hotel in Irkutsk where I was supposed to be staying.

'I'm sorry about all this trouble. You know the Irkutsk Consul's gone on holiday. Your visa turned up in Moscow the day after you left. The Foreign Minister here has instructed all border guards to let you in. You must come by train. Everyone on the border knows all about you and you'll have no trouble. It's an unprecedented business: nothing like it has ever happened before. I've brandished about the name of Churchill and everyone else for months. You'll be all right now.'

I got through to Valodia in Irkutsk. I never learned if I made these calls through the sanatorium, a post office, a local or district operator. I just picked up the receiver and began speaking. Valodia was pleased for me.

In an hour Valodia was back: Intourist would not issue a train ticket unless I had written evidence that I could enter Mongolia.

'But it's not their business,' I said. 'They take me to their border, the rest is up to me.'

'I can only tell you what I have been told to tell you.'

'Tell me this: can you send a telegram for me? Telephoning doesn't seem any good.'

'Yes, I can do that.'

I dictated a telegram to Sullivan.

Gone was any desire to enjoy Baikal; I was obsessed with getting into Mongolia. I wasn't going to leave the vicinity of that little surgery. Outside that odd little room was a giant chess set on a giant table. The pieces were twelve inches high. I found a boy of nine and asked him to play with me.

Why not? I left the boy to arrange the pieces, went back to the phone, and without any idea to whom I was speaking, said I wanted to speak to an Indian friend, Surya Kumari, in London.

The boy was a monster. He never took a piece but knocked it flying like a soldier in a battlefield. The floor became strewn with twelve-inch knights and bishops. I won. But that's only because he was nine. At ten I wouldn't have a hope. A strange lack of humour: he was ferocious. We had three games. It mounted all the time: he used his pieces like clubs: wallop! my poor pawn had gone twenty yards.

When he went, I played against myself, and then was joined by a battle-axe. It's unkind to call her a battle-axe because there never was a more well-meaning battle-axe. Her room was opposite the surgery and sometimes we sat in it. Someone looked in to tell us we shouldn't be in the room alone together after eleven, it was against the rules. It was then seven.

Soon I was telling her of my expected calls. She was all for Surya and had begged for a minute to speak to her herself. I stood guard over the phone when she went to supper and she stood guard while I went to supper—only to tell me that someone had come through and—instead of telling me!—she had explained that I was eating so would they phone again?

Did I like it there? I said the breakfasts were big. 'Fish and potatoes, followed by mutton and potatoes, followed by porridge and milk, then eggs stuffed with vegetables and meat and potatoes, then yoghurt . . . plus other snacks lying around. It's all so heavy!'

'This is a sanatorium. We build people up. You must eat it, it will do you good. Your friends who left you said you write. I write too. I am a Tartar. I wrote a book showing the hardships of the Tartar minority in Irkutsk. A small printing.'

'How many?'

'Only 30,000.'

'Our first printings are usually 3,000.'

'I don't believe it. You are the father nation for literature. I was paid badly.'

'How much?'

'Only £2,000 advance royalties.'

'We are lucky if we get £100. The Society of Authors states that of 1,500 authors, 500 get less than £1.10.0 a week for their writings, and 500 get less than £6.'

'I don't believe it. It cannot be true. I am not a recognized author. I am a schoolteacher. I have just retired at fifty-five and get £53 a month pension. My husband gets very good money. I will tell you about him if you'll come on a picnic with me tomorrow to see the views from the tops of the mountains.'

'What did you do with your £2,000?'

'I bought my house. It cost £1,250. And I took our family on a long holiday to Moldavia. But they should have reprinted. It was sold out in a month.* Everybody loved it. Everybody cried so much. People used to write: "I so loved your book. I have never cried so much." We in Russia are never more happy than when we are sad.'

Phone call. London. And although the Tartar authoress couldn't speak a word of English she clung within a yard of me and hung on every word. 'Tell her I send her my love. Tell her she is beautiful. Have you told her?' Surya said she was leaving for Madras and I said I'd telephone her there again from Tashkent.

The Tartar made tea in her room. She oozed friendship in a steam-roller way. She bludgeoned me with generosity: gave me her book, reviews of her book, apples, sweets, planned a dozen picnics.

Phone! 'I am John Hutchins. I work with Michael Sullivan. He asked me to give you this message.' Again I had got Mongolia: again no operator-introduction: again in that little surgery room at the end of nowhere. 'Look, Michael says there are two Queen's Messengers leaving for Irkutsk by air. Try and be at the airport at 8.30 in the morning to meet them. Much better if you do it personally. Michael has got the Foreign Minister himself to write a letter saying you are to be let in without a visa. The guards have all been told all about you.'

To get to the airport by 8.30 in the morning! There

* The Soviets do not print according to demand. A publication of *Alice in Wonderland* sold out in three days. There was no further edition. It's as if they decide in advance 'this work merits x thousand copies, no more, no less'.

were no buses, trains or cars . . . I got through to Intourist. Valodia's wife and his little child had arrived from Yakutsk and he had thrown a party. But Intourist would try to send him out to meet me in the morning.

I felt certain there'd be no Valodia and no car.

But there were both. 7.15 and waiting. Valodia had thought I was desperately ill. No one had told him why he should meet me.

We drove to the airport. I was not allowed to meet the English couriers. Valodia went in. He came out: 'I have the paper,' he said. 'It's in Mongolian. I'll show it to our border guards on duty at this airport. You can see your friends now.'

I shook two pairs of English hands. They had touched down for twenty minutes and were flying on to London.

Valodia said: 'That's the best and surest document the guards have ever seen. You're in for a certainty.'

Valodia, correct like a knife from the Russian point of view, took infinite delight when things went right for his tourists. He was more delighted than I was. I still held myself in check. I would believe nothing till I had crossed that border.

The Russians issued my train ticket, promised to phone up the Russian guards to tell them the story and offered me Valodia as a companion and witness, to explain things if any hitch cropped up. I accepted all with pleasure.

It always happened like that. Every time I made a conclusion about the Russians something happened next day to prove me wrong. I had been convinced that the Russians had blocked this at every point: now I was convinced that my suspicions had been ridiculous. Later, in Tashkent, I decided that the architects had failed the revolution, there wasn't one worthy building in the land. Then I saw three in a row. Big things and small things . . . my conclusion about the Soviet Union will be that there are no conclusions.

41

Valodia was not to come. His office had called me in. It would take more than three days for him to see me to the border and come back: whatever way they worked it out he would arrive back half an hour too late to meet seventy-four German tourists. Intourist were sorry. Valodia was sorry. I was sorry. To the last, Intourist were trying: they said they would tell the personnel on the train my situation. Actually they told no one on the train, nor anyone at the border, nor anyone anywhere: but I am certain a link in the chain went wrong and that they had been genuine.

Valodia was furious he could not get me in the First Class and that it was a slow train. I said the worse the class the better the people, and the slower the travelling the nearer it got to the only true pace at which a man should travel, which was walking.

'Not cycling?' he asked.

'Cycling is good because that way the cycle carries the luggage: but anything faster than walking is an insult to the territory you pass over.'

My seat was occupied. He flung two other people's luggage out, then the people out. There were screams. Everything except blows. Valodia stood like a rock, heard nothing, occasionally said a nicety to me. If I was to live in Russia I'd model myself on Valodia. Almost all Russians shout and scream: if you keep track of one for just a few hours you will see him or her shout, scream, cry, whisper, whimper, laugh, ogle . . . every emotion that it takes an Englishman a year to get through is experienced by half this race in hours. No wonder they are good actors, they only have to be themselves. Valodia played his part, but he was always right. Those other two had no proper tickets. And Valodia had no fear. He bulldozed his way through any situation he felt was correct: something else he had done for someone else had infuriated half the station. He stood unperturbed, tall, powerful, a fortress silent among a howling mob. A certain young lady from Yakutsk had got herself a damn good husband. A man so strong he could afford to be weak.

'What about your future plans?' he asked me.

'Cancel Baikal, Bratsk, Irkutsk and Novosibirsk. If I get into Mongolia I must lose out on all of those. That's nothing. Your country is easy to come to, Valodia, all I have to do is to win the Pools' (they have State Lotteries in Russia). 'But winning the Pools a dozen times over might not get me into Mongolia.'

Slow train to Ulan Bator. We pulled out.

In less than ten minutes the scenery grew exciting.

Would I cross the border?

42

It was to be a thirty-six-hour journey and there was no restaurant car: knowing that, I had fed myself up like a snake in Irkutsk, having two ample meals one after the other.

The two men Valodia had slung out slunk back again

and settled. A boy was asleep above my head. First stop already! A place called Goncharov. The scenery was beginning to look like the Tyrol: then it got more stretched out. There came a house painted white and veridian green, and another white and Oxford blue: why don't they all do it? It was so rare to see any paint on a house and so happy a sight to see.

When the dark came I lay down to sleep with my head towards the window. Above me the boy had his head also towards the window and his father, sharing his bunk, had his own head towards the door. Then I changed ends. The father asked me why. 'There's a draught by the window,' I said. Like a shot from a gun the father was up and turned his boy round. He might face the draught, but not his son!

I lay, eyes open, listening to the beautiful singing going through the loudspeakers. A forty-year-old engineer burst in. 'Hallo, Englishman, when are you going to build your tunnel?'

I said I hoped, never: I wanted to reach France by bridge.

'Do you know, Englishman, they are going to build a bridge from North Africa to Spain? Is our Metro better than yours?'

'Leningrad's Metro is fantastic and more exciting technically than Moscow's. But all of yours should be better than ours: they are so recent. We were at it 100 years ago.'

'I know. The Metropolitan through Baker Street 1863. You know, Englander, when this line was built? In 1937. No railways in Mongolia before then. Ulan Bator, then called Urga, was just a monastery centre in those days.'

'Are you English?' the two 'intruders' asked.

And we were off. First the personal questions and then London. Everyone wanted to know about London.

I have already doubled my salary and procured an English wife and two splendid children since beginning this journey. I am mostly a freelance in life but telling Russians of my salary when employed I grew tired of agreeing with everyone that the salary was abominably low and so I have doubled it to match up with theirs. I grew tired also of explaining my matrimonial affairs and found that a loving English wife and a boy and a girl, sometimes infants and sometimes teen-aged, dispensed with the subject quickest.

'Why haven't you brought your wife with you?'

'I couldn't afford to. You are supposed to be a country with a love for the poor man and the working classes: do you know in your country now you charge me a minimum of £10 a day and I have never done any other long journey in our wicked capitalist world on more than £3 a week?—twenty-three times cheaper.'

'That's impossible!'

'It isn't. I camp out. That's free. You make me stay in expensive hotels. In 1935 I bicycled to Russia: it cost me £1 a week. Then I entered Russia and it cost £1 a day—seven times dearer. You had your revolution for the working classes. Do you realize you have never had a poor foreigner, one of your kind as it were, here in fifty years? Only the wealthy or the near wealthy can come to see you.'

'Is it our fault if our country is dear for outsiders?'

'Of course it is. You make the rouble any value you like. When I was here in the war you gave us in the Embassy 100 roubles to the £1. Journalists, who you less wanted, got 50 to the £1; a military mission got 25; but fur buyers and sausage-skin buyers, who you wanted very much got 200 to the £1. Now the rate is 2 to the £1 and your net is for rich tourists. If you wanted to show your land to our poorest classes, which is after all what your revolution was supposed to be about, you could make the rouble suit their pockets. That's beautiful singing on the radio.'

'It's not the radio! Come with me!' the engineer cried.

He took me down the corridor, the music increasing in volume. We entered the small room of the two women guards. It was them singing!

'But you sounded like a choir! The Piatnitsa Choir,' I said.

The samovar was on. Tea was on. And singing was on. The gay engineer played with his fingers like castanets: but it blended, it helped. And others came to the doors. Soon it was a full house.

And singing went our train through the night to Mongolia.

43

The sun was up betimes and the terrain played glorious. The samovar boiled at the end of the corridor and we all got tea.

Biscuits and apples and tea and a woman opposite talking. I wanted to stand by the windows to drink in the skin-soft hills but I sat and listened to the sorrows of the colonel's wife. At some time in the night the 'intruders' had got their final quitting orders—they hush whispered to me that they were getting off at dusk on a fishing exploit anyhow, so not to worry—and a Red Army colonel and his wife with an Everest of luggage came in.

'Always, always moving!' the thick-set, formidable colonel's wife was saying. 'When will we have a settled life? Years in China before the war, years in the Arctic, years at Baku, now we're off to the Gobi.'

'At least he takes you with him.'

'Oh yes. But then we are stationed. Ten years here, five there. Home is in Kiev and that's where my children are and there's where I want to be. I want to be with my children's children: there are two of them now.'

She showed me their photos. I lied: I said they were bonny: but there have scarcely been a dozen in history who, at minutes old only, haven't looked like squirts out of a tube.

'Then you must look forward to your husband's retirement,' I said.

'He *is* retired. Seven years on a pension.'

'Then why this move?'

'It's all this trouble. All this Czechoslovak trouble. Everyone has to help.'

The Gobi? They were going to a camp 500 kilometres west of Ulan Bator. The government must have expected more trouble than had as yet accrued: their making a special announcement of it on the radio had indicated that.

Among the luggage were a hundred eggs.

'My husband knows the camp. He knows everywhere. He says in Mongolia there's mutton, mutton, mutton, and scarcely a thing besides. Eggs are rationed, and at that not always obtainable. I thought Mongolia was hot, did you?'

'I was certain of it. Even in Irkutsk everyone asked me if I could stand the heat.'

'It isn't hot at all, you know?'

'People on this train have been telling me. But cold doesn't fit in with the picture I had always had.'

The colonel joined us. An extravert, stocky but of a fair height too, wearing glasses: thorough, he organized everything, the monumental luggage, his wife, we fellow passengers, he took us all on. Sixty-two and guardian, father and friend to everyone. Even the 'singing guards' must have lost some of their 'guard' influence when we took on this newcomer.

'Cold it can be,' he said. 'Minus 60° I have had there. The average for the year is minus 2°. It can be hot, scorching: but two items are constant, winds and sudden changes. Winds are always blasting through, dust and sand-storms too: while, change? you wait, you will not believe it: you can be hot in your shirt one minute and screaming cold for your overcoat the next.'

'How do they get about in the winter?'

'Oh, no snow-shoes or skis or sledges. Oh no. Very little snow and the wind blows that around. No, oh no, it's the horses: they can manage. Hard ground, soft ground, grass or ice, they can do it. The only horses in the world who don't alter their pace going downhill. Take you down a mountain at the same steady pace they will. They run, you know. Don't gallop or trot. They run: level, you know; tailored into the landscape: keep as level as this train we're on now. Look more like ponies than horses. Shaggy they are, shaggy. Tails to the ground they have, to the ground. Kids of three ride them. An annual race every year in the capital: who for? For ten-year-olds and under. Never grown-ups. Why not you ask? Yes, you ask? Because they're testing the horses, they say: all Mongolians can ride: there are none better than others: there's no sense to testing riders. There's not one will fall off breaking-in a new horse. Tell that to your American comrades eh, my friend? Not one. Ever. Kids of three ride, kids of four chop wood, kids of five fix up a tent. Ah! here! you should photograph this!' He was up, hurrying me to the corridor window. So the colonel didn't know the rules! I photographed it. Woods a tornado had torn through. Cedars down like nine-pins, and the way that at one point all trees had fallen to the left on one side and to the right on the other, it was as if a giant cyclops had scythed through.

The wood got left. In an hour we were back to hills as never-ending as a chain of sausages. Sometimes we passed some geese and very often turkeys. But never in ones: always in hundreds.

A wheatfield scrambling up a blue hill and at the base a thousand—there couldn't be less—goats.

Everything was in herds or hordes. Cows, horses: someone had been rounding up the West for a mammoth movie. And more turkeys: out and about: what would they be talking about four hours from Mongolia, with the sun, spacious gossiping areas, and not an enemy in sight?

Our fourteen-carriage train thrust its nose into space, space, space. Steam all the way: the titan engine exuding fat white giant woollen sheep putting them out to graze in tapestries of everlastingness.

This was big. What an extraordinary adjective to give to landscape. But this was so big. Pushed back, pushed out, no doll's house or pretty pretty postcard scenes these. Grey hills, green hills, blue hills, shadows of clouds like dinosaurs over them: 90 per cent beauty and 10 per cent awe. Awe because these scenes were not of us . . . a broken heart in England can seek some balm walking in the countryside: break your heart here and find another shoulder for your tears, for this landscape wants none of you, you are a neuter, you're with the ants or a grain of corn, you are a part of the landscape, a neuter mote with all the other neuter motes: this is removed from you, will give no solace, will tell of eternity and cares for no other subject.

Almost my favourite book is *The Wind in the Willows*. But I could not have read it here.

Climb a hill in Wales and you know that corner of Wales and feel you belong. Climb a hill here, and it would be the same as climbing any of a thousand, and you will never belong. The vineyards can change the look of Italy, the orange groves can change the face of Cyprus: but farmers and cultivators galore here could leave no more effect on the scene than pimples on an elephant's back. Change here comes in aeons of time, not in decades.

So soft the colours now. Brass and silver and platinum sound like glossy metallic colours: and there was much of brass and silver and platinum in the brown fields, the grey hills and the long rivers: but these browns were warm as rugs, the greys were dovelike, the white rivers ran with silk.

I have never travelled across Eternity in a train before.

44

Approaching the border now and I was getting apprehensive.

'How's my dear Epsom?' It was the engineer who had come to join me by the window. 'I'm in love with Epsom,' he said, 'and would like to die there. I'm mad on horse-racing. I've been in England, spent every minute of my time I could at race meetings but loved especially Epsom. I don't bet much. The atmosphere of places like that just suits me. Do give my love to Epsom, will you Englander? You know, Englander, I'm not Russian, not really, in spite of my name, Ragosin. It's a very long and complicated story; I'm only sort of Russian. Do you mind if I talk seriously to you?'

What a curve our train was making. I resisted the urge to photograph it; border territory was no territory for my camera now.

'About Czechoslovakia. You are at it again.'

'England? What are England at?' I asked.

'Never giving the Russian point of view. I've been in England. Can I explain myself?' He had become another man and very earnest. 'Fifty years ago here we had a revolution. Now if you could look at the whole from another planet or another point of history, it was a worthy revolution for a worthy cause. We here will for ever find it incomprehensible that endless millions throughout the world did not see it as worthy. Christ, Buddha, Mohammed and all the great do-gooders of the last milleniums if they exist would be sitting somewhere and saying "Ah, now this is something. This is a real revolution: a hammer-stroke for humanity." But the followers of all those do-gooders, and the followers of all other worthy creeds, were against us at that moment and still are. Now you might say we haven't lived up to our pretensions: that as I see it, Englander, would make no difference: the world was against us in our fantastic gesture for the benefit of all mankind and still is and still would be if the Soviet Union had been turned into a paradise on earth. We make a move in Czechoslovakia and out comes all your scorn, all the clichés of condemnation that have been in your hearts since our beginning. Clichés like the Russians setting their sights on world communist conquest when you know well that it was because of Trotsky's world communism and Stalin's saying that communism in one land would do that Trotsky had to leave our country. Since then the old cry is dead except that you won't let it lie down. Because you know that it is a cry that creates tension. If we had given every Czech a million pounds you would have found some way of condemning it. What I am hitting you for, Englander, is not whether our country does right or wrong, but because, whether we do do right or wrong, you in the West consistently insist that it is wrong. I will explain Czechoslovakia in a minute. May I continue? You are not angry with me? I want first to explain how I mean. I mean that you in the West, even especially England, are proud of the fact that you think you always hear all points of view. You kid yourselves. Englander—I call you that, I don't know your name—I told you mine, didn't I? Ragosin—there has not been one issue ever on which your people has been told the Russian point of view. Your facts can be right: but the interpretation never and they are mean and intentionally deceiving. A small thing first: Mr Kruschev goes to an exhibition of modern art in Moscow and slates it. But he went! He honoured it with his presence. Do your queens and Prime Ministers go? You hinted all the artists would be banished. What nonsense.

The exhibition continued successfully for ages. Now a big example. Hitler invaded Poland in 1939 and Russia attacked from the other side. Your whole outcry was that we stabbed Poland in the back. Why did you say that? Your press knew the truth. After the Revolution Russia was weak and Poland stole our territory up to Minsk ignoring the line, the Curzon Line, that your own Lord Curzon had laid down as a just border. In that section of Poland up to Minsk Russians outnumbered Poles by 4:1. When Hitler attacked Poland the Red Army moved up to the Curzon Line, up to our lawful territory, and not one step over. After the war Roosevelt and Churchill, I believe, unhesitatingly accepted the Curzon Line, which had for more than a century been the true border. Yet you called it, with all the abuse and venom possible, a stab in the back. Call it that too if you must, if that's your point of view, but why must you never once also put the Soviet viewpoint?'

Half an hour to the border.

'Now: Czechoslovakia. We have created what we think a political unit of socialist nations. Some people in one nation want to pull their country out of it. We think, and we think the majority of the Czechs think, that would be a mistake. What did you do when India wanted to leave the Empire? You put Gandhi and Nehru and others in prison for ten and fifteen years. You kept the established state of things by force.'

'It was a long time ago.'

'That is nonsense, my friend, and you must realize it is so. All countries are in a different point in history. What is a point in history for you is different for an American, an African, a Russian. You are an old nation; we are young. We want to establish our order and not to see it toppled. What did you do in Cyprus? Supposing Hong Kong or Gibraltar rose up tomorrow and you sent your troops in. Would your papers scream about the brutal British occupation of Hong Kong or Gibraltar? Of course not, they would say that elements inside were being encouraged from elements outside, and your troops would fill the place up to ensure order for what, you would claim, the majority wanted.'

Fifteen minutes to go to the border. I interrupted: 'Politics and chess,' I said, 'are games milleniums old. The players change, but the rules remain the same. And in both there are pawns and there are kings and queens. A pawn starts off on one or the other side, is used, then sacrificed for the kings and queens. But all true men—which I hope includes you and me—feel for the pawns. Russia and England are not the pawns. The only people who matter in the present dispute are the pawns, the Czech people. I have heard there is uranium in Czechoslovakia. Have you heard that?'

'No.'

'If it's true it could explain some of the concern from both sides, couldn't it? Because politics are just a blind. They are façades for which wars hot and wars cold are waged. Behind the façades are power, avarice, aggrandizement: but no populace will die for such causes so they have to be fed façades, now politics, sometimes religions, sometimes patriotisms. Fascist Spain today has great trade with Russia: what's happened to the politics? America has little trade with China and refuses to recognize it: yet recognizes almost every other dictatorship: what's happened to the politics? Why this tremendous upsurge about Czechoslovakia? Few are dead: though both the Soviet Union and the West treat it with more moral indignation than Vietnam and Biafra where millions are dying. There's probably something behind the façade and it may be uranium. To hell with façades and to hell with politics. What matters is this: if there was a free vote tomorrow almost certainly 95 per cent of the Czechs would vote for an independent development in a state of peace.'

'But you miss the Russian point of view again. For instance, if Wales wanted to be free from England, England dare not allow it.'

'Why not? We've dared to accept it for half of Ireland. The Welsh are realistic people: if there was a vote I think 95 per cent would stay with England for reasons of logic. If you've heard any noise to the contrary it's because the 5 per cent are very vociferous. And perhaps because you'd like us split.'

'You still miss our point.' We were drawing in at the border station. 'We are a young bastion of socialist brotherhood in a new ideal. We must defend it if it weakens in any cornerstones, because we have always had the world outside against us and still have.'

'Certainly, we rarely, perhaps never, put your point of view in our press,' I said. 'Yet we might also ask, how often in your press have you put England's point of view?'

'Always!' he half shouted.

'Always?!'

'Yes always if it's the World Cup!' He was laughing loudly. 'We were with you to a man, English point of view to a man, against Germany in that final! Can't have Germany winning at that! Can I buy you a beer?'

The train had stopped.

45

The colonel, I felt, was trying a little too hard to help me at the border.

When asked what I had photographed he replied for me: 'Just a few scenes here and there. Nothing to worry about.'

When asked if I had many films he replied for me, 'Only a few.'

If they had searched they would have found enough for a thousand pictures, half already used. I felt uneasy and that I would lose them all.

When asked how much Russian money I had on me, I said seven roubles, and the colonel explained I was returning and would need it. At this point the officials were getting annoyed with the colonel, said they must take my money: he spoke up saying I would need a little to buy food with before meeting up with a bank when I returned. They stuck to their point and from then on, for all his perfect intentions, I felt glad the colonel didn't interfere. I told the authorities that I knew I must surrender my money in return for hard currency but it had been the Irkutsk officials who had said I should keep anything less than ten roubles.

I now realized for the first time that I was losing my Russian visa: leaving the country meant its automatic cancellation. Mongolia had China on one side and Russia on the other: and I, soon to have no visas for either. Interesting.

'You have a visa for Mongolia?'

'Yes.'

I lied. If they had asked to see it I would have said my document equalled a visa, but I was relieved they never asked.

They didn't look at the luggage. They rarely do: but if they do, they do it minutely.

They took my passport and disappeared for an hour. They would see there was no Mongolian visa, but Russian visas were on loose sheets never stamped in the passports, so perhaps Mongolian visas were too.

The taller of the women train guards invited me to join her in the restaurant for a meal. The meal was very wonderful but there was not a thing to drink, neither water, mineral, beer nor spirits. I showed sorrow at this. And there were nineteen bottles of lemonade awaiting me from various passengers when I returned to the train.

The 'singing guards' . . . I must describe them. Imagine a female Laurel and Hardy. Spit and image Laurel and Hardy.

Then imagine that Hardy has the falsetto, the soprano voice; and Laurel the deep, the alto. Then imagine that they never sing without staring each other fixedly in the eyes. Hardy offered to pay for my meal thinking I had surrendered my money. But I still had my meal coupons.

More than two hours we waited in that station!

Then we pulled out through thick jungle through a very long no-man's-land. How long? Possibly even seven miles. Possibly more.

I was out. But was I in?

46

What a change! The Mongolians! They looked like barbarian bears. And then they smiled. And smiled. And smiled. And never stopped. Children, all. Yes, they were all Jenghis Khan: in appearance. But in fact they were great homely, welcoming children.

The officials came. They took my Foreign Minister's paper.

The mosquitoes were enormous, vicious and millionfold. Couldn't stand on the station though we tried to: the mosquitoes drove us back to our train.

So we waited. Another two hours we waited.

Three officials came back. Gave me my passport, shook my hand, gave me the Foreign Minister's letter and smiled and smiled and smiled.

I'm in!!

'Have you got a cigarette?' I asked the engineer.

'I thought you said you never smoked?'
I don't. But how hell else to celebrate? Tobacco: I love you: even if you are my rare one. What a cigarette!

47

An umbrella, flapping loose, its owner in grey flannels, hurrying—with a stoop because that's the way he had of hurrying—hurrying because the train was in and he had scarcely time to park his Land-Rover . . . Michael Sullivan is no Terry Thomas but he stood out among those milling Mongolians on the platform as every bit as much an Englishman as ever Terry Thomas has.

It was another world and that was good because there had been too much of sameness in the Soviet Union.

The Embassy was in a hotel: only three were in it at that time, the Sullivans and John Hutchins. But that was more than other Embassies had. The British to their credit had not only been the first western Embassy in Mongolia (in 1961) but it remained the only one with permanent residents. Forty-two countries had some sort of representation but the Americans (why not?) didn't recognize the country at all. Sullivan was Chargé d'Affaires and the Ambassador was in London and I was given the Ambassador's suite, grand piano, car, golf clubs (which I didn't use), detergents (which I did use). I also had the Ambassador's photographs of Harold Wilson, and the Queen sometimes crowned and sometimes not, watching over me from every wall. And I had bacon and eggs. And coffee. Perhaps the stomach should not have pride of place in life but the young and beautiful Jennie Sullivan's cooking made me think it could have if she was to play host to it. There was not much to cook with: for seven months the Sullivans had not had greens, the markets offered little beyond meat, and little meat beyond mutton, the necessities of eating as the English knew them were difficult to come by, and what did reach them did so mainly from Copenhagen. Even rice, potatoes, milk, bread, all were rare. The Polish Embassy hadn't even got water: water was delivered to them every morning by a water-cart and, as Sullivan said, the procedure looked like London in the eighteenth century.

The Sullivans were mad. Mad about music. Oh happy madness. Two pianos, a silent key-board to practise on, tapes galore and records galore.

John Hutchins was going out so I went with him. In the Bank I waited seated at a table filled with magazines. But every magazine turned out to be a *Labour Monthly* from London and every copy was pre-1964: so I read what Palme-Dutt, Ivor Montagu and Bernal thought of our world long ago.

In the post office I spent my time entranced before the clock. In this, perhaps the most cut-off capital in the world, was a wonderful clock within a wonderful clock, the inside one registering the time at twenty-four different other corners of the globe.

In the store I spent my time bewitched before Mongolians. There was little to buy: no eggs, which was what John had hoped for, a great amount of bread which was selling fast, and little else. But every Mongolian was a prize. National costumes still, national features the same down the neverending centuries, plus the ever-ready smile which the portraits of Jenghis and Timur had never shown.

In the bookshops two-thirds of the books were in Russian.

In the streets half of the houses were tents. The Mongolian tent is a yurt, a large circular affair with one to five layers of felt inside as walls according to the temperature, and the Mongolians, disdaining apartments that the authorities were encouraging them to accept, brought their yurts up to within 200 yards of the central square of their capital—wigwams off Times Square.

In the city, still in embryo, most of the fascination was in the faces and the costumes of its inhabitants. Why do we delight in finding corners which won't accept our 'civilization'? Perhaps because of the joy of finding people who insist upon remaining themselves. That the Japanese and the Indians wear shirts and trousers means they have lost a little of being Japanese and Indian. Go to Mongolia: and see where the national costume is still every day's for every man.

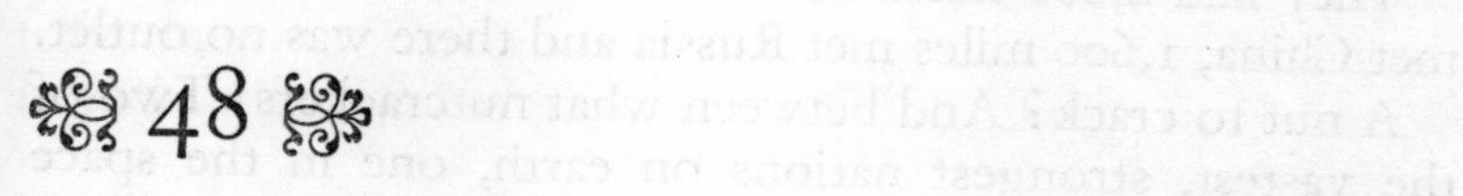

We left for the motor-cycle scrambling. John Hutchins, half Dane and half English, golden blond hair and on his first post abroad, filled his Land-Rover with foreigners and drove us over. Good that we took the long road round; three lorries attempting the crossing of the low river Tola got stranded forty yards from shore and spent the afternoon there.

Czechoslovakia and Poland and Russia and Mongolia were to compete with teams of twenty in each. Three races of ten times round the course. The course went everywhere, up hills, round them, down them, diving to hair-raising dips, rising off heights so that the machines took off as from springboards, man and machine flying upwards united as one and coming down sometimes disunited as two. Crowds four deep here, ten deep there, wound around and about forming the edges of what looked like monster-sized nets with the action caught inside. Horses joined the crowd, staring nonchalantly at these barbaric machines from the modern world, an intrusion on their dominance for millenniums. No cheering or shouting from the crowd: just clapping as motorized beetle ran rearing roaring raring after motorized beetle in this battle of the nations.

Higher hills towered round, some horses awaiting owners mustering in a cluster up one: yurts for competitors like a row of white cotton reels up another.

100,000 watched. Battle was being done.

100,000.

Less than 1¼ million Mongolians in the world and a twelfth, a Wembley Stadium load, were here. Twelve Wembley Stadiums' full equalled Mongolia.

They had 4,000 miles of border and no sea. 2,400 miles met China, 1,600 miles met Russia and there was no outlet.

A nut to crack? And between what nutcrackers! Two of the vastest, strongest nations on earth, one in the space race, one in the atom bomb business. And this 1 million still with its horses and its tents. Surely the easiest nut to crack? At some time or the other one of the nutcrackers has temporarily subdued the nut, but the nut at other times has cracked both sides of the nutcracker together.

6,000 years ago these people grew wheat out of grasses by the Gobi desert and gave wheat to the world.

4,000 years ago these people gave the tamed horse to Europe with the saddle which they invented.

In its entire history scarcely any Mongolians have been known to leave their country at their own instigation and the one notable exception who did conquered four-fifths of the known world. Jenghis Khan.

700 years ago from these very tents with such horses he, with his Mongolians, made all men tremble for more than a hundred years.

Now, in our time, they are being shown the blessings of twentieth-century civilization and being courted desperately by both sides of the nutcracker, China and Russia and half of the rest of the world besides and they are resisting all as the world's ever toughest most incredible nut.

Twelve Wembley stadiums' full, of which one is here watching with solid, stolid, childlike, titan-like, hero-like joy, four countries helter-skeltering over its hills on solid, stolid, titan hero-like motor-cycles.

This country, besides being strategically placed, is rich in gold, iron, zinc, copper, oil, coal and asbestos, and other countries would like a little gold, iron, zinc, copper, oil, coal and asbestos, but unfortunately for them the Mongolians are more interested in smiling, smoking and savouring the passage of time. Mongolia also has the world's greatest supplies of dinosaur skeletons but having collected one for a museum for Ulan Bator from a valley by the Gobi the Mongolians see no point in collecting a second.

They have no postal service. How could they have? They have almost no streets and almost no houses, and both street and house (being a yurt) could be up tomorrow and away. They have started a Poste Restante service in the capital's post office.

They have no roads. How can they have, when streets and houses move how can a road know where to go? Even a car, like the Ambassador's, takes to the fields after a very short spell: it can keep vaguely to old caravan routes marked at great distances by gigantic cairns—everybody has to add a stone as he passes—and the only way to know the way is to keep your eyes on the next cairn a skyline distant.

Motor-cycles get around. They are bullies of machines and look incongruous parked outside the yurts. I poked my head in a yurt and saw two brass bedsteads out of a novel by Dickens looking more incongruous still. Yurts are almost all fifteen feet across, mostly without beds or chairs, a fire in the middle, a pot, a tureen, a jug, one wooden box for everybody's wardrobe, mats for sleeping and sitting on, no other furniture, no utensils, each Mongol carrying his own wooden cup inside his bosom and his own knife. No toilet services ever. All sleep in their clothes.

There's little water and most of what there is the animals need. People drink mare's milk. There's little fuel. Cow-dung, smell and all, burns continuously in the centre of the yurt. There's enough mare's milk and enough cow-dung because there are at least thirty head of cattle per person.

Until recently half of all Mongolians born died before three. Medicine creeps in slowly.

But observers vary in assessments. Some say that houses are fast replacing yurts, factories are being filled, nomadism is being replaced by settled co-operatives. Others declare that as soon as the foreign experts leave the factories the workers are away and the factories fall to ruin: that there never has been and never will be a Mongolian who sees the point of work: that medicine makes no progress and central heating and brick walls and mod-cons are unwanted and unvalued.

Experts argue. Communists claim they have made a further conquest: though one Soviet official told me: 'All Mongolians and Cubans are lazy and we cannot continue to carry them for ever.'

I could only listen to both sides and look. I saw yurts all over the main city: I saw strong and happy faces: I didn't see one person 'enjoying' work. It remains the last stronghold of the wild horse. It remains the greatest remaining stronghold of national costume and custom.

This surely is an independent people?

But there are not only those who question the state of the present, but those also who question the state of the past. Has it really always been yurts and horses? There are legends of wondrous cities and there are ruins of some and remnants of others. When the country came under communist influence in 1921 there were 1,818 temples and 747 lama monasteries, lamaism being a binding force, and one-third of the population were priests. Now there are 300 priests.

Another mystery are the reindeer races, the Tsatangs, in the north-west: the only place where white reindeer are natural white and not so from winter camouflage. The Tsatangs build tents identical to those of the Lapps. So did the Lapps and the reindeer come from Mongolia? Some say yes. Many a European Lapp looks Mongolian. Also European Lapps like to be called Samma, while the word for a Siberian-Mongolian is Samoyed.

So much mystery in this beautiful, hard, remote land, with the bluest blue skies ever known.

And the motor-bikes roar up and down and over, and a Russian has won the first race and a Pole the second, but the Mongolians are leading in the last.

I set off over the hills photographing. A white horse with sandy mane and sandy tail to the ground was surveying the scene and I turned to take his picture. He turned too and posed a perfect silhouette filling half the frame and the scrambling races and the 100,000 crowd were caught tiny between his mouth and foreleg. The two leader motor-cycles rushed up near us and the Mongolian had now dropped four yards behind a Pole.

'Who is winning?' a group asked me, speaking Russian. And I explained the colours of the jackets denoting the nationalities.

A young soldier in khaki with forage cap stood with his arm about an Amazon in a lush green satin del.

The Mongolian dress is called a del. It is worn by men and women. It is tight about the neck, held at the waist by a sash and drops well below the knees. In the summer it is of silk, cotton or wool. In the winter it is lined with sheep-skin, goatskin or wolf's fur. The dresses are richly adorned, more so the younger the wearer, and still more so if the young wearer is married. Furs usually line the sleeves and often the base of the dress. Sleeves are long. The dress is double-breasted buttoning on the right. Brocade is common especially about the collar.

In the winter a wadded coat of lambskin or sheepskin is worn. Pelts from corsacs, lynxes, wolverenes, raccoons, foxes, sables are used. Outside, the whole coat might be covered by silk, satin, cotton or tussore.

It was still summer but only just, so that I was able to see some autumn and winter clothes among the thousands as well as the summer ones.

If Bernard Shaw had been with me and if he had known as much about Mongolian costume as about English dialects and accents he could have told me by observance of the colour, style, ornamentation, width and fashion and trimmings of borders, the variance of waistcoats worn over the dels, and the difference in ear-rings and jewellery, the age group of the wearer, the season of the dress, and the race he or she came from: that blue and brown meant a Khalka, that blue alone meant a Buryat, that the darkest colours were of a Khoton, that a thin strip of black velvet trimming the border if cut rectangularly might be a Turgut, if obliquely cut perhaps a Barga, that if a woman's sleeves had horizontal pleats they would be of a Khalka and if vertical pleats then of a Mingat.

A heavenward-pointed peak of a cap on a cupola-shaped base symbolized joy and prosperity: an eyelet on an upper part of a cap symbolized the moon, and a knot on a cap meant simplicity and strength.

Coral ornaments were worn by the Uzumchins and the Darigangas, gold, silver and pearls by the Khalkas.

Even more distinctive than the costumes were the hats and boots, though almost all boots were high up to the knee and had turned-up toes.

For national occasions the Mongolians liked to portray animal features in their costumes, hair forced out as cow horns, shoulders padded and humped as bull shoulders.

The finest designs of all were in the tobacco pouches. Almost all men carried tobacco pouches, and sheaths conining knives and, to this day, steel for striking fire.

If a person wanted to he could see traces of Chinese, Japanese, Russian, Polish and even Viking influence in the costumes: but it was more possible that all those peoples, and others besides, have all learnt from the Mongolians and not vice versa.

The Mongolian motor-cyclist had regained the lead in this last race and the Pole was again second but I hardly noticed as I tried to photograph without being observed.

Men walked like ducks, the women waddled, all were ungainly except when on horseback. All had leathern faces that centuries of sun and driving wind and cold had fashioned. Old men often had beards and if they were not philosophical then appearances have lost all meaning. No one under fifty had a beard and it is even said they would have difficulty growing one. All had high cheekbones, oblique elongated eyes dark and piercing, flat noses, large ears and strong black straight hair.

49

I am an authority on Embassies having been a nightwatchman in one for years. I don't know why Whitehall thinks that their Ambassadors know best the Embassies they work in: it's the nightwatchmen who really know. I was courting a Russian girl once when she was called in for questioning by the N.K.V.D. (Russian Secret Police). They said, didn't she know, all foreigners were spies? She burst out laughing: 'Him! a spy? He's only the nightwatchman!' 'Our top man in Paris,' they said, 'is the nightwatchman.' We, the nightwatchmen, knew who the Ambassador's friends were—and Sir Stafford Cripps didn't have a quarter as many as he thought; we knew the keen of work—and there was one; we knew the lovers of the land they were in, Russia—and there were none: and Bill, my mate, and I sickened at the affectation of the diplomats at the hardships of their jobs—what no chocolate bourbons? what no pâté de foie gras? what, no Bronco? Christ what a war!

The Sullivans however made no bones about it: they loved Moscow, they adored Ulan Bator. No greens for seven months? If that was the price for being in Mongolia it was worth it. They were English to the core; pukkah to the core; yet unaffected to the core.

The English have a knack of bringing a happy incongruity to a scene. And here was Sullivan with his Chopin *Studies* and his Schubert *Impromptus*. Precise, serious, sensitive playing . . . incongruous because it was an opposite sanity to the sanity of Mongolia. The sanity of Mongolia is its outdoorness. Most countries have come in from the out-of-doors, got snug in houses and created an art which is part of the snugness. Chopin is drawing-room matter, not steppe and desert matter. Look at the costumes and the faces and the yurts and the decorated saddles and the love for the horses here: and then think of Canaletto, Fragonard, Chopin, Galsworthy, and you realize that almost all our creative endeavours are wrapt around in a sort of shelter-cover: they are cosy. Henry Moore wants his sculptures shown out of doors: is it an instinct to get back to the point where we began? Mongolia is not cosy: it's Life with scarcely a single trapping. Mongolia must be the greatest outdoor nation there is. Chopin and Schumann are at the heights of the indoor world. That's why Sullivan's playing in Ulan Bator had a double force, a double need, a double sanity.

On the radio that night we picked up four announcements. The United States President announced that the bombing of North Vietnam would continue and was highly congratulated: France had made a new bomb test in the desert and was highly congratulated: Nigeria was to continue to get her arms supplied and should finish off Biafra and was highly congratulated: the Soviet Union had called the leaders of Czechoslovakia to Moscow for talks and were highly condemned. Hallelujah! more will be killed in Vietnam: hallelujah! France has increased our already overloaded skies with more killing fall-out: hallelujah! another million will be bombed to death in Biafra: boo! the Soviet Union are talking instead of killing. How wrong was Engineer Ragosin?

I tortured myself till 1.0 a.m. trying to keep a contact going with the Far Eastern Service of the B.B.C. because England were beating Australia in a Test Match. With Australia 118 for 8 in their last innings and with only twenty minutes to play, the Far Eastern Service closed down. And they did it so nonchalantly. I tried endless Chinas, Russias, Indias, even Germanies: no one it seemed was alive to the drama being played out at the Oval. How could I sleep?

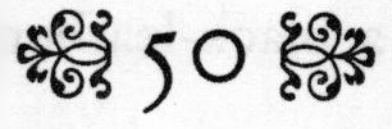

The Chinese Embassy appeared isolated as a walled city. The high wall was a quarter of a mile in length on each side of its flanks; there was a knot of buildings in a compound inside. There was no sound and no sign of inhabitants, though certainly it was inhabited. Its occupants had shut themselves away and the atmosphere pervading it was eerie. There was no one in sight outside either till a most incongruous something came along. It was a sensational black leather-sheathed skirt. It was a shock as if striptease had come to a church.

An hour later I went into the hotel restaurant and sat at the next table to the possessor of the skirt and her companion. The Head of the Restaurant came and took a hand of each, clasped them together, then kissed both hands, both heads, then both hands again. He continued with this and other attentions for twenty minutes. I didn't believe he was the Head of the Restaurant because he had taken my order, done nothing about it, and had gone from table to table being intimate and friendly. I thought he must be a popular habitué. Sullivan told me that when he had come to Ulan Bator nine months before that rotund piece of jocundity had been porter at the hotel. Now he was Head of the Restaurant and soon he was to become manager of the hotel. He was kissing the hands again, then the heads again. The pair turned to me: could I sell them dollars to buy some American cigarettes? I couldn't. They were a Polish couple from the Polish Embassy and bitter for the things that hard currency could buy and they couldn't.

I left, begged some cigarettes off the Embassy upstairs, and returned to present them. The man was overcome: what could he do: he must have my address so that he could send me Mongolian stamps. Alas, if he had but known the truth: I never have been able to resist a black-leather skirt.

The restaurant wouldn't let me pay. They said it was too much trouble to make out a bill. Her Majesty's Embassy and the Sullivans won't let me pay either, so this country that should have ruined me was proving all gratis.

Gratis or not, the restrictions were formidable. Travel was limited to one trip up one road which died after fifteen miles in hills and birch woods, and a second climb with the Land-Rover up hills where roads died in less than a mile, then up a few grass ups and down a few grass downs, then getting out and walking into the vastnesses for some hours alone. Permits to travel to the interior were as rare as gold in a pauper's pocket. And photographing was no straightforward matter. Photographing factories, statues of Sukhe Bator and Lenin were correct: but old people's faces (masterpieces) were insulting to the young regime. New buildings, yes: yurts, no: a co-operative of women at work, yes; a thousand years in a stoic's face, no.

When I left for the hills with the Ambassador's chauffeur, a Mongolian, we drove first to the old Lama Temple. This lama temple was on the edge of the town: four or five buildings within a compound wall about sixty yards long each way. This almost dead world was colourful, picturesque, with many half asleep 'layabout' priests and worshippers. The factories and official offices in Ulan Bator might have ten times the vitality and life: but where has all the colour gone? In Russia too: why must the communist strongholds of activity be cobwebbed with dreariness while the old churches, full of cobwebby people, are alive still with their colour and glory? Perhaps it is something inherent in goodness. The communists, the socialists, the methodists, the baptists . . . they all mean well: but where is their art compared with Jenghis Khan, the wicked old aristocrats, the ritual-loving Catholics, the degenerate, blood-sucking Greek Orthodox Church and the syphilitic and parasitic lamas of Mongolia? (90 per cent of priests in 1870 had syphilis and two-thirds of the male population were attached to temples and monasteries and therefore parasites.) Have we got to want to be wicked to have any exciting art?

The priests were wearing saffron robes and wandering about like crabbed ghosts in search of a shadow.

Children came into the temple with parents and turned prayer-wheels two feet high. These wheels were full of written prayers stuck on in paper to wooden frames: turn the wheels or walk once round them and that was equivalent to saying all the prayers.

Many men were telling beads.

The temple was 'alive' in a 'dead' way. It was 'dead' because the priests were uninspiring.

The State had allowed prayer-boards back, long boards five feet long on which worshippers could prostrate themselves wholly. I saw three men aged about forty doing this.

The Temple dazzled with its reds, oranges, blues: there were curling blue-tiled roofs, pink doors, tortoiseshell and ceramic ornament, dragon carvings, fretwork abounding, a white yard in stone squares on which a hundred pigeons descended, a strong air of wealth and art, of gilt decoration, brass knockers, silver peacocks . . . and, as a contribution from God, flowers and fir trees.

51

After the car had done a little grass hill driving I left the Land-Rover and the chauffeur and set off walking.

Almost immediately, and for some miles, vicious and noisesome insects appeared. I think there were horse-flies, I think there were cicadas, I think there were grasshoppers, but those that made the most fierce attacking sound—a sort of 'Got you! take that you bastard!' racket—I never saw, and if they hit against me it was accidental and they were off before I could say 'Got you! take that you bastard!'

It was late August. A pleasant heat. I was seeing that section at a good moment: no scorching sun, no driving ice, no winds from hell.

Marco Polo came this way.

The high hills varied from shades of green to shades of

grey, from gall to the juice of crushed doves' feathers, and all were skinned over with films of sea and cloaks of gossamer. Thus a valley of verdigris was creamed with tears and a hill of cool stone grey was lacquered with mercury. It was all so gentle. Yet tremendous and everlasting as well. Above me the sky crazed a man with its essence of a million million sapphires, darting blue glorious to all heaven and the beholder.

I have never walked in dinosaur territory before. 60 million years since they were here. It makes the 6,000 since the Mongolians grew wheat by the Gobi less than yesterday.

From 6,000 years ago to A.D. 1200 the races in Mongolia, as far as is known, were nomadic, living mostly on meat for food and mare's milk for drink. (Marco Polo said mare's milk tasted like white wine.) They lived by pasturage and hunting and sometimes war. Towards the summer they drifted northward to reach the pasturage as the snows melted and towards the winter they drifted south to enjoy the extra warmth. For long periods they were subject to China. Before the end of the twelfth century they were victorious with Jenghis Khan in an insurrection against the Kin peoples of north-east China. In succeeding they learnt much military science. Jenghis Khan's first successes were not in conquest but in assimilation. First he organized the Mongol tribes together then extended westwards to induce the Tartar Khirgis and the Uigurs to join him. Throughout his career coercion was his strongest weapon: a share in the spoils to those who voluntarily surrendered, utter destruction for those who dared raise a finger or sword against him. (Should we be thankful that some recent dictators, like Hitler, didn't learn 'coercion' from him? Like the Balkans, many lands had been ripe for a liberator in 1939.)

In 1214 Jenghis Khan attacked the Kin Empire and conquered Pekin. He immediately wooed the Kin peoples, won them, and they aided him greatly thereafter. So

Jenghis Khan turned his attentions west with settled harvests, trade and peace in the east. His first envoys to the west were put to death and, in modern jargon, 'that did it'. Fury went with Jenghis Khan over the Pamirs and down into Turkestan and guns and gunpowder with him learned from the Chinese. Kashgar, Kokand, Bokhara and Samarkand fell, the Kharismian Empire fell, and the armies swept on west to the Caspian, south to Lahore. A Russian army from Kiev appeared; the Grand Duke of Kiev was taken prisoner and the armies swept as a wave of locusts to the Black Sea. Panic arose in Constantinople. But with his Empire stretching from the Pacific to the Dnieper Jenghis Khan died suddenly in 1227. No one knows the spot where he lies buried. It is probably near Kilien. Most graves of most khans of the great days are unmarked and unknown and the probability is that there are wonders a-fortunefold awaiting archaeologists. Jenghis Khan, like Budantsar the founder of the Mongol people millenniums ago, had the legend attached to him that he was the son of a virgin. All the best chaps are . . . unless they are bastards like Leonardo. Jenghis Khan has written such a page of terror into the history books that it should be noted that no conqueror ever had such complete tolerance in religion.

Ogdai Khan, Jenghis's son, continued the conquests. He advanced further south into China and further west into Russia, sacking Kiev. Almost all Russia, then Poland, was ravaged by the Mongols. On to annihilate an army of Germans and Poles at Liegnitz in Lower Silesia in 1241. Strategy, always a stronger point than usually accredited to the Hordes, took the Mongols into Hungary. Punctuality, organization, tremendous vision, thorough information through spy networks of a country's internal strengths and weaknesses, nasty touches like attacking a city with captured inhabitants of that city in the fore, regular and utter ruthlessness . . . method and not madness was the strength of the organized, not disorganized, Hordes.

Beyond Liegnitz were woods which were not the

Mongols' forte, so they did not march on after their victory but spread out in the plains of Hungary.

Ogdai died suddenly in 1242. There was disputing about succession and khans great and small scurried back to Karakorum like hares.

For years dynastic troubles in Karakorum continued and eastern Europe began to breathe. Then there were splits: and successes became greater in China than in the west; so the Mongols, with Kublai Khan Governor-General of China—brother of Mangu Khan, the great Khan at Karakorum—became more and more influenced by Chinese culture, art and learning. Tibet was conquered: Persia and Syria invaded. Baghdad was captured by another brother of Mangu Khan, the entire city being massacred.

In 1259 Mangu died. It took the leaders one year to reassemble from their corners of the Empire. Kublai was elected Great Khan. He immediately made his capital Pekin and this act led to considerable independence for the distant places, Hungary, Russia, Syria, Persia. Thus when Kublai died in 1294 the title of Great Khan disappeared from Karakorum's and the Mongols' pages. Four separate Mongol Empires were set up instead and also extra States such as Siberia and Turkestan.

One remarkable effect of this Empire had been that it had opened all roads between Europe and Asia: free and open intercourse had been enjoyed between peoples: all men's minds had been broadened. Representatives of every nation had appeared at the court at Karakorum: envoys from the Pope, Buddhist priests from Tibet, French, Italian and Chinese craftsmen, Turkish and Armenian merchants, Arab mathematicians, Iranian and Indian astronomers and astrologers, all found themselves at the Mongol Court.

Charlemagne was an energetic illiterate, Alexander the Great was spoiled by egoism, Hitler was a tyrant with a little mind, Jenghis Khan a tyrant with a big mind, Kublai Khan a conqueror with an insatiable appetite for learning. Observe the failures of the religions before the Court at

Karakorum: the Mongols had had no prejudices, but all the religions that had wished to convert them had. The Mongols might have been touched to have made their kingdoms part of the Kingdom of God, but not part of the earthly kingdoms of Rome or Constantinople or Baghdad. Kublai Khan in 1269 sent to the Pope for a hundred men of wisdom and talent to be sent to his Court, and the Pope despatched two Dominican friars to insist that the greatest Empire until then known should be subject to his religious sovereignty. But even those two missionaries of God couldn't endure the toughness of the journey and found excuse for abandoning it. For hundreds of years the odd priest and Pope's emissary turned up, but to convert to the mumbo-jumbo of Christian doctrines was the only fire in their hearts and was not enough to stir the Mongols.

In that first mission including the two Dominican friars was the traveller Marco Polo. He went on where they turned back. It had been his father and his uncle who had previously been the bearers of Kublai Khan's request for a hundred Christians of learning: '. . . intelligent men,' Kublai had asked, 'acquainted with the Seven Arts, able to enter into controversy and able clearly to prove to idolators and others that the Law of Christ was best . . .' Marco Polo came this way and might very well have come across these very hills I was alone in now. It took him three and a half years to reach Kublai Khan, who took to the young Marco, made him governor of Yang-Chow and retained him sixteen years. Argon, monarch of Persia, grandson to Kublai, lost his Mongol wife and promised her on her death-bed only to wed another Mongol. Kublai decided to send his grandson one from Pekin, but she refused to travel unless she had the company of the Polos: otherwise, maybe, the Polos would never have been released by the Khan to return to Europe.

The original religion of the Mongols was animism, Shamanism. They finally came to accept Lamaism and Buddhism from Tibet. Buddhism was pacifying. That, with pestilences, and a growing impotence, led to the falling apart of the Mongolian Empire.

Karakorum was two hundred miles away from me now, a ruined temple, an immense stone tortoise in a field, a piece of wall and the rest buried in the dust.

High up an eagle flew over. Something fell from its beak; it swooped suddenly and in a nose dive the eagle re-caught its prey. Up it flew again to my right. Again the prey fell, again the eagle swooped, and again it re-took it. I had forgotten all about the bird when I saw a dot in front of me. It was the bird again; the prey, a very tiny dot, once more fell but this time the eagle merely veered right and away over an ice blue hill. I watched very carefully the prey fall. I kept my eyes pinned to it and went forward. Would whatever it was have any life left in it? I could see it, a smudge on the ground. I reached it. A bundle: some twigs and bracken.

The Mongol warriors could hit a running hare while at a gallop; they could shoot at half a mile's range. In their contests they could stand with their backs to the objects, swivel round at a command and fire without hesitation. So confident were the judges of the contestants' skill that they often stood within a yard of the target which was to be hit. In Greece and Persia they drank the blood of their enemies from the skulls of their enemies, and Timur in India allowed his soldiers to purify themselves in the blood of idolators. Mongols can eat, sleep and drink on their horses. They start off with some tough meat under the saddle, the heat and the pressure makes it tender, and they pull it out and eat it. They can ride at top speed holding a glass of water filled to the brim and never spill a drop. Trotting, galloping or standing in the stirrups, they ride motionless and go across an horizon like a zipper. The horses almost as much as they themselves won for them their empire. Tireless, the horses can go for days in boiling heat or freezing winds. No opponents' horses could do such a thing. A Mongol has been known to freeze solid to his horse into one piece like a chessman, so that they have to thaw apart inside a yurt.

In 1368 Chung-Lo, Ming Emperor of China, drove the Mongols back and razed Karakorum to the ground to an extent that would make Guernica seem a half attempt. All countries then under Mongolian oppression revolted and regained their freedom. And so Mongolia went back to being Mongolia.

Out in the hills and steppes, and in the larch and cedar forests to the north, herdsmen and shepherds have found ornaments of gold, trinkets of silver, bangles of bronze, jewels of all varieties, weapons of iron, and more than 200 ruins 600 years old. Yes, there have been towns in nomadic Mongolia: all part of the giant mystery of this small people in a country which now at one inhabitant per square mile, has, as far as can be known, its largest population ever. I myself, looking for nothing, just missed treading on two pieces of ceramic painting inches wide only, and a mile from each other, and with nothing else but grass in sight.

The town of Kara-Balgasum in the Hotong district had covered ten square miles and been surrounded by a thirty-foot wall. Inside had been monasteries and palaces with towers forty feet high. Central heating by pipes on the floors was in many houses.* It had thrived in the eighth and ninth centuries, 400 years before the contact with the outside world brought about by Jenghis Khan. Mongolia had had ten written languages and when they wrote on stone they often wrote in two languages.

Marco Polo and the monk Plano Carpini and the Franciscan William of Rubrouck were not believed in their descriptions of Karakorum but are tended to be believed today. Surrounded by walls, a little of the three miles of which still stand, Karakorum received ambassadors and princes in temples and palaces. There were two Mohammedan mosques, two Christian churches, Lama temples. The great palace was supported on sixty-four pillars, and

* Jorgen Bisch: *Mongolia*, Allen & Unwin, 1963.

is the palace where Marco Polo and Rubrouck were received. A silver tree was built, at its foot were four silver lions, and out of each lion was built a duct out of which gushed mare's milk. Four other ducts led up into the tree. These were fashioned like snakes. Out of the mouth of one poured wine, out of another caracosmos, a milk spirit, out of the third bal, made from honey, and out of the fourth the potent terracina, a mead from rice. Four silver basins stood at the base of the tree to collect each drink. On the top of the tree sat a silver angel with a silver trumpet. When the court assembled the trumpet blew and the beverages poured to the basins.

Karakorum lay forgotten except by creatures of steppe and desert till 1889 when a Russian explorer, Yadrintsev, went there.

There were two horses grazing on a hill. They were sand-coloured. The hill was steep, and in a ridiculous way it looked as if the horses should fall off. The horses were a quarter of a mile apart and at one point in my walk they stood silhouetted against the sky. The hill was mildewed-gold in colour, that is, mottled green over an unpolished gold base. The horses looked like the tiny handles of a giant upturned bowl which was the hill. Behind the horses and behind the hill was the violent fire-blue sky.

In 1912 a treaty between Mongolia and Tibet was signed 'by the President of the Mongolian Council of Ministers and the Patron of 10,000 truths on the 4th. day of the 12th. month of the 2nd. year of Him who is Exalted by All. And signed on behalf of Tibet according to the Chronicle of Tibet on the Same Day and Month in the Year of the Water-mouse.'

In 1918, Sukhe Bator, a printing worker from Urgh, now Ulan Bator, united with Choibalsan, a friend, educated in Irkutsk, to form a resistance movement to the Chinese who had taken overlordship. But then 'The Mad Baron', the German Baron Ungern-Sternberg, turned up with an army of 10,000 White Russians fleeing from the communist

Revolution, murdered all Russians in Mongolia, then all Chinese, and then set himself up as dictator with the help of the Living Buddha, Bogdo Gegen. He made the Living Buddha King, whereupon the Living Buddha made the baron a saint. Sukhe Bator got a letter from Lenin through to Bogdo Gegen secreted in a hollow whip handle, and thus they raised a revolt together from without and within and with the help of Soviet Forces drove the baron out, till two months later he was captured and shot. Bogdo Gegen got his kingship back. Sukhe Bator died two years afterwards, very young, many say murdered by the lamas. Next year the Lama King himself died and Mongolia became declared the first 'People's Republic' in the world.

Sukhe Bator, the Red Hero, lies buried in a tomb with his friend Choibalsan, the mausoleum being an exact copy of the Lenin Mausoleum in Moscow. His statue in the main square is a half copy, with Bator instead of Peter, of Peter I's monument in Leningrad.

In 1955 China sent 10,000 workers and technicians to assist Ulan Bator, paying all wages themselves. In 1957 Russia built two airports, gave 2,500 tractors, 550 harvesters, 3,000 trucks and £10 million worth of machinery.

In 1958 China lent Mongolia £10 million and sent 20,000 more workers and technicians. Russia immediately sent more combines, tractors and added some experts.

In 1959 Chou-en-lai personally visited Ulan Bator and offered £17½ million (which he had borrowed from Russia) to be spent on foundries, a circus, and blocks of flats. The blocks of flats remain the finest architectural works in the capital. The Russians then offered £55 million of credit, an oil refinery and more technicians. They sent Molotov along as representative.

The Russians are winning the wooing probably because of a historical fact. When the Chinese have moved into Mongolia previously they have stayed on as conquerors: when the Russians have marched in it has been to help dispel an enemy—like the Japs in the last war—and they have then always withdrawn.

It was so silent today under the sky ablaze in blue among the valleys emerald on gold two hundred miles from the dust that sleeps on Karakorum.

52

Back at Irkutsk a third time and it was a break in the train saga.

I had planned this mile journey from St Pancras to Euston so that, excepting that England is an island and excepting a Black Sea trip from Odessa to Istanbul, the whole could be done by train. But no more trains! In so far as a guess can be made trains went too near too many borders. I must do all the little hops from Irkutsk to Odessa by air except for being permitted a road journey from Tashkent to Samarkand and another from Samarkand to Pendjakent. Come peace, come a death to all suspicions, and this journey can be made by train, but for now I must bow to circumstance and take to the air.

Trains would become my companions again from Istanbul to Euston.

The *Morning Star* had stopped appearing in Russia the day of the invasion of Czechoslovakia. Which meant no Test Match results and no football results. Thus an Englishman's last life-line to things that mattered had been cut. 'Bournemouth 1, Southend 6' had said the last *Morning Star*. For one who has supported Southend United spiritedly from one doldrum to another throughout the ages this was a cruel moment to be cut off.

But I took to the air to Tashkent where they were still talking of Cardiff City's visit. I remember some English sports journalists inferring that this city was, as it were, the last thing in barbarism. Another cause for Ragosinism? It was all civilization and sunshine and well-being in Tashkent.

I waited at the airport with an American while an Intourist guide searched for a Frenchman, then to take all three of us to our hotel. A Sikh, just in from the Punjab, kept saying: 'And the Custom man he asked me, and very serious he was, are those snakes you have in that basket?' Then the Intourist guide mentioned the Frenchman's name. 'That's my name,' said the American. And we had been waiting two hours for a Yank who had flown in from Paris and who was with us all the time.

53

I went to the terrace garden restaurant on the sixth floor of the hotel and ordered schashlik.

The terrace was elegantly lit. A strip of ceiling was held above the seating by a colonnade and the remainder of the terrace was open to the sky. Overhead strings of red, white, blue and orange lights looped from table to table.

Below, across the road, played a grand fountain with wide strips of water shooting skywards like sheets of running metal.

There was a half a moon in a cobalt sky.

Behind the gardens behind the fountain was the entrance to the Theatre of Opera and Ballet.

It was there Violetta had danced. It was from there she had gone to Kuibyshev and it was in Kuibyshev we had met. We married in Moscow.

When the diplomatic corps was evacuated in 1941 it went to Kuibyshev. Half of the Bolshoi Theatre went also but Violetta, straight from school, turned up with her mother here in Tashkent. Of the 200 who had originally started the vigorous Bolshoi course only three were passed out, two girls and one youth. She was one of them. Immediately upon passing her examinations she came here and immediately was given leading roles. At the close of the season she was sent to join the larger group in Kuibyshev where she was immediately given soloist roles and thus became one of the tiny number who have ever danced with the Bolshoi and not been through its Corps de Ballet.

At some time in our courtship I tried to explain to her my work at the Embassy, that she should not think I was a grand person, that in fact I was the lowest of all. She couldn't understand why I was telling her. She didn't care.

When we became engaged I warned her that after the war I wanted to try to become a writer and that might mean financial difficulties at first. She didn't care.

We are not together now, but all the time we were married, however wretchedly low we were in funds she never once reminded me I earned so little or suggested I might do better.

When I got my first book accepted all the skies of London shook with her joy.

Odd the sentiments passing through me as I stared down at that theatre tonight.

Violetta remains the best person I have ever met. I cannot see how there can be anyone better.

54

The bespectacled Intourist young man who showed me Tashkent was keen.

Someone had been killed, 'by gangs of counter-revolutionaries and reactionaries acting as agents in the pay of bloodsucking foreign saboteurs and capitalists'.

Some houses had been built 'by the love of our great Pioneer movement inspired by the heroic deeds of our guide and teacher Ilyich Lenin'.

Some people were playing chess in a park 'in the leisure time given to them after their working hours by our government of brotherhood and comradeship with all the working classes of the world'.

An earthquake three years ago had flattened one area and one block was being rebuilt: 'by the workers and comrades of the Armenian Republic to show our solidarity of purpose. . .'

'Wasn't there a world-wide collection at the time of the earthquake?' I asked.

'And this block,' he said, 'shows the solidarity and love of our comrades in the Belorussia Republic . . .'

'Wasn't there a world-wide contribution?' I asked.

'And this factory,' he said, 'built as a gift to our great peoples by the . . .'

'Wasn't there a world-wide collection?' I asked.

'Yes. And this school . . .'

'If there was a world-wide contribution,' I said, 'why don't you say so?'

He didn't like my saying that.

We came to a monument of Karl Marx. For twelve feet there was an outsize in handles for a torch. Then came the two-yard-high head of Marx and his hair for one yard more was carved as a flame. 'That,' he said, 'world experts have declared is a breakthrough in sculptural conception and representation. They have evolved new ideas. A torch with the hair carved as a flame. It shows . . .'

'It all began in London,' I said.

'What began in London?'

'Well, all this business, Karl Marx, Engels, Lenin: you'd have been nowhere without the British Museum. That's where it all started. Lenin called himself Jacob Richter. It was the Secretary of the Federation of British Trade Unions, J. H. Mitchell, who got him his Museum ticket. What's the next line?' I read from the monument: ' "Workers of the world unite" and then what? "You have nothing to lose but your chains" isn't it? Why isn't that put?'

He didn't know. And he wouldn't grant any honour to London. It's a hopeless situation: being asked to marvel at other people's gods. What do visiting foreign football teams think of the message written colossally across the length of the Dynamo Stadium in Moscow: 'Lenin dead? Lenin has lived, is living, will live.'

'I know many people,' I said, 'who met Lenin.' *Now* he listened. 'I know one good soul, a Mr Charlton, a Labour M.P., who used to play with Karl Marx. Marx used to come home from the British Museum and play in the streets of Islington with Charlton who was just a boy.'

He wrung my hand. Nearly wrenched it off. I didn't tell him what Karl Marx was supposed to have said about the Russians: 'give the Russians a good idea and the devil comes in at the back door'. Or that in 1882 he was heard to shout out 'I am no Marxist!' The guide had taken out his notebook.

'I am so honoured,' he blurted, 'so overcome, I am glorified, to meet such a great man wh has such great friends who knew our founders and leaders of our inspired movement for brotherhood among the nations. The press will want to hear of you, such a great man, and your friends, such great men, and they will want to know the names. All our people will want to correspond with your great comrades who have known . . .'

'Charlton is dead,' I said. 'He died when he was eighty.'

'But those others, those who actually met our great founder—their names so that our peoples shall be aware . . .'

I held my fire. I got the subject changed.

I had wanted him to show me some old living quarters. For two hours he said he would. But he didn't.

55

I was to visit Fergana, but almost all the time I should have been there I spent waiting for the plane to get off the ground at Tashkent. Fergana airport announced furious winds which would tilt any aeroplane over after it had landed.

When I was taking my third meal in the airport restaurant the manageress and chef came to me: would I visit the kitchen? I went there. Now would I show them how to prepare certain English dishes, starting first of all with toast? Grills are non-existent in much of the world, and certainly are not to be found in Tashkent. I thought and thought. I explained what a grill was. How could they manage so many English dishes without one?

Intourist left many booklets around in the waiting hall for tourist consumption. One was called *Spy College at Château Pourtalet*. It was the only interesting title I ever saw

It told of a college in France where Americans trained spies. It told chiefly of Negroes being approached while at universities in Russia, offered better and more generous education if they would go to the States instead. The material did not live up to the title. And is it all worth it?

For the Americans to go to all that trouble to get a few Africans over to the States?

It would seem obvious to laugh it all off as a tremendous to-do about too little. What, after all, is there in the modern world of peace worth endless time and expense for foreign agents? A few nuclear formulae? A few military set-ups? Surely all this concern about Mr Everybody is ludicrous?

It's common to invest your enemies with your own sins. If the Russians are that concerned about such activities of the Americans, probably the Russians are engaged in such activities themselves? But are they? And are the Americans? And, to repeat again, is it all worth it?

In 1958 I bicycled the length and breadth of Thailand and Cambodia with an Indian friend. We never met a communist or a Russian. We never heard the words mentioned except when we met up with Americans and then we heard nothing else. 'Communist infiltration' was on their lips like saliva. The Americans were helping train the Thai troops against the scourge, building Friendship Roads to help link village to village, yet in actuality linking no villages but pointing straight at Pekin. American missionaries told us that before being sent to Thailand they, and all their families including tiny-tots, were sent to special schools for a year to make sure that first they were fine American citizens. They were then given cameras and unlimited supplies of film and told to photograph anything and everything and send it free to Washington.

Ramesh, my Indian friend, and I had the feeling that the Americans were injecting an enemy into an area, then injecting the methods for combating it. It was America, not China or Russia, that was introducing communism there.

And we all know about Vietnam since.

So how with *The Spy College at Château Pourtalet*? Africa is a hearty fat chicken which the English and the French and the Dutch and the Belgians let loose in the world. Pray heaven that the Africans find it in them to say: a plague on all your houses!

Meanwhile people like me and the millions of innocent tourists like you have to accept the ignominy of being suspected of being spies little or spies big because of the games our Powers and politicians are playing.

Or must we? When will Mr Ordinary Man rise up and say, Enough: we are friends all: to the furnace with your passports and your barriers?

56

'What have you come to Fergana for?'

It was a small office and the Intourist manager of Fergana was asking me. I had arrived at 6.0 a.m.

'To see your historic architecture.'

'We haven't any.'

'I had picked it up somewhere,' I said, 'that I should go to Fergana to see Margellan, Urgench to see Khiva, and Samarkand to see Pendjakent. Isn't there something wonderful to see at Margellan? I had heard of new archaeological discoveries.

'There is a silk factory at Margellan.'

'Did Alexander the Great die there?'

'They might tell you so in Margellan. There is the legend. But nowhere else in the world would they believe it.'

The manager, Isakov, was called out. An Uzbek who spoke English came into the office. 'I am called in,' he said, 'if any English speaking people come. I speak here the best English, but my work it is not. The manager he has been so excited about your visit. He, he has been talking of nothing else for months.'

'Why?'

'Because no one ever comes this way here. They opened the office in June of this year: a rare stray he comes through. You are the almost the first Englishman. He's been so worried these last two days that you not turn up. It was the winds. And now you must go back the night? Less than a day's visit? It will break his heart. He's been wondering what he can show you. He's reckoned that if he can get one tourist per month he can keep his office open. He's very excited about his job, he is. He's longing for it to be a success, he is. So do send one tourist a month to us will you?'

The manager, Isakov, returned. He was about forty, knew the travel agency I sometimes worked for and wanted only to talk about how to get bus-loads of tourists to Fergana. 'I lie awake at night,' he said, 'and see coach-loads of tourists arriving here. Kokand!' he blurted out. 'Come on, let's go to Kokand!'

The Uzbek was against it: he argued hotly and suggested Isakov was stretching hospitality too far, that Kokand was not on the tourist map. But we were going and the young Uzbek was coming with us.

So I never saw Margellan and still wonder what the information I had received was all about. But Kokand . . . yes Kokand was important. Throughout this vast area where a thousand years means a young city; where civilization was a real thing years before Christ, the four greatest cities of all were Kokand, Khiva, Samarkand and Bokhara.

We left: one Russian manager, one English-speaking Uzbek, one Korean chauffeur, and myself.

It had often been said that the absolute end of the west and the absolute end of the east met at Kokand.

57

From Fergana to Kokand was a flat road. It was all insid
the Valley of Fergana, which is like a valley drilled into th
Pamirs. My companions regretted not having the time t
run me off route into the mountain scenery. They need hav
no worries about having little to show the foreign visitor
possibly the greatest mountains and the greatest scenery i
the Soviet Union were on hand. From this valley began th
great caravan trek up the Pamirs and over into China an
Mongolia. Marco Polo was here. I looked out of the ca
realized the situation and knew I should have had a wee
here, not a day: but the frustrating stupidity about trave
in the Soviet Union is that to change a plan is a nightmaris
upheaval, Moscow has to O.K. it, reasons have to be give
all future plans go awry, the costs are enormous, and th
chances of permission not being given are ten to one—
suspect chiefly from laziness. I had succeeded in changin
plans in Irkutsk by extracting a lump out of my programm
for Mongolia then rejoining my schedule at Tashkent. Bu
I cannot cut out a lump of the likes of Samarkand an
Bokhara.

It was to these areas that Jenghis Khan had sent his not
and got his envoys murdered. The kingdom (Khanate) c
Khiva had stretched from the Caspian to Delhi. Jenghi
had asked for the Khan of Khiva's daughter's hand i
marriage. The Khan said he'd never recognize Jenghis, wh
instantly destroyed Khiva's only city east of the Pamirs

then stormed over the mountains and stormed down into Kokand with all his first fury and razed it mercilessly to the ground. Then he tore into Khiva.

We drove mainly past maize and cotton: maize always being grown the year before a crop of cotton is desired. (A pleasant word is the Russian for maize: kookoorooza.) Isakov, looking less Russian than our Uzbek companion, seeking all avenues for my complete entertainment, asked the car to stop. There were three cubes four feet wide on each side. They were of stuccoed brick. There was a leaning tree, some tables and as many as a hundred teapots all beautiful in design. On the top of one of these cubes sat a young man cross-legged. Isakov asked for 'One'. The bulk of the top where the man was sitting was a circular lid. He opened it. The oven—for it was an oven—was spherical inside. Hanging down off the top walls were pasties—like flying foxes hanging down asleep from caves in India. The young man took something like a trowel and scraped one off. 'A speciality of our parts,' Isakov said and handed it to me.

Four people were drinking. Tea is a serious business in Uzbekistan: everyone's at it and everyone regards it as an art. The trees were playing ping-pong bat shadows on the tables and on the four Uzbeks with their tibiteikas—skull-caps. How easy was life in the south, in the sun! To catch as splendid an atmosphere in Siberia needed warmth, a finely designed café, effort and cost. Here, some rickety chairs, a tree, tea, the warm sun, a friend . . . the finest café with the finest design with all effort and all cost could not equal this.

I said I'd eat the pasty in the car. I'm one of those pernickety people who are put off food unless it is pleasantly presented: if I was blind I would enjoy more food than I do: and after the appearance of this, one bite of it and I was completely put off. It was a meat savoury with tomato and some bitter filling. I said later I wanted to photograph cotton, having never seen it before. I took the pasty to the cotton-fields and left it there.

We had a third stop. People were crawling all over a
house. Isakov said: 'In these parts, if someone wants a new
house, he puts a notice up. Everyone gives twenty-four
hours gratis. That's enough; the house is built; and rounded
off with a party.' We passed this one on our return journey
and it was two-thirds completed, a hundred and possibly
more, people working at it like bingo. They stopped to
talk with us, then were back at it immediately: it was joy
and music while you work.

'It's for newlyweds,' said Isakov.

We then, in a discussion, disposed of my marital affair
and got on to theirs. Isakov had two children and was
happy man though his children were over boisterous and
wore him out. In the winter he would have months a
home, for four months there would be almost nothing to
do in the office and he would be fully paid although mostl
at home. Did my travel agency pay me when I was no
working? Imagine that! He knew hundreds of Intouris
personnel who had one month's certain holiday and anothe
three to four months likely holiday, always on full pay.

The young Uzbek had only been married twelve days
which no doubt explained why he hadn't wanted a whol
day with us. If the winds had kept up a little longer h
could have had all this time with his beloved.

'My wife,' he said, 'was, how do you say, unspoiled
undeflowered, when her father sent her to me. If she ha
not been I send her back. It is, how you say, the way w
Uzbek do. Now she must do everything I tell her, she mus
always exactly obey me. But I on the other hand do and wi
always do exactly as she tells me, that is the way I will wan
it so. That is the way it must always be, it is so. She wea
long plaits and I love it. An Uzbek girl can have as many a
forty plaits at the same time. My wife a student is. She wi
a student be for three more years. And then she will wor
do. She is a student of Russian literature and history. Mo
Uzbek marriages are—is it so you say?—love marriage
though some marry in the old style of the parents do th

choosing. That was the law until our Revolution. If an arranged marriage is and does not—how do you say it, does not work, is that right?—if an arranged marriage is and does not work there can be divorce but that is very hard on the woman for no man wants the woman who is spoiled, deflowered. She can never, do you say it, approach a man. She must await for a man to approach her.'

'Do you live in Fergana?'

'My wife comes from Bokhara and we can find no flat here, so we must pay for one very dear. It is 11 roubles for each month for two rooms and the shower and the kitchen and one very large verandah, isn't it. We live on the verandah, isn't it, and we sleep there and we eat there. The rent, how do you say it including gas and electricity and water, do you say it, but it is too dear. My salary, it is 100 for each month but 5 per cent I must pay to the Income Tax. I could take the one room less and then it would be 7 roubles for each every month.'

The Korean said he had never been to Korea, had married in Moscow and had been a driver in Fergana for twenty years. He grew very serious about cars and between the three of them they told me that everyone they knew was rich, everyone had nothing to spend his money on, kept his money at home and dreamed of buying a car. A Volga could cost £2,500. There were cheaper cars but none were easy to come by. An Uzbek they said would have no interest in having more than one shirt and one pair of trousers but he would have a dozen or two dozen or three dozen carpets for floors and walls just for the pleasure of having them, no money in the bank and a hoard at home waiting for that glorious day when he could buy a car. Private cars in the Soviet Union were almost non-existent: Fiats had built two factories and cars should be coming off the assembly line soon. From lists it would seem half the country wanted a car.

'What will you do with your car when you get one?' I asked Isakov.

'Drive it up and down to flaunt it in front of my neighbours.'

I was told elsewhere that all people watch out to see who wins the State Lotteries. Sooner or later such winners usually garner a car. Then everyone bargains with him to buy it off him. It would be illegal for him to sell for a profit but . . . what most of the world can find a way around, the Uzbeks can.

We passed plane trees, poplars, cherries, apples, plums, peaches, pears, apricots, pomegranates and cotton. 'You seem to have every fruit except bananas?' I said.

Not one of them had ever seen a banana.

Isakov said: 'In this district on 14 February 1483 a baby, the fifth descendant of Timur on one side, the fourteenth descendant of Jenghis Khan on the other, was born. His name was Babur. Our City of Fergana is a modernish Russian city but the district of Fergana has been a kingdom for endless centuries. Babur's father went to visit his pigeons and to brood with them over an invasion and the whole house collapsed on his head and killed him, and Babur, aged only eleven, became king. His kingdom was being attacked from two sides. He summoned his grandmother Aisan-Daulam Begam and between them they banished their enemies. Babur was never able to rid himself of the lust for wanting the kingdom of Samarkand. Twice he conquered it and twice he lost it. Then he lost his own kingdom and went as a hunted beggar from valley to valley with 200 and sometimes 300 followers. One day 4,000 men came and offered him their lives. A king without a kingdom, he ignored his own birthright and marched on Afghanistan. He captured Kabul and set up kingship there which he held till his death.

'He turned again to Samarkand. Again he captured it, again he lost it. He turned towards India. And after four attempts, in April of 1526, at the battle of Panipat, he was victorious and gained Delhi. He was met at Agra by his son Humayun who gave him the Koh-i-noor diamond, given to Humayun by the family of the Rajah of Gwalior for his generous behaviour in Agra, and considered then equal to half the expenditure of the world in any one day. Babur returned it to his son. Humayun fell sick and a saint declared he could only recover by surrendering to God the most precious thing in the world in his possession. Babur said: 'I am that, and will surrender myself to God.' He walked three times round the bed of his son drawing forth the sickness; was dead in three days and Humayun recovered. Thus began the Great Moghul Empire in India, with the Taj Mahal, with Akbar, with the Muslim religion, all replaced eventually by you British. So hereabouts 500 years ago was born a very famous baby, famous believe it or not, also for his poetic and high literary gifts.'

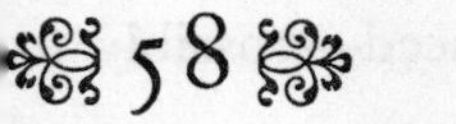

Into Kokand.

A city in the process of reduction. It has been the last thorn in the Russian side during many campaigns; it was the last to surrender to the Russians in 1876 and the last to surrender to the Red Flag: it has already been reduced from what it obviously is, the capital of the area, and little Fergana has taken its place. Like making Harlow capital of England, while London carries on cloaked in a cloud of not being what it is.

Over the last 300 years there have been many khanates—kingdoms—in Central Asia (as kings rule kingdoms, khans rule khanates), the chief being Kokand, Bokhara, and

Khiva. From time to time they have swallowed each other. Kokand khanate, 1,500 miles in breadth at several point and including Tashkent, was ruled by the khan from hi city. None of the khanates or any of the lands around ther ever had stable boundaries, the outlying peoples of thei territories, often even nomadic, felt only those allegiance that cajoling or the sword could bring about, and th Russians making their inroads into these territories wer helped by no area having much love for another or for it ruler. Russia itself also had no very definite frontiers but i had a sense of wanting them and it was Russia who finalize the boundaries with Afghanistan, China and Persia.

Chinese historians mention the existence of Kokand i 100 B.C. Arab historians say it was in existence in 1200 B.C The word itself means City of Wind. It was captured b the Arab armies in the eighth century and they replaced th Zoroastrian religion with the Muslim. In the thirteent century it was conquered by Jenghis Khan, who left it religion intact though not many of its population. Jenghi Khan, like Napoleon, gave his conquered territories muc administration and censuses were introduced—possibly t ensure that no one was missed for taxes.

Kokand was captured by the Uzbeks in 1505 and the are still in the majority.

A Chinese visitor in 1840 (China is 400 miles away) found 600 mosques, 15 madraṣas—religious schools— 15,000 students, 80,000 people and a city that had bee mainly erected in 1700.

Kokand began growing tremendously in 1802, had it first Uzbek khan in 1808 and its last in 1875. Its gran palace was built from 1840–1860 and we were driving to it

Its two most famous inhabitants have been the poe Navouitch and the doctor Abu-Ali Cino of the tent century.

It was 1934 before the Kremlin could feel sure o themselves in Kokand. The priests could not abide th freedom for women that the communists granted and i they saw a woman in the streets out of purdah slit her throat, and it was six years after women's suffrage that the women walked the streets open-faced without fear.

And now the President of the whole of Uzbekistan is a woman! Mrs Nasredinova.

The government commenced restoration of the Grand Palace in 1962. Little was done yet except to the entrance, a hall and a few rooms. What had been done was masterly done. Are there finer restorers than the present-day Soviet Union workers? They work slowly but with care, love and ability: I wonder if there has ever been a more incredible restoration than the Russians have made of Pavlovsk near Leningrad?

Here in Kokand the ceilings were colourful precise geometrical abstractions, the interior walls and gateways and the rare room or two were epitomes of cleanliness with the certain stamp of authenticity. We should have had hours of browsing. We had half an hour of listening to a guide. We saw a grand and noble entrance to the Palace. We saw a divan in a high room where the young khan lay by his window watching forty of his harem bathing in the flimsiest of garbs, then selected the meat of his choice and had her sent up.

We saw the house of a local Soviet hero stoned to death by the populace in 1928. We saw pictures of his body dead on a cart. His birthplace was in the old town and it was pleasant to get among the daub and wattle houses and streets. Streets narrow, streets winding, one-storey houses with grapevines over every entrance—what an entrance to a home, a grapevine leading to the front door! The side alleys and streets of Kokand were all charm.

One fact should not be retained in the mind as a memory of a city: yet I cannot forget one. There was a picture in a museum of a criminal nailed to a mosque door by one ear and guards standing by watching: if one worshipper entering the mosque showed one glance of sympathy to the bleeding man he or she would be punished immediately.

In the horrors committed by man to man this area can boast some of the grimmest. Thirty-foot stakes pointed at one end: that end driven up the prisoner's rear by a mallet, then the whole stake raised upright the prisoner pinned in his agony at the top. Prisoners being forced to drink the blood of their loved ones after the heads had been cut off before their eyes. Prisoners over forty, being too old for work, blinded, the executioner standing on their chests, wiping their knives afterwards on their beards, then in terrible pain the old rising, groping about. Others too old for work, nailed to the roadway and allowed to die from slow starvation moaning and groaning and begging their way to death. Young soldiers impaled in their coffins and buried alive.

There were categories of dying. A very simple crime might mean simply death, the larger the crime the more protracted and horrific the dying. The argument was: 'You will appreciate that a straight death would be too good for you: it would not be justice. I therefore sentence you to . . .' and then the imagination went to town.

Vambery* reported that the khan in 1840 punished a man for looking at a woman although she was veiled completely. The man was hanged and the woman buried to the waist beneath his gallows and stoned to death. Vambery also reported that as he stood in a square 100 horsemen arrived with men, women and children prisoners tied to their horses' tails. The khan appeared. Each horseman removed sacks from each side of his saddle and emptied them, servants kicking the fallen into heaps at the khan's feet. They were human heads. Each horseman took a receipt for the heads and three days later was paid.

* A. Vambery, *Travels in Central Asia,* John Murray, 1864.

59

The aeroplane flew down the Fergana Valley, then turned right—or north as the erudite people would say—straight to Tashkent. A four hours' flight.

Immediately I flew on to Urgench.

An official in the plane asked me what I was writing. Before I had answered he answered for me: 'Oh! It's your diary?'

'Yes,' I said.

In the war I had been caught in the suburbs of Moscow in an air-raid. I had gone to a cellar in an apartment block with a hundred Russians. After an hour I had taken out pen and paper. Someone reported me. In minutes only a warden asked me to go along with him. He asked to see my passport. He took it. I asked for it back every five minutes and never got it. He took me to another building, then to a militia station. They kept me there for three hours and no one spoke. If I went up to an official or anyone else in the waiting room, if that's the word, they behaved like wood to me. They did not hear. Soon their wooden behaviour had become a concrete behaviour. I kept thinking, I must tickle them, if nothing happens then, kick them. Their officialdom had a weak spot: it was a crime to be late for work. I went to the desk where there were three slabs of concrete that had once been men and said: 'I am the nightwatchman at the British Embassy. I must be on duty at 9.0. It is now 8.0. If you do not release me you must telephone through and explain why I am late otherwise there will be a scandal.'

No one answered, but after a minute one slipped away. In another minute I was taken to a room for questioning. Another three men.

They spoke to me in German. I said in English: 'I am English. For hours I have been demanding that you get in touch with my Embassy. I am on duty there at 9.0 tonight.'

Ten languages they tried on me for half an hour. Then came Russian. I insisted on English. It looked like an impasse.

But then one began speaking perfect English.

Soon the matter was cleared up. I got my passport back. They asked me to sign a paper. I refused. They asked me to sign to say I had not been physically manhandled. I said I would sign no paper but write a few words in English to that effect. I did that. They then gave me a car and with all the energies of which police are capable they rushed me through the streets as if the war depended on it and put me down outside my Embassy at one minute to nine.

All that for putting pen to paper in public. Here agair on the aeroplane . . . the fourth time so far I have beer questioned about my writing. What unholiness woulc happen if I started sketching? It was the lack of sense that was worrying. What would I sketch that I could not photo graph? What would I write down that a trained mar couldn't memorize? And would I, if I was a spy, sketcl or write down under public gaze something that woulc give me away?

On one of these hops on this journey a young lady short-skirted, fresh as an opening flower, sat next to me She looked out of the window and said: 'No bicycles! Thi country should be full of bicycles yet I hardly see any. can't understand it. Bicycles would be a godsend.'

It was one of those hops with a stop halfway and we al got out for twenty minutes. She behaved like a youn woman shopping in Oxford Street about to return in som minutes to her home in the suburbs. She was dressed too as if home was only half an hour away. She was handsome, as natural as spring water, unaffected, unsophisticated, and blooming.

Back in the plane she spoke of Marilyn Monroe. She resented that she had been looked upon as just a sex-pot with little or no acting ability. She considered her one of the most talented actresses Hollywood had produced and hoped the world would come round to granting her that much one day although, sadly, posthumously.

My companion had been representing France at a film festival and her name she said was Anna Karina. That most brilliant young French actress!

Intourist give no guarantee of such companions on every trip. If they did there might be point to air travel. Air travel to get a person from one town to another in a hurry is a miracle: but as a means of knowing the world it is ridiculous. I had just been into the Pamirs and out again and might as well have walked on Salisbury Plain for all the feeling of mountains I had had.

From Irkutsk to Tashkent we had flown high. I saw Irkutsk and I saw Tashkent and I saw nothing in the 2,000 miles between. What sort of travel is that?

Now we were flying low. It was in a new dimension of experience: we were not earth bound, we were air bound. To know the earth I should be down on earth, and this was intended to be an earth journey. Even a desert, and we were over one now, needs going through to realize it.

There are levels of living. There is being awake, there is dreaming, there is being in love: and flying low in an aeroplane is so much a different dimension from ordinary experience that attempts at descriptions seem inadequate; how can earth-bound adjectives and similes get inside a bird's world?

The air hostess called the desert we were over 'Red Sands'. Some books I have read call it 'Black Sands'. In the atlas it is called the Kara Kum Desert.

I could not understand whether the water we saw was above the desert or below it. The sands were mirrored through water and yet they protruded from it also. Weird. Looking further towards the horizon, was it blue sky or blue water that ran away to distant bluer clouds or bluer mountains? Weirder. People who take drugs can get unworldly yet beautiful visions. This was a vision, it was unreal, it was sublimity: I wonder if the drug-takers get anything its equal? There was not one thing I was looking at I could name for certain: that might be sand, that might be sea, that might be cloud, that might be river, that might be mountain: Turner had never made things half so indefinite as God was doing now.

There were enormous crow's feet markings in the soil: there were shallows like stepped-on snakes so turned and turned about it took twenty miles to cover one. There was a sudden accumulation of greens so galled and gut tortured, it could be jungle except that jungles and deserts do not stable together. There was now a river, perhaps a tributary of the Oxus. It looked flowing into living matter spunk and rheum, and running nerve and vital mercuries and spirits and oil and heart and tissue and, in parts like a bared vein it was glistening gristle up at us, and the sun neoned up a curve of red, or an electric line of purple or a rabid run of gangrene. The sands shelved up.

The odd feeling persisted. Was I seeing the land through water or was it a trick of sight? If you look in a shop window you can see the goods in it, or you can readjust your eyes and see the people reflected on the other side of the street. It was like that here: I could see the water or I could see the sand, only when I saw the sand the water wasn't there.

There was Cellophane and chiffon and silk and angel mist, catches of sparkle in seas of colour.

As forbidding as hell down there.

Like an abstract from paradise up here.

New Urgench was nothing except itself. It, like Fergana, had nothing to show the tourist: it had its own small unpretentious existence and that was its charm. I have a Swedish friend who goes regularly for holidays to England: he will never go to anywhere that has anything specific to show him: Hartlepools, Andover, Leigh-on-Sea, Sheffield. 'My joy,' he says, 'is to see the English being themselves.' Then were he to come to the Soviet Union, he would enjoy Urgench and Fergana.

From Urgench and other places I tried to phone Madras. 'We have no one,' I was told, 'to listen to what you are saying. There is therefore no possibility for you to make the call.'

My guide's name was Dubovitsky. If the Party checked on him they would find they had no more loyal son, but he never once broached propaganda, he was all knowledge, all help, loved his subject—Khiva—loved tourists, had a touch of the dreamer and the poet: an ideal guide.

We left by car for Khiva.

On a straight stretch of road was a little man on a little donkey. The donkey, in a hurry yet refusing to rise above a walk, looked, from the rear, like Marilyn Monroe in a hurry. The man had a two-foot wide fur hat on so that man and beast together appeared like a T-square with a wobble.

'Tadjik,' said Dubovitsky. 'Only Tadjiks wear such hats; and don't try to purchase one, no one knows where they

come from. The only way to get one is to marry a Tadjik
woman and it's not worth it.'

'But they must be so hot: fur hats in this heat!'

'They argue that after an hour the hat sets up a resistance
to heat and that in fact they are cool. Khiva is very old,'
he continued. 'No one knows how old. It was not always
the capital. It became its biggest and strongest from 165
till 1920. Before 1695 Old Urgench was the capital. In 187
Khiva became Russian. After the Revolution Samarkand
became the capital of Uzbekistan; now it is Tashkent. You
are interested in ceramics? Many inventions in ceramics had
their birth in Khiva. And there is a large ten-inch tile used
here that I will show you, invented in the eleventh century
and not known outside of Khiva for a hundred years. The
religion was Zoroastrian, but the Arabs brought the Muslim
religion in with the sword in the ninth century. Jenghi
Khan destroyed the city; Timur destroyed it. Zoroaste
himself at some time lived here. Omar Khayyam is said to
have seen it, Marco Polo, your own Antony Jenkinson too
in 1559—and he lived a month in Old Urgench—it has
produced more than its share of brilliance and more than
its share of darkness—the greatest slave trade has been here
Russia said they freed the city to free the slaves and then
found that the greatest number of slaves were Persians, not
Russians. The Russians used to be caught by the Caspian
Sea. It's market day and we'll go straight in.'

O I fell in love with Khiva. At last here was the past to
stare at. Countries do not realize that more than half of the
joy a visitor has is in staring at the past. The Russians do
not realize it. And almost all the nations of the world are
in a continuous state of tearing up their past. London is in
the process of obliterating Bloomsbury, yet if London could
have held on to the best of itself even since 1900 it could
have brought tourists flocking in for 500 years. Tourists all
if you visit the U.S.S.R. go to Khiva! You enter the past
The past which is still the present: Khiva as it is today as it
has been for many a thousand yesterdays. No wonder

Dubovitsky was proud of it. He was always discovering new titbits, masterpieces of doorways, picture-book alcoves, frolics in tiling and carving.

They say we don't want to live on in our old places. But we do. My house—which is the bead on the string this book is hung on—was built in the St Pancras section of Bloomsbury in 'the last street in the then London' in 1799. It could have stood 200 years more. The demolition squad had difficulty knocking it down. No one wanted to leave the area. Eleven acres—and much more close by—of London was axed and gawd knows why. Flimsy universal and nondescript buildings (I nearly wrote 'architecture': but that's what went) buildings have began to mushroom in their place. London becoming as it is in France, in Pennsylvania and Australia. To the utter end in this seven-year massacre not one of 700 tenants was able to find out what was going on beyond the fact that he had to go. We are a democracy. Listen to a dictatorship at work:

Dubovitsky: 'The government want to clear the centre of Khiva but no one will move out.'

I: 'Aren't they compelled to?'

Dubovitsky: 'They are offered terms and if they won't accept they won't. They are told of the advantages of modern flats: terms for purchases are raised. But the people won't budge. The government daren't do more: there'd be too big an outcry.'

Democracy: dictatorship: dare we look up our dictionaries?

61

'Khiva,' Dubovitsky said, 'is fed by a canal from the Amu-Darya River known to you as the Oxus. The Oxus is 1,578 miles long. It is the joke and the nightmare of the kingdom and known as 'wayward'. It's always changing course. It was said that if you took a steamer on it you might be two days or two months on your journey, goodness knows where the river would get to. It drowns cities, it floods agriculture. We are in an oasis of the Kara Kum desert. The old citadel of Khiva, the Kuni-Arq, had four gates, but in the nineteenth century an outer wall was built with ten gates. The inner city is called the Ishan Qa'leh and the outer city the Dishan Qa'leh. You'll be pleased to hear that the government have recently decided to preserve the Ishan Qa'leh as an ancient monument. They want the people to go but I can promise you the heart will remain architecturally intact. The population of what was the old kingdom of Khiva is 400,000 of which 90 per cent are Uzbek. The Uzbeks conquered this area in 1512. The district was mentioned in 600 B.C. but existed before. Cotton is our greatest trade, though the silk-worm industry stands high. You are one of the first visitors. The very first was Mr Jones. Can you guess where he came from?' Dubovitsky smiled.

'This kingdom had an undying feud with Bokhara which only ended when the Russians took over. Here we are at the entrance to the markets. In the old days Khiva was noted for hemp, oil, animal fats, wheat, rice, apples, sheep, fur coats, poppy-seeds for intoxicating liquors, and Russian pots, pans and sugar. Cattle also and, of course, slaves. The Persians claimed, probably misclaimed, that only 100 years ago one in two people here was a slave. The slaves had three days' freedom a year after Ramadan and all crowded into Khiva to meet, eat, discuss their trials and tribulations and imbibe their ounce of freedom. So, here we are, here's the market. You will see what you will see. But, sorry, no slaves.'

62

We entered under low arches. A man was leading a nigger-brown sheep who wouldn't be led, so the man carried him in.

It was the Bible inside: Bible beards, Bible robes, Bible characters squatting, Bible fruits, Bible buzz and Bible peace. Two boys were pushing a donkey around; they loved him, kissed him sometimes, he knew their love, but he was tired of their antics, their ridings, their loading him with nonsense for the sake of loading. Food, food, everywhere, in outrageous quantities. Melons and pumpkins, football-size and in hundreds, daffodil yellow, burnt red, staring orange, sea-bottom green; yards full of stacks and mounds of them. Onions, carrots, garlic, peppers, potatoes, maize, artichokes, rice, tomatoes twopence a kilo: all sumptuously spread out. Grapes pond-dark black, large and alive with nutriment . . . attempting to rival my Surya's eyes.

Dubovitsky left me to wander alone.

Two young people were taking photographs. I guessed they were Scandinavian.

Then I turned in a doorway to raise myself on two steps to improve my view when they came to the doorway also and started the ritual of cutting open a melon.

'Will you have a piece?' they asked.

'Yes. Thanks. Are you from Sweden?'

'We are from Moscow.'

'I thought you were foreigners.'

'We are. From Russia. This is very foreign here. The militia think we are from abroad too. They've stopped us twice to ask what we are photographing.'

'It's your dress that deceives them,' I said to the woman. 'It looks foreign-made. And your hair and features are Viking.'

'Perhaps we're all Viking,' she laughed. 'Rurik, who gave his name to Russia, whom many look on as our founder, was a Viking. I made my dress myself. It's from *Vogue*. I belong to a club where we hire the magazine out at a rouble a week.'

It used to be a rouble a page. Violetta's mother took it in the war and made all her daughter's clothes that way out of any old clothes the relations could uncover. Violetta always looked the best dressed in town. Her mother's results were so striking that scores of relatives and friends ordered clothes, even offered advance money sometimes. The mother meant to make them: a year went by, two years . . . she never made one, not even for herself. Only for her daughter. Love was the only goad the mother knew.

'This melon should not be called a melon,' I said. 'It's taste is so exquisite it should have a new name all of its own. It's a delirium of deliciousness.'

The couple's names were Elena and Eugene. Elena said: 'Arab documents of the tenth century recorded that the melons from these parts were as fine as any fruit on earth and by far the finest melons.'

All goods other than foods—carpets, cloths, books—were in kiosks or enclosed shops or stalls run by the government. The food was all capitalistic enterprise.

Elena and Eugene offered me more melon. Alas, it was a melon that had given me unholy dysentery in India, and I funked it.

63

Dubovitsky returned. Outside, the streets curled like swans' necks, heat swam in layers about the stuccoed buildings, tile-towered minaret led to tile-towered minaret, mosques crowded about, carved doors were a thousandfold—apricot was the favourite wood—carved as sweetly as if butter had been the material; colour and quiet and history alive hit at every turn, shadows shawled, faience and majolica glinted and glittered—at the most heavenly mausoleum, Dubovitsky told me 'Paklavan Makmud died in 1326. He was a Hercules. He was also a philosopher, composer, poet and fierce critic of the regime. For twenty years he lived in India. He considered he had an affinity with Omar Khayyam. Both wrote rubaiyats. When he died, an enemy of the powers, people flocked to his grave. The government began to charge for the visits. Still the thousands came. So the rulers saw their chance to build this so beautiful shrine and then with all the money still pouring in, to build their own mausoleums around it. And they are the others you see. I could translate one of his quatrains if you'd like it:

To go through a hundred mountains
To be locked up in the jail for a hundred years
To colour the sky with the blood of your heart
Is easier than to speak to a stupid man.'

64

We would return to Khiva on the morrow and left for Urgench.

In the park in Urgench I had seen two long tables like hall tables at a university, full of chess-boards with people playing.

I left with my camera hoping unobtrusively to take some pictures. I got held up by a thousand doves in an avenue of ash. The trees were so filled it was difficult to see the leaves. The trees flickered as hundreds of birds hovered beating their wings inches from the branches.

'Why are you looking at him so much?' a stranger asked me.

'Him? Oh the monument? No, I wasn't looking at the monument. But that's Kirov isn't it? Was he from these parts?'

'We think he was murdered unofficially officially. We think his murder was sanctioned and that all the thousands who suffered because of it were fish in the net too. We thought it so strongly that we had his monument here.'

'Why do you think all that?'

'Too close a rival to Stalin. Certainly he could have been his successor after his death if not before. He was a Leningrad man; he never came to these parts. Something else we question down here. Why did Lenin and Krupskaya have no children?'

I jumped to Lenin's defence. 'There are many people—

Bernard Shaw's another one—who fill their lives up with other activities and just don't have children.'

'We question here. We have more children than anywhere in the Union: seven per family is our average. You come from abroad: I wondered if you had heard any reason given about the Lenins.'

This was heresy. Lenin was God, and to hint that he might have erred was unheard of. One of my tourists once suggested to an Intourist guide that Lenin had been responsible for a death or two: the girl all but had apoplexy.

Dusk had come; I had missed my photography so I turned back to the hotel. Elena and Eugene waved from the hotel restaurant window and I turned in to see them.

'It's Eugene's birthday. Won't you sit with us?'

'Thanks. Then what about some vodka?'

'There is no vodka. There's scarcely any alcohol. We don't know what to do to celebrate.'

And I didn't know what to give. So I gave all my English coins. Eugene collected coins so that was well.

'Are you newly-weds?'

'No. We've been married six years. Eugene's thirty-one, I am twenty-five. This is our first holiday that we haven't had at the Crimea. It's expensive travelling! Is it expensive for you? It's 20 roubles per day each for us. We booked three weeks going round from Moscow. Then we'll end with a week in Sochi. It will cost us 1,200.'

I would be in Sochi at the same time. They took my address and said they'd call on me.

'It might be cheaper,' I said, 'when you are able to buy cars.'

'Oh we had a car. We sold it. And are having this holiday on the money. Eugene's an engineer. I teach English. Can I try my English on you?'

I listened. 'I would say,' I said, 'that you are not Viking. I would say you are English.'

It was a very English English. She lived for English. She had two radios, both permanently tuned in to different

B.B.C. stations. She had read three times what I had. There was not a word of Somerset Maugham she had missed: she looked upon his language with holiness. *Of Human Bondage* she read once a year.

Eugene spoke no English.

'We are buying our flat,' she said. 'That's taking a lot of our money. It will cost 4,500 roubles. We put 1,000 down and pay 20 each month. It will be ours in fifteen years. We have heard that in England if you buy slowly you pay more in the end? Can it be? It seems very unfair. Why is that? We pay 4,500 now or 4,500 over fifteen years. That seems fair. Another thing: if you sell in England you can sell for more than you are paying? Is it true? Why is that? That seems most unfair. We can sell in fifteen years at 4,500 or we can sell now for as much as we have already paid and the new people continue payments. That seems right. We might at some time live in the Crimea, so might want to move. We might sell to Eugene's mother. We were buying another flat, but this one is better, so we sold that for what we had already paid and continue with this. We are forbidden to make a profit: and if we lived in the Crimea and wanted to keep our Moscow flat, we would be forbidden to sublet at a profit. We will buy another car; it will cost us 2,200 roubles.'

The waitress had come with some vodka and wine! Eugene said: 'Let's have the vodka here and the wine upstairs after the football match.'

They were inviting me to their room to continue celebrations. 'What football match?' I asked.

'Manchester United versus Wolverhampton Wanderers on the TV.'

'Really?'

'Yes, really!'

Eugene was anxious to tell me about his small study in Moscow. 'I have an English corner. These are my photographs: Stanley Matthews, Matt Busby. Bobby Moore being presented the Cup by the Queen. Churchill's grandson

—I don't know why, because Churchill did bad to Russia, and my favourite Englishman, Sir Bernard Lovell. He helps us with our travels in space with his Jodrell Bank telescope and he takes such marvellous pictures and gives them to us.'

Elena joined in. 'We are members of the Flying Saucer Club in Moscow.'

But I had already chipped in: 'It's a pity we English are not in the Space Race. We've been in on every advance for man for 500 years, even revolution. We must have turned out more inventions than any nation; we've still got the brains, and Sir Bernard Lovell is one: yet here it is, the world's reaching out for the planets and we, reduced to an anybody financially, are for the main part just looking on.'

'What have you invented?' asked Eugene darkly.

'Football,' I said.

Eugene grunted.

'It's a very important invention,' I said. 'Very important. Then there's penicillin, radar, hovercraft . . .'

'What's that?'

I explained.

'Ppp! We've had them for years!'

His wife explained that they had had hydrofoils for years.

'Well, it's the same, it's better!'

'But we didn't invent the hydrofoil, dear.'

'Who said we didn't? What else?'

He had grown very dark. Elena, struggling at the same time to keep her husband calm, helped me in my list. It's preposterous what inventions have come out of tiny England! I am a poor patriot, but I was oozing with gush now. Our inventions, Shakespeare, afternoon tea and football: what else can you ask of a nation?

Eugene took the inventions one at a time, denied many outright, minimized the worth of others, granted nothing: would not admit that England had contributed a mote to the world: and Sir Bernard Lovell's contribution was that he aided the Russians. Elena tried to be a reasoning umpire, though it looked as if she came down on my side the more often. She said of radar: 'I heard at school that King George VI walked through an armaments factory in 1939 and gave scientists the idea which led to radar.'

If I have met a hundred Russians on this journey, ninety have been Eugenes and ten Elenas.

65

The football was a Eugene leg-pull: the match was Kiev versus Baku. Kiev were in their third year as champions of the U.S.S.R. They beat Baku 3–0. There was a lot of ballet in the game, pretty dancing over the ball, sophisticated entrechats and pirouettes, an elongated much ado about a wonderful nothing, then, like foreign matter injected, three explosive moves that led to three explosive goals.

The TV set was in the lobby of the second floor. Twenty watched. And the seventeen that remained watched as I followed Elena and Eugene to their room. I could feel their eyes in my back.

Violetta and I once met in the street. A shadow picked us up, followed us to a theatre, never lost sight of us through a four-hour opera, shadowed us to a hotel, came up hot after us to the floor on which I then had rooms, hurried to the woman-of-the-keys on duty there, demanded instant information. 'You are six months too late, comrade,' she said, 'they married last week.'

Elena and Eugene's room was not as classy as mine.

In fact they had a single room and I had a double room. So I offered to exchange. But they wouldn't. None of their water was functioning. We had grapes, melon, varieties of cakes including doughnuts—'I had always thought,' I said to Eugene, 'that the English invented the doughnut, but it is so popular here that if you like to claim it as a Russian invention . . . But tell me how serious are you in the Flying Saucer Club?'

Eugene was at all times light and bright unless I claimed some prowess for England or hinted that all was not complete perfection in his People's Paradise.

We had a sweet Georgian wine and had brought the remains of our vodka up. We had one glass, one cup and one saucer. Elena insisted on the saucer and I got the glass.

'Very serious. We had a woman tell us of a flight she was on from Moscow to Kiev; they were approached by "something". All lights went out. After some minutes all lights came on again and the "something" had gone. Gagarin was convinced that there was "something" out there. He worried as to however we could communicate with "it". I'll tell you one thing about our relationships with the West,' said Eugene, 'between 1950–1955 we were convinced there was going to be another war, that we were going to be attacked. Now we are convinced there is not going to be.'

'There dare not be,' I said, 'nuclear warfare is such that it has brought all leaders, except the completely insane, to an almost absolute point of hesitation.'

'Nuclear warfare,' said Eugene, 'has forced common-sense upon us.'

'By the way,' said Elena, 'our woman cosmonaut has had a baby.'

'Nothing!' said Eugene, 'will stop women having babies!'

Eugene looked shy: but possibly with intimates he'd be very far from shy. Elena was extraverted and lively.

Eugene was proud of his watch. His grandfather had

visited Paris and brought it home in 1900. It even had an inbuilt alarm.

At one o'clock Elena procured some hot water from someone on night duty and we had tea.

We gossiped, we argued fiercely, we laughed a lot, we drank a dozen healths and Eugene's especially. I invited them to London; they invited me to Moscow. And we'd meet at Sochi.

At three o'clock I left them.

66

On the road to Khiva next day Dubovitsky told me: 'The Khivans used to be so keen on chess that they carried it to war with them, the board being a sort of handkerchief on which the squares were drawn. They had no doctors. A hundred years ago there was not one doctor in the whole territory. Sufferers went to their learned priests, the mullahs, and that was all. Blood-letting was the cure-all. If not, then verses read from the Koran. Leprosy was common: and rheumatism from too much sleeping on the ground. It's all desert, desert, desert everywhere about and water was so rare that there is a proverb that one drop of water given to a thirsty man in a desert absolves you from a century of sin. Brides used to be purchased. A good one would cost £200—a lot of money then—and a squint eyed, smallpoxed one £15. A slave could cost as little as £4. You know the two sects of the Muslim religion: the Sunnites and the Shiites? Well, almost all slaves were

Shiites—like as if your Catholics having only Protestant slaves. Often slaves bought their independence, then were waylaid by those they had paid and murdered after all had been stripped from them. Sometimes the slaves learnt of this and only agreed to pay after they had gone a certain distance. Then the owner would journey to another tribe and watch out for his 'runaway slave' then lead him back weighted down with wood, lead and irons. Then more slaves got more cunning still. Having bought their freedom they stayed on in Khiva. At one point 40,000 slaves bought their freedom and all stayed on to live in Khiva. Khiva used to be the most important of all the khanates stretching as far up to the gates of Baghdad as terrain allowed and well into India. One conqueror, Allah-el-din, titled himself 'God's Shadow on Earth' and his mother 'Mistress of the World'. In 1716 the Russians under Prince Cherkasski defeated the Khivans. The khan made his peace but said to assist matters for housing the victors the Russians should divide into five groups. They did so . . . and were slaughtered one at a time.

'You should know of the bouran. It occurs out in the steppes, in the deserts. It's a north-west wind accompanied by snow—it can be 32° below zero out there, though it's a furnace in the summer and the winter is only short. It affects men so much that they can be found frozen only yards from their homes; in town streets or villages they can be found exhausted having strayed in circle after circle. The cattle run with the wind for 100 miles without stopping and sometimes rush straight over precipices and steep banks of rivers. No Khirghis will be your guide in a bouran. In 1827 it was recorded that in one bouran 10,500 camels were lost together with 280,500 horses, 75,400 head of cattle and million sheep. They all rushed northwards in the direction of Saratov.

'The great Russian invasion of Khiva in 1840 was precipitated by you, the British. You were stretching out beyond India and Afghanistan. In those days it was called spheres of influence. And we looked upon this as our sphere of influence especially as you had settled in China as well as India. You sent emissaries chiefly to Bokhara, trying the foolish idea of uniting the khanates against the common enemy, Russia. You did not know their first hates were to each other. Your emissaries were put to prison and although they kissed the Koran and swore to the Muslim faith they died there. The Russian invasion was a disaster and the troops turned back with no result and no enemy seen. 7,000 camels started: 600 returned. The cold defeated them.

'Have you discovered how Uzbeks love the poets? More than in anything they revel in poetry.

'Don't think that it is only the Soviets who work their women. Uzbek women, since time immemorial, have tilled the soil, collected and prepared the kiziaks, which are the pats of cow-dung used for fuel, spun, weaved, made clothes for the whole family, made sheepskin dresses, tanned and dyed leather, made pelisses, raked the beds in the gardens, reaped, winnowed the corn, and done the household work. The woman was always the ox of the family. She also always paid for the household out of her earnings. The man paid out on festive occasions. Children and parents rarely respected each other. The Uzbeks worked their children irrespective of their potential talents as soon as possible and the children hit and punched their parents as soon as they had the strength.

'In Khiva you will see 2 palaces, 17 mosques, 22 madrasas a caravanserai, a covered market and 260 shops dating back 300 years.'

We went to the mosque of Pulnan Ata, built in 1811 in honour of the saint Khan Mohammed Rahim. It was buil of brick with a green cupola gilded at the top. A coppe railing surrounded the tomb of Rahim and chandeliers hung over the tombs of a Khirghis khan and an Uzbek khan who died in 1842. The saint Pulnan Ata was buried in a tomb seen with difficulty through a grating, a tomb twelve fee long and four feet high. We saw the mosque Send Bai buil

12. Samarkand: Uleg Beg Minaret and Madras

13a. Bokhara

13b. What was it? At Afrasiyab, site of the first Samarkand

in 1835. We saw the palace of the khan in front of which was a pit fifteen feet deep where criminals were punished. Dubovitsky said: 'The Khivanese did not consider torture as cruel. Inhuman behaviour was considered natural, being in accordance with law, custom and religion.'

The caravanserai was built in 1823 in the western part of the town and had forty-six shops, and above them forty-six rooms for travellers.

There were no open squares in Khiva. The streets tortured about, then suddenly there was a grand palace, the stately Khoja Islam minaret, or the incredible Kalta Minar minaret meant to be the largest and widest in the world, to be built so high that Bokhara could be seen from it, but never finished, standing a majestic colossus of nothing.

I saw Elena and Eugene. I called out to them. It seemed they didn't hear so I left Dubovitsky and hurried away to them. They gave me a lukewarm greeting and Eugene hardly gave me a greeting at all.

'Come and meet my guide,' I said, 'he's got keys to some wonderful places. You'll never see them unless you join us. There's a place with 215 wooden columns some of them dating back to the twelfth century.'

Elena turned to Eugene to reply. 'I don't think we will,' he said.

'But these are marvellous things. And he knows everything. He's a fine fellow. You'll miss some of the best if you don't join us. Come on, I'll introduce you.'

I dashed back to Dubovitsky thinking they were at my heels. When I looked round they weren't there. I called out. At last Elena came forward from behind a wall to show herself.

I went to the wall. Were they hiding from us? I brought them forward. I introduced them. There was a coldness between the three.

I repeated that the pair should join us. Eugene showed his notebook and that they had a plan to carry out. They had better stick to it. I thought he was stupid. I thought he was unfriendly and forcing his wife against her will also to be so.

I'm very dim at times and things can dawn on me insanely slowly. Elena and Eugene left us. I was piqued especially with Eugene . . . penny, penny when will you drop?

They had been got at.

'All foreigners are spies. Keep away from them.' This is no communist innovation: Russians have been suspicious of foreigners for 500 years: in Peter the Great's time they reckoned on three Russians to watch one foreigner. It's an inborn pathological trait. Elena and Eugene would be all right. Even under Stalin one warning was always given and the wise accepted it and there'd be no more trouble. It was only the lovers who were unwise. A salute to the unwise!

There was no meeting in Sochi.

My evening last night had now become soured. The young couple would be thinking: 'Ah maybe he was O.K. last night, just sugaring us up for something . . .' What had been healthy was now sick.

67

The mosque with the 215 wooden columns had a flat roof and no cupolas, which was most rare. Five of the columns were from the twelfth century and the remainder from the seventeenth. The bulbous, abstract-carved and never fluted columns were wondrously handsome. Occasionally there was a hole in the roof to let a tree go through, a tree ıysteriously growing inside the mosque. In the centre of ıe mosque was a fire altar for sacrifices.

Dubovitsky said: 'Because the government are to turn the eart of Khiva into a museum they are offering high cash or ancient carved columns and doors and the people haggle ery much for better prices.'

Out in the street again we almost immediately faced the reat unfinished Kalta Minar minaret. 'There are three easons given for it never having been finished,' Dubovitsky aid: 'One because its builder Islam Haja was killed at war nd his successors did not want to glorify him. Two because e wished to build it so high—100 metres, it is stopped at wenty-six metres—that he could see Bokhara from it and okhara tempted its craftsmen away to build a still higher ne there. Three because the chief builder fell in love with ıe khan's daughter and the khan had them both flung from ıe top. It is fourteen metres wide at the base.' This great nfinished work was as recent as 1908! Nine years before ıe revolution they still built so nobly. 'Did I tell you that enghis Khan and Timur both destroyed Khiva utterly xcept for the one mosque you have just been in? We know ıat because it is two metres below present ground level, ıe sand having built the level up.'

Many of the houses in the streets had no windows facing ıe streets but opened on to the courtyards within. I was taring into one interior, and seeing carpets and mats pread everywhere instead of chairs, when the owner came ut to talk. He said he only had two rooms and his caked ıud house was only sixty years old. The government had ffered him 2,000 roubles to leave and it was a rotten offer. Ie said taxes were high: as a single man he must pay 16 per ent in income tax whereas married men only paid 10 per ent or 6 per cent if there was one child. We talked by a ne of mulberry and acacia trees. Dubovitsky joined our ıx conversation. He said that he paid 6 per cent and 10 oubles a month for the crèche for his children. He got 5 per cent added to his salary because he agreed to work

outside Tashkent. He said his salary was low, 250 rouble
a month, but he was allowed to take extra work as tourist
were still rare bods. The man by the mulberry tree told m
that the likes of him considered a hundred roubles a mont
a wonderful salary.

It was not that the individual showpieces of Khiv
shattered the senses with their greatness: it was that Khiv
with centuries of fame behind it was still itself; like th
centre of Salisbury, like Milton Abbas and Wroxton, lik
sections of Bath, it was alive among the buildings of its pas
Stevenage, Basildon, and cities where the new regime of th
Soviets have made their imprint, do not and cannot giv
this feeling. In all this journey only Khiva, and later Tbilis
gave this atmosphere and if a visitor could stay a month
cocoon of centuries would wool about him and he woul
be overcoated around with an enthralment that would neve
leave him.

68

Sweet to ride forth at evening from the wells,
When shadows pass gigantic on the sand,
And softly through the silence beat the bells
Along the Golden Road to Samarkand.

We travel not for trafficking alone;
By hotter winds our fiery hearts are fanned:
For lust of knowing what should not be known,
We take the Golden Road to Samarkand.*

* James Elroy Flecker: *Hassan*, Heinemann, 1922.

The car was ready outside the hotel at nine o'clock at Tashkent which was the starting point for all these visits in Uzbekistan. The driver, Mikhaelov, had brought his son Stepan, aged twenty-two, with him. Samarkand was 270 kilometres away to the south-west.

The strength of the lines in Flecker's play perhaps means that half the world has a longing to visit Samarkand; and half of that half a desire to turn up by road.

I have bicycled in thirty countries and had had a private dream to enter Samarkand on my bicycle, then pat my bike on its saddle with thanks, then put it out to grass. That was to have been our ending.

Perfect would have been to have entered in a camel caravan.

Some wishes are only dreams. I was fortunate enough. My companions were down-to-earth, practical . . . to use a phrase stinking with sanctimonious condescension, they were 'honest men'.

I asked a few questions about food for the journey and was told we would be stopping at Dzjizak halfway. Through the broad avenues of plane trees, past the nine-storey building they were so proud of, now to become a hotel, that had stood firm throughout the earthquake with all else tumbling down about it, past tall pre-revolution timber apartment blocks, past the mud and wattle suburbs with plate-and-saucer-shaped-shadows down the walls, past the red and yellow and green and white down-striped costumes of the Uzbeks wandering with their wearers in and out and among acacias and poplars, past a flock of geese, then a line of willows, two donkeys taking time off to nibble in a ditch, one last low hut, now fields of maize, now a mile of cotton, some children squatting waiting for a bus, a pool and a broken fence and nothing to indicate a reason for a fence, one lone camel, blue doves flying . . . no wonder the Soviets use the dove so much in peace demonstrations; the most common bird I saw throughout my trip was the dove, and often looking abnormally soft

and peaceful, abnormal because it's a rigorous land fo
climate, and the doves looked sophisticated, towny, warm
comfortable, more as if taffeta-coated than feathered, mor
suited to a boudoir than the devil's own cold and heat an
wind.

'You didn't mind my bringing my son? He has neve
seen Samarkand.'

'Have you been often?'

'I have been six or eight times.'

We drove in a Volga.

The road was asphalt. All roads (and all aeroplanes an
trains too) were more superior than my expectations. I
this instance today I was sorry. I wanted a camel-track of
dust of a road.

'I had heard,' I said, 'that the U.S.S.R. would never hav
good roads: it would go straight from river and trai
travel to aeroplane travel: that distances are too great t
justify the cost of road building. But as far as I could se
you could even travel by good road all the way t
Vladivostok.'

'I am not sure,' Mikhaelov said. 'Are you married?' H
passed me the photograph of his wife. He had thre
children.

'Lovely face your wife has. It's very nice for us tourist
that we can see your women's faces now. Are you pleasec
the Revolution freed your women?'

'Yes.'

'Will you ask your father before you ask a girl to marr
you?' I asked Stepan.

'We are a Russian family,' he said, 'and never have done
such things. I sort of asked her and she sort of said yes.

'And then they told my wife!' the father joined in. 'Anc
then they told the town! And then they told me!'

'But she is an Uzbek girl,' said Stepan, 'and before the
Revolution it could not have happened.'

'You would not even have seen her, my son!' called the
father.

'This is her photograph.' And Stepan passed the photograph forward to the front seat.

'Plaits,' I said.

'They all have plaits. She was late and said she had been doing her plaits. I said next time she could come with them undone, and I would do them. She said, nothing she wanted more than for me to do her plaits all the time. I said if she wanted that she'd have to marry me. And she accepted and I hadn't meant it. She saw my surprise and she said she'd let me off—after marriage she'd wear only three plaits instead of eight.'

69

It was arid. Stone and dirt and dust and sand, flat to the horizon; a paper sky with a lick of blue and, at the side of the road, one donkey. On the donkey was an Uzbek man, bent and already clothed against the winter still one month away. Behind was a cart that the donkey pulled: a two-wheeled cart of such odd contraption it looked like a framework for delivering plate glass. Why the man rode on the donkey and not in the cart was the only mystery in a scene that could call for no other mystery.

Some tufts of desert grass, blobs of green on a scene yellow to ending and then, stabbed like stubs a mile away, a line of wattle houses ochre yellow, and above them a sky of Chinese blue. Nothing else in that scene in any direction.

Then, further on where Mikhaelov called it the Hungry Steppe, the colour had been drained out. Take a sheet of white paper and up to halfway think of it as white sand; and above halfway think of it as white sky; and just before the white sand joins the white sky draw a thin pencil line across for a line of a thousand cattle far away. And that is another scene.

The road ran blue through the white desert. There were whirlwinds of sand often rising. The whirlwinds formed in spirals—Mikhaelov suggested by two currents of air meeting—dashed for a hundred yards or spiralled on the spot where they formed—dust, sand and dried grass all rising up in a whirligig more than lamp-post high, often such whirligigs going at it together, then suddenly they stopped spiralling or dropped dead—usually just as my camera was at the ready. The atmosphere all round was tranquil but Mikhaelov said that very close by the columns the wind might be heard whistling around caught in the centre.

Beauty is in the eye of the beholder. Beauty is in the stomach, mind, warmth and condition of the beholder too. Take an Arctic waste and view it on a satisfied stomach, in a quiet mind from a snug cinema seat and you will see its beauty: view the desolation of Angkor under a fiery tropical heat from the pages of *Exploration* in an armchair and you will stagger at the marvels . . . take a Volga and two good Russians and fruit passing back and forth and a pleasant heat and a blue road as a ribbon from Tashkent to Samarkand and you will revel in the graduation of colours, in the glory of vast nothingness, in a hill or wattle hut so perfectly blended in that you cannot say where hill or hut ends and desert or sky begins. Yet Alexander the Great came down this road, and Jenghis Khan and Tamberlane, and a hundred times in 2,000 years this very road could have been carpeted with corpses. Even in times of peace men have died from thirst out there, perished from the cold, died from the cobra or from the asp, starved to death.

Zenkovsky used to say, how could a man with a full stomach pass judgement on a hungry thief: how can I from my de luxe view assess these scenes that bring only delight to the eye? There was nothing grim or stark or forbidding in them: there were always soft and gentle colourings and an inner feeling of tremendous wonder.

My 'cinema seat' view of the road to Samarkand had taken on an aura of warm awe.

At Dzjizak we stopped for lunch.

70

We drove into a dirt yard. A dozen lorries had pulled in. There was a corrugated iron roof down one side and tables under it. Most seats were soap boxes. There was spittle, oil, noblets of tough meat men had spat out on the grimy ground. We ordered schashlik and beer, only Mikhaelov, driving, would have no beer. There were no potatoes, but onions. The schashlik was on yard-long knives: eating was holding the knife each end in the hand and pulling off piece by piece with the teeth trying not to split a lip on the knife's edge. All was tasty, but because one hunk in four was inedibly tough and because the extra onions were served on broken saucers on an unswept rickety table, this detracted from the tastiness. The beer was weak. Strong beer, which is rare, would have made a right combination. Often, at workmen's halts like these, food can be better than in first-class restaurants: but it is not often tastily served. My food throughout this entire trip considering the exorbitant prices averaged well below West European standards. Most Russians, like most British, do not love their stomachs enough to put love into their cooking. The temptation was to steer clear of places like this one because of the unappetizing presentation, but often the garnishing and the sauces surprised.

We had tomato patties. There were peppers and garlic in them.

As we left I said to Mikaelov 'Any chance of tea?'

'In a minute,' he said.

We left the car near a railway line. Stepan stayed with it. Mikhaelov and I went to a rambly place. It was full of 'ping-pong' tables with legs sawn off to bring them down to sitting height. Men squatted there, legs crossed. There were bolsters and arm-rests. Men eased and lazed and sipped tea. These were all Uzbeks. The pull-in restaurant had been filled mostly with Russians. There was music, very Indian, there were chickens, sweets like red lollies, pumpkins and melons multitudinous, a halva served by a man with crutches. Over the brick enclosed fires were copper chimney funnels.

The tea we had was green tea and we drank from bowls. There were various varieties of tea and teapots stood about on stoves in platoon-like formations of twenty and thirty. Biblical characters with prophet beards like sages through the ages, most with skull-caps and a few with fur hats—skull-caps were Uzbek, the broad fur hat Tadjik—robes and never suits, conversation and never argument, contentment and never anxiety, savouring the passing of time and never rush. Most ate melons or grapes. We bought both. Mikhaelov borrowed the proprietor's knife and set about the ritual of melon cutting. Some very poor men went round sweeping the seeds and skins and wastes of melon-cutting into sacks which they carried away with them.

All was ramshackle, the table-seats sprawled around yards, a timber store was at one end, a garage at another, the road at another: a feeling of taking your ease with friends in your own backyard. Every face would have left Rembrandt spellbound.

For twenty years Flecker's lines had sung in my ears 'We'll take the Golden Road to Samarkand'. I yearned for a build-up to match the pictures the lines painted. This corner helped. The schashlik stop had been too much of our times: while the asphalt road had taken the gold out of the road.

Dzjizak too had known Alexander and Jenghis Khan and Timur. It was at the junction of the road to Fergana.

71

'For lust of knowing what should not be known' . . what had Flecker referred to? I don't know. But I do know that it was not for poetic content alone he called it the Golden Road. For a thousand years people have said there is gold in these deserts.

The militia stopped us. There was a high glass tower at the edge of the road and from this we were summoned to stop. Mikhaelov had to explain his English cargo.

There might have been more checkpoints. I did not look out for them. Rumour is that there are militia stationed at every forty miles throughout the country. As a car passes, they phone the next place who look out for it. If it doesn't turn up a search is instigated. Like all done for the foreigner, things are double edged. A sympathizer with the regime will say, isn't it wonderful, if you break down on the road assistance will come in no time? A non-sympathizer will say, hell, you can't even stop for a snooze or a picnic or a rolypoly in the grass or a vodka in a village but that they are on your tracks in an hour.

Seats in restaurants are reserved for Intourist, that is fo foreigners. It means better service. It also means you don' sit with Russians.

I asked to do this journey by bicycle. I was told I mus keep to main roads, never to turn off by more than 2½ miles only to stop at camping sites or hotels which could be 100 200, 300 miles apart (some cycling!), never to accept th hospitality of a Russian, and that bicycles, scooters, motor cycles weren't allowed anyhow. It could be said they didn' want me to get lost in their vast country. It could be sai they didn't want me to see their off-track villages. 'Fo lust of knowing what should not be known' I had asked

72

Out again into the open road, out into the Hungry Steppe Marmots were the chief population. From the far distance hills began to march towards us.

From the colour box came a pink, and a wash of pal carbuncle came over the road, over the desert, over th gentle hills and began to enter the sky. There was an aur of chintz in the warm glow.

This was the road that curled in from Kokand, Asia' old highway built for trafficking in salt, handling down th centuries spices from the east, sandalwood carvings fror the south, Bokhara carpets from the east, and furs and skir and slaves from Russia and the north. It knew civilizatio when England knew barbarism. It knew barbarism whe England knew civilization. The souls of the too-soon dea hover over the area where they are slain: and for 3,000 years the souls of the too-soon dead have held ghostly concourse here. The Revolution fifty years ago brought in its wake the last page of that fearful canker, war. Since then lorries have driven where camels used to go, asphalt has been placed where the natural earth had served.

The hills were set all round us now. We stayed level but twisted through the gentle valleys. One pink-coated hill had a breast pocket of pure purple. An eagle held timeless in the sky. A stork passed over like a lazy arrow. We passed a hundred sheep with ebony black faces protruding out of deep nigger-brown curly woollen bodies. Once far in a valley appeared perhaps a thousand head of cattle with one jerky horseman against a weep of green.

Our white car sped along our now mauve road to hills away.

All nature was mounting a grandstand finish for entrance into Samarkand.

Out of nowhere, out of a sudden mound, shot a waterfall spitting diamonds and in the rush of verdure about it stood seven willows in a row.

We slipped through a damask gorge.

I was excited as at a race, almost cheering at the mounting glories.

And then . . . it faded. For forty miles I tried to will the road to live up to the poem. The hills began to desert us. For a while the great strains of the desert stayed stretching far to the distance to the edge of the climb that led up to the Pamirs. Across the wide across, up the high up, over the wild over, to neverending and to Turkestan.

Then the humdrum began replacing the desolations. Cotton was with us again. Then maize. Even elms. Then cherry and apple. Then carts towering high carrying loads of briar.

And it was flat. And the hills had gone. Wattle cottages right on the roadside. The down-striped Uzbek costumes. Even a dog.

At every mile of the last forty I hoped the poetry woul
come back to the road. It grew dull. Miles out only w
reached a hill. I asked Mikhaelov to stop.

We climbed to the top. Over the trees, beyond the fe
miles of pink-gold hills, were lines of warm blue grey. Ou
of them two scars were against the sky. They were th
remains of the Bibi-Khanum mosque. Samarkand was befor
us.

The colours remained warm and welcome. The scene
became ordinary.

As we drove in, back there across the Hungry Steppe th
shadows would be passing gigantic on the sand.

73

Samarkand was grandiose. Its avenues were sumptuou
and grandly shaded with old plane trees. 'I went to London,
said my guide, 'and could not believe my eyes. What wer
plane trees doing there? I thought we only had them here.

There was a park in which everything seemed happening
Three orchestras, two dance-bands, forty table-tennis tables
a hundred chessboards, thirty netball courts, sixty finely kep
billiard tables, and all sports in full use: then there wer
walks, fountains, flower-beds and benches numerous: a hiv
of joy—'wholesome joy' as the authorities would like i
pointed out.

The past of Samarkand existed as monuments to visit, a
in London or a thousand other cities. In Khiva history ha
been still the present day. Here tourists set forth and di

their rounds, and the city itself was very much of our century. It was in every way pleasant: it is just that Samarkand being what it is in the public image it might have had a stronger impact had it still been as Khiva, asleep and alive in its past.

There is a poem by Langdon Smith* which begins:

> When you were a tadpole and I was a fish,
> In the Paleozoic time,
> And side by side on the ebbing tide
> We sprawled through the ooze and slime,
> Or skittered with many a caudal flip
> Through the depths of the Cambrian fen,
> My heart was rife with the joy of life,
> For I loved you even then.

About that time Samarkand was born. It was called Maracanda and was the capital of Sogdiana. In 329 Alexander the Great captured it and like all great men he mostly flattened it. He also killed his favourite, Clitus, here. In the ninth and tenth centuries it was captured by the Arabs and they in their greatness did more flattening. In the eleventh century it was conquered by the Karakhanids, then the Seljuks, then the Kara Kitais and in the thirteenth century by Khiva. All contributed their share of destruction. Then the greatest of them all came along, Jenghis Khan in 1220, and he could hardly bear it if a stone were left standing. In 1365 the Samarkandians said 'enough' and kicked the Mongols out and built a little. Then Timur captured it and knocked it about to ensure his name in the history books (that's the least the historians demand: Shah Jahan built finer than perhaps any monarch and did little destruction and the historians call his reign 'dull and uneventful'. Another ingredient that historians demand: that is that no great people have fun. Henry VIII and Nero are to be cartooned. Top of the chart men do not smile: Great Timur

* From *Treasure Trove* by John O'London, Newnes, 1925.

passed laws forbidding joviality and humour). Timur returned and made Samarkand 'his' city. He rebuilt a few miles from the old city and the glory of Samarkand is very much the glory of Timur. There followed so many conquerors that they can't all be named as I have been asked to keep my book to under 100,000 words: but at one point the inhabitants got utterly tired of great men destroying it and from 1720 to 1770 not one soul inhabited it. The Russians took Samarkand in 1868, destroying the six gates and the eleventh-century five-mile walls that surrounded it, made it capital of Uzbekistan in 1924, made Tashkent the capital in 1930; and now Samarkand is a living pleasant place, with history in every cubic inch, active and a joy to stop in, no doubt to live in too. It has a university, an Uzbek and a Russian theatre, a railway and an airport. Only the waiters are alarming: they serve you immediately.

Samarkand was on the Silk Road, the junction where China met India. It contributed itself to the caravans with wine, dried and fresh fruits, carpets, cotton, rice, silk and leather.

Samarkand stands 2,000 feet above sea level. It has been sung as 'The Mirror of the World', 'The Garden of Souls', 'The Fourth Paradise' 'The chosen above of all the arts that adorn and sweeten life'. Timur called it 'The eye and the star of the earth'.

Timur's sepulchre is known as the Gur Amir. It is reached down a double avenue of poplars ending with a gateway covered with faience and flanked by ruined minarets. The Gur Amir itself is octagonal and the dome above it is deeply fluted with cerulean-green tiles; a ceramic wonder. Inside is a vaulted corridor leading to a thirty-five-foot chamber with a cupola 115 feet from the ground. The walls are covered with six-sided plates of transparent gypsum. Timur's tomb is severely simple. Muslims so constantly create miracles of simplicity. 'Only a stone,' said Timur, 'and my name upon it.' It is the largest sheet of jade in the world, one slab 6′4¼″ long, 1′3¾″ wide and 1′5½″ deep and dark green. Many adherents came in to offer prayers while I was there and I put my camera away as I felt they felt it an offence that I was not religious before such a spot.

I went out to sit in the garden in the sunlight ready to feel the breath of Timur. But a gang of boys gathered round and wouldn't leave. They wanted to know about my children. I said they were twelve and ten, a boy and a girl. They asked if they ate bananas and what presents had I given them. 'Why did you give your son a watch and not your daughter?' They wanted to write to my son and my daughter. So I gave them my address and now I must find a Charles aged twelve and an Anne aged ten to give the letters to. They performed fencing battles with long rods and asked me to photograph them to show Charles and Anne.

74

The Registan is the main square of Samarkand. Of noble proportions and surrounded by three madrasas, huge and one-time wonderful, now mostly down but being repaired by the authorities. These, on three sides, the fourth side remaining open. One madrasa, on the south, was built in 1648 by Iman Kuli Khan and has melon-shaped domes and tall minarets. Inside a courtyard were cubicles and class-rooms of two storeys. On the north side of the Registan is the Tila Kari, and the third and smallest on the west is called the Shir Dar, founded by Uleg Beg, the astronomer grandson of Timur. An Uzbek came up to me and said he came once every five years from Tashkent to view the progress in the renovations but the progress was so negligible he might as well have made it every ten years. There were always artisans around and they chipped a few blocks and polished for weeks on end but he hoped he could live two hundred years so that he might see a real development. It was the size, the majestic proportions of the buildings of the Registan which gave it its great character. At some time it must truly have been awe-inspiring.

I had begged the authorities to show me a ceramics factory or craft shop and was always told 'In Samarkand. In Samarkand.' I was about to see such a place and was excited, for Central Asia, and Samarkand itself, have given more to this craft than any other spot. Behind the central madrasa in the Registan we went, the guide and I. There was a yard, like a tiny stonemason's yard. At the end was a room and in it a smallish kiln. Rectangles of 3″×1″ were being glazed in monotones: these to fill in the gaps in the thousand mosque walls throughout the land. I was expected to be thrilled. I was alarmed. Has all that come to all this? 10,000 schools in England with no aspirations could have shown me more. Dear Kremlin, why have you murdered the crafts? Not even designs here: just monotone glazes: not even tiles just dog-biscuit bits! I was assured this was the all that went on in this field in the entire country. It would have been insulting to have left a tear behind: a nuclear bomb of rage and fury is necessary. Crafts they say are individual joys, and to be individual, they say, is to be a capitalistic petit bourgeois. I once went through endless endless rooms of ceramics in London's museums and selected as my favourites works from Samarkand. I was yet, on this journey, to be made aware that unequalled masterpieces were forthcoming from here right up to the day of the revolution . . . But since then, silence. When will they learn it? When will they learn that the greatness of a country is the sum total of its great individuals? Haven't Shostakovitch, Prokofiev, Eisenstein, Botvinik, Ulanova,

Pasternak, Soltzeniken, Oistrakh, Pavlov, Tolstoy proved that to them yet?

It was the size, the majestic proportions of the buildings of the Registan which gave it its great character. At some time it must truly have been awe-inspiring.

75

I went to the theatre. There were three one-act ballets. The last was Ravel's *Bolero*.

The curtains opened on a pale light on a female form. Others were on the stage, but felt more than seen. She danced slowly, but so slight was the light on her that it was a pale apparition in movement. Gradually it could be seen she was wearing red and black. As the music gained power so did the lighting. She danced over the entire stage, ending at a rear corner from which she brought out two other figures. Then she left. The two brought out two more. Almost unnoticeably others came and almost unnoticeably they joined in. The only three the audience were very aware of were the female lead who had reappeared and her two male lovers, claimants to her hand.

Then the music and choreography took over and all became one with the action. A corps of thirty dancers were on the stage and it built up to sixty and all became of the action, yet never intruding absolutely. The corps de ballet were separate dancers in themselves, unaware of the drama which only gradually took command of the centre of the stage over the pattern-weaving of the multitude. The swirling skirts, the stomping, the strong gut-filled colours, remained more a part of the music than of the dramatic triangle, and never became fully involved: at the same time the immense orchestra, the growing flood of dancers and the battle for the lady's hand were uncannily ever one.

The brass came in, the music grew, the lights flashed full, the corps de ballet beat about like moths, yet very much Spanish dancers also, and then the audience too got trapped inside the spellbinding.

The rivals glorified themselves and it was a terrible crescendo that was mounting.

Is there any greater drama in ballet than the end of Act I in *Giselle*? And yet there the drama rests with the principals, with the other dancers in the main trapped in the agony of what they are witnessing. The music gloriously adds its dramatic contribution. The audience suffers and watches. But all are extraneous to the principals.

In this *Bolero* today the corps de ballet and the music were the pulse of the action: and just as in life our pulse is involved with us yet it is not consciously involved in our actions, so the pulse of the sixty, of the trombones and drums, became of the fever yet never absolutely cognisant of it.

The music, the flashing rhythmic dancers, the three the story concerned, and the audience too were sucked into an inevitability, terrifying, terrific, larger than three lives, as large as all life. And all were driving the three and they were driving themselves. There was not one being on stage or in auditorium who was a bystander: and yet, dreadfully, like a reader of a book, the corps de ballet were only connected to the drama as limbs to a body, as an umbilical cord, as something slightly extraneous, as observers on a fringe.

In a moment of absolute drama in any person's life that person feels a surcharge of outside forces, as if what is happening to him or her is of cataclysmic emotions one thousand times larger than his normal living: as if he or she is not experiencing a personal thing but something which is a part of all life, so much bigger than just his own life.

So in this ballet all else beside the three leads: the corps de ballet, musicians, audience, became that outer life of which the struggle of the rivals was the inner. And this outer life was of all-emotion, all-fighting, all-heart-and-soul strife: and the three were three who had detached themselves from the umbilical cord, to dare to death their private drama.

One rival had won. To reach him the woman stepped across the path of the other, the loser. The loser drew a knife and stabbed his beloved as she crossed in front of him. Sudden silence. All cacophony, all movement was frozen. There was petrification and stillness.

The curtain lowered.

I could not applaud and no one else could. I have never heard silence speak in the soul like that. Someone attempted a little clap. I tried to join in. I couldn't. The someone stopped also.

I hope the performers understood.

If only Ravel could have been there.

76

Pendjakent was in Tadjikstan fifty kilometres east from Samarkand. 'Was' is the right word, because 'is' it is not. It was destroyed in 723 A.D. and has never risen again.

I went with a driver so mad for speed and so uninterested in pot-holes, chickens, sheep, barriers like road repairs, that my only excuse for remaining alive is that I must be a cat. There was however one barrier which barred the whole road and a turn through a village was indicated. The driver would not accept it. He went through the barriers, got stuck in the tar, argued for forty minutes with a foreman, came out aflame in fury into a hundred cows which he began to treat as dodgems at a fairground. Then he continued in the steppes of Jenghis Khan.

We went to a museum named after Rudaki. Rudaki was the founder of Tadjik literature and lived in the ninth century.

A guide took us one mile outside the present village to a hill among hills. Then we walked the last hundred yards to see what the Arabs had done. Pendjakent had been a flourishing town in the country of Sogdiana of which Maracanda, now Samarkand, had been the capital. Pendjakent was here in the fourth century B.C. when Alexander came through.

Now we walked among its scars in a scorching heat. The city stood waist high. The roads were ten feet wide: we saw the drainage, some mosaic walls covered now with paper and then mould (both of which were removed to show me) which archaeologists had put there to serve as protection for the mosaics until removed to the museum. The walls were of earth: lavatories were holes in the ground which fell to considerable depths; we saw old stoves, open spaces which might have been theatres. 5,000 coins had been unearthed, ornaments, pots, but not arms. There had been three-storey houses. We went down a street where it could be seen that each house-front must have been a shop as in a bazaar. The religion had been Zoroastrian. This meant no cemeteries. As the Zoroastrians (Parsees) do today the bodies of the dead were put out for the birds to pick clean to the bone. The inhabitants had got warning of the Arab invasion and had fled almost to a man. The Arabs destroyed the empty city utterly.

With the Aksu River beneath it, and caught between the Suzan Garan mountains to the north and the Kara Tau mountains to the south, Pendjakent had had a fine setting for a city. Snow could be seen far away on the mountain tops. 1,100 years after Alexander came through it was destroyed. 1,200 years after its destruction Soviet archaeologists began to unearth its stories.

Our guide said: 'A quarter of the nineteen-hectare town has been uncovered. Temples, byways, artisans' shops and houses upon houses have been bared. The Tadjik Expedition led by A. Y. Yakobovsky decided to select this as their site to find cultural links with East Turkestan, Afghanistan, Iraq, Pakistan and India. They have found much Buddhist influence. The Moscow and Leningrad expeditions have shown chief interest in studying the irrigation, problems of contact with other parts, ethnic origins, rituals, economic and social structures. It is a site selected. It could have been any of a hundred other sites in these parts. Away to the east you see the Pamirs, that part which we call the Bum-i-Dunya, the Roof of the World. From there came out this man Zoroaster, unwanted there but listened to here and his very great religion caught alight throughout all these vast areas.'

77

The most impressive group of buildings in Samarkand are the Shah-i-Zindah (the living saint). Kasim Ibn Abbas, a saint, endured martyrdom in attempting to get converts. Some claimed him as the grandson of Mohammed. He picked up his severed head—as they did in those days, like the Green Knight—and retired with it to a well whence he will emerge at Islam's triumph. The Shah-i-Zindah is entered by a brick gateway rich in blue and white faience opening on to a street of tombs—a minor Appian Way. There are a series of mausoleums erected to Timur's family and generals and servants, many with sublime majolica and mosaic decorations—the best in Samarkand. The vista closes with the saint's own tomb.

The most sad group of buildings is the Bibi-Khanum built by Timur's favourite wife to welcome him at his return from a war. It never got finished and conquests and earthquakes—the greatest in 1897—have shaken the heart out of it but it still clings up to some form and is the landmark from outside the city as St Pauls used to be for London.

I went outside Samarkand to the hills called Afrasiyab. That's where it all began and there has been found evidence that Samarkand stood there certainly in the eleventh century B.C. The guide was so off-putting that I expected to find nothing: 'I want to go,' I said, 'to put my feet on such famous soil.' She saw no point to it, said there was not a thing to see, and she did not join me. I was therefore astonished when mounds began shaping themselves to fire-places, steps, latrines—one big drop. For hours I wandered thinking I must have seen all. But arches came, then streets, avenues in rifts by cliffs, gigantic hollows which could have only been house forms. More and more, as if the more I walked the more history grew up to meet me. Because of the pronouncements of the guide I now felt I was in on a wondrous discovery. These were the places where Alexander trod. Jenghis Khan was here. Wells appeared, then a list of inexplicable inlets into walls, perhaps hot steam jets for baths; valleys which had held streets, gigantic arches and, suddenly, a ravine and a river rushing far below. Two sides at least of all this considerable territory had had natural barriers against attack. The cliffs were sudden sharp and finely deep. Mud rooms galore were everywhere now. Then corridors two to twelve feet high. Then gorges; much crumbly soil; then remnants of 3,000 years bygone-fortresses, then suddenly 20-foot-high walls appeared and, more suddenly still, a 200 feet drop. I had to watch my step, holes that could have been more latrines or dried wells became plentiful, and it was night which drove me away; these hills pockmarked with holes were no place for no light. Suddenly thirty boys and up to many hundred sheep were with me. The boys begged for ball-pens and chewing-gum and I had neither.

78

Bokhara, 150 miles west of Samarkand, was a short plane light away.

Because of the greater learning that has come from it and because Islamic fanaticism has nowhere reached such depths (or heights according to your outlook) Bokhara is held by many with more reverence than any of those other Central Asian cities. Bokhara, like the other cities, began no one knows when. Cyrus I of the seventh century B.C. conquered it and the Persians held it till Alexander of Macedon turned up. (The history of almost any country, even England, we are expected to believe, begins when someone conquers it. The poor child learning history begins with a conquest and is then spoon-fed on them.) Bokhara is a Turanian word meaning 'a place for the collection of knowledge'.

When Jenghis Khan entered 20,000 defenders fled from him. He pursued and slaughtered every one. He entered the great mosque and asked if it were the Sultan's Palace. On being told it was God's Palace he flung the Koran beneath his horse's hooves. He was about to pardon all other

inhabitants when word reached him that some of th
Sultan's guards were hiding in the city. So he burnt th
city to the ground and Bokhara ceased to exist. Timu
about to re-destroy it, was told that the iodized waters
a certain mosque were curing his soldiers' goitres, so h
spared that mosque, though to his chagrin the waters faile
to cure his lameness.

There grew up 103 madrasa schools for learning. But i
bazaars brought Bokhara its greatest fame. Unintentional
it became, as it were, the wholesale clearing house for Centr
Asia. From there goods were bought and sold in th
markets of the world. Bokhara carpets to this day hold the
acclaim. Carpets, rugs, shawls, snuff-boxes of polish
gourds, cutlery, trinkets, literature and lithographs we
Bokhara's own contribution to all other wares brought
on the Silk Road, and the Cotton Road, and the vario
camel caravan routes from Cathay, India, Russia, ev
England. The bazaars, which I walked around empty in t
cool of evening, had booths on all sides made of clay la
upon undressed timber. Slaves had had a pride of place
the open places of the bazaars: 40,000 were once sold
a day. A labourer cost £29 in 1840, an artisan £64 and
pretty girl £100.

The places of bazaars were reached from the north-we
corner of the Registan. They were filled with shops, square
always, as today, cleared at dusk, and bounded on one si
by a great tank shaded over by trees. A last stall just closi
sold apricot stones. These had been cooked boiling hot f
fifteen minutes, highly salted, then eaten cold—very tas
because of the salt in the hot climate.

There were four mosques still active: and to this d
Bokhara is a place of pilgrimage for the devout. The wom
wore the veil here till well into the 1930s.

It has worried me that Uzbek people look so villaino
when they are obviously not so—now I see it is the
moustaches; they droop to thin waxed points like those
early Hollywood villains.

The Rahin Khan's gateway led to an open vaulted corridor leading up to the Emir's palace, treasury and State prisons. There Jenkinson had been received.

Prisoners sometimes were riveted to the walls for years where they slowly reduced to skeletons, finally to be impaled. Women caught in adultery were stoned to death. If there were insufficient prisoners to make fodder for the lice and ticks and rats and vermin, these would be spoon-fed like pets to keep them alive for greater days when humans could again be on the menu. Bokhara's greatest contribution to man's fearfulness to man was the great minaret in the Registan, from which criminals were hurled blindfolded, with their arms bound behind their backs.

A little outside Bokhara stands the palace of the last Emir. He built it from 1917 to 1920, lived in it three years with 400 concubines, then escaped with his favourite, a German, and much jewellery, to Kabul where he lived out his days. The palace was considerably of pre-war Lyons-Corner-House architecture, but then suddenly showed Dutch stoves or wood panelling of extreme elegance, as if a bad pavement artist and Rembrandt had got mixed up together.

The palace was a museum now. There were twenty to thirty plates and bowls exhibited. They are the greatest I have seen ever in the whole world. Melancholic: 'heavy': masterpieces in old green and tired brown and autumn yellow. In design, in conception, supremely bold, subtle inspiration thrusting like bared veins out of heavy souls. I went back and back and back and back to see them and re-see them. I could not leave them. The young lovely eighteen-year-old guide grew angry. And I grew angry with her anger. She refused to see anything but bourgeois degeneracy in work created in the last years before the Revolution: and these were dated between 1917 and 1919. To think that sublime works like those, that art lovers have come to expect only from age-old centuries ago, were made here up to 1919!

79

Over the hills and deserts away.

It was a shock to come down at Tbilisi airport. Surely I was going to be among picturesque mountains at last? But it was as flat as a mat. I complained to the driver. 'We are twenty kilometres out,' he said. But all the way, to the very door of the hotel, it remained as flat as a bat.

But across the street, yes, only on the other side and stark behind it began the giant climb.

'What do you want to see?' Intourist asked me.

'Scenery, scenery, scenery,' I said.

They decided to take me down the Military Highway on the morrow.

Outside in the street, two funerals passed within twenty minutes of each other. The dead men had been 'prepared' in their Sunday best, raised shoulder high in an open coffin which was tilted at thirty degrees so that all could see. It was not macabre. Something splendid about it. Looking at their best for their city to see them for a last time. When our friends die in the west, unless we see them dead, they have an uncanny way of remaining alive to us, with that one horrific proviso, we can never see them. If we saw them dead it would have a less disturbing effect upon us, we would accept it better, instead of going around muttering: 'It can't be, it can't be, I just can't believe it.'

The first was the smaller procession of the two, about a hundred followers. Yes, he was dead, he was sallow, tallow, but not too much. The coffin was draped in black velvet and pulled back to uncover the top half, so that we saw him from the waist up, flowers mostly covering the lower portion. In front of each cortège was a large portrait of each as he had been in life. This open coffin angled up seemed right for the man himself too: it was less barbaric than making his last journey utterly nailed down. The second had an assembly of about three hundred following. He must have held authority; there were officials and menials present and Party banners. The widows were there. The two men had been about sixty and seventy.

Rustaveli says: 'Death enshrouds and draws out the sting which was our birth and we become whole within our shroud.' During the moments of death even the biggest atheist would be forced to admit that 'something' exits: call it life, call it soul, call it spirit, call it Mr Smith, call it sting, but minutes after death, the living, for all their love, know that they are confronting a shell. Seeing that, the realization is complete, that there is no coming back. If you do not see your loved one dead there is the trepidation that he or she could knock on your door tomorrow. Better be quiet, better the Georgian way, better we see it as a fact, there'll be no more knocking at the door.

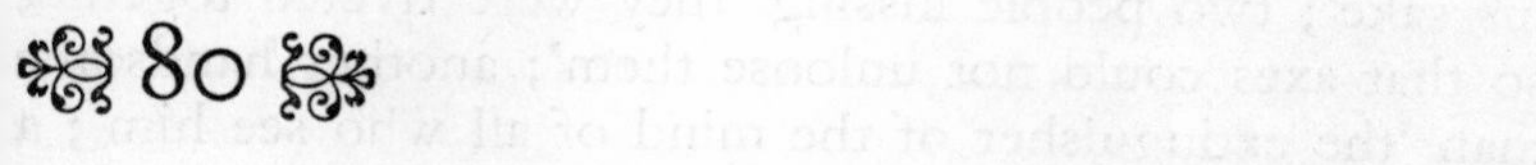

I went into a bookshop. 'I am a friend of David Dickens, great-grandson of Charles Dickens. I want to get him a copy of his ancestor's work in a foreign language, Georgian, Uzbek, Russian.'

They said: 'You can tell your friend his great-grandfather is still a bestseller. Any printing of a Charles Dickens work is sold out instantly. There's a secondhand shop further up, try them.'

I went there. Two brothers said they had that morning received some Dickens in Russian. I asked if I could have *Pickwick Papers* and *David Copperfield*. As I left they said: 'And this is for you.' Beautifully bound, translated into English, was Georgia's greatest literary work *The Man in the Panther's Skin* by Rustaveli written in the eighth century. An Englishwoman, Marjory Scott Wardrop, had commenced translating this work. She gave her entire life to it. She would never allow it to be published as she said all she had achieved so far was a direct literal translation: much more work was necessary before it would be worthy of publication. Born in 1869 she died in 1909 and her brother then delivered it to be published as it stood: 'a close rendering from the Georgian attempted by . . .' Result: a miracle. First there is the translation: Marjory Scott Wardrop's work is so simple, unaffected, direct, that it is far more enjoyable than others who have attempted poetic translation—not every translator is a Fitzgerald or a Scott-Moncrieff. Then the work: love all the way, man for woman, man for man, woman for man, woman for woman: is there any work that has so much hyperbole? If a woman weeps all the land about her is flooded: if a man is brilliant 'they who gaze at him account it an honour to swoon for his sake'; two people kissing 'they were riveted together so that axes could not unloose them'; another handsome man 'the extinguisher of the mind of all who see him'; a sorrow 'the sun wept tears of blood more abundant than the sea'; if a woman is beautiful whole cities go down blind as of sight of her. It's a dangerous book for writers to read because the hyperbole is so powerful and so right that it would seem there is no other way of writing. A masterpiece.

81

It took me an hour to fall in love with Tbilisi. It took me two hours to decide that if I had to live in the Soviet Union I'd prefer a slum in Tbilisi to a mansion anywhere else.

Why, it actually had an art and craft shop of local artists! The only one I have seen in the U.S.S.R. Nikolai says there is one in Leningrad but I have never seen it.

Tbilisi had a poetic, dreamy, enjoyment-loving music mad people.

Georgia even was one of those countries like Iceland and India who have nearly never invaded anybody.

It had a romantic, dramatic setting. It had sunshine. It actually had good modern architecture, a new hotel, the Iveria, being the best modern building I was to see. The Russian 'V' is the Roman 'B' and this should have been Iberia: someone had blundered. Not only do the Georgians think they have a link with the Basques but before Georgia was called Georgia it was itself called Iberia.

Tbilisi has bohemian corners, picturesque alleys, wooden story-telling balconies, an air of well-being—my own hotel, built in 1900, Victorian, but the finest on my journey.

It has 1,500 years of history to talk about. Forty times destroyed by invaders it has always risen again.

I had a large room. A bat came in. How could it fly so and not hit anything? It was unnerving, miraculous. I turned the lights out to let it find a window.

Out in the street was a sign. It was on the pavement but turned to face the road at an angle so that all passing motorists could read it. It began 4′ high then towered up for 6′ more. After it was another sign of similar size, which said the equivalent of 'AI, 3rd on the left'. So it seemed obvious that the first must be a motorist's sign too. But what did it say? It said in French:

> '*Va, mon cheval, alle par les routes du monde,*
> *Livre aux souffles de l'ahr* [*l'air*?] *ma secrète pensée!*'
> ('Go, my horse, go throughout the ways of the world,
> give to the wind my secret thought!')

Why such a road sign? The explanation is simple: it is that once in every three days in the U.S.S.R. something inexplicable has to happen—such as my telephone calls in the surgery at Lake Baikal—and there had been nothing lately. So we got this 'road sign'. And why in French?

I went wandering. And the streets and the alleyways went wandering. And the houses went wandering—as in old Hampstead. In old Hampstead architecture has no law, no symmetry, no order: result: architecture which sucks you in and you feel at home. Here balconies have been stuck on as afterthoughts, then enclosed as an afterthought, then turned into a greenery and dining-room combined, then used for lounging: conversation would hang around in nooks there—talk of moonscape, old friends, or Georgian wines and the conversation would still be hanging about on your next visit. There was no reasoning in the architecture: six broad steps would lead you to a door, then six narrow steps would lead you to an adjoining door: both doors were of one room, one set of steps would have done, or the two could have been joined as one wide set. Wrought iron stuck out anywhere or filled gaps between archways to no purpose. Lamps lit up nothing needing lighting. A column of wood would rise to hold up an unnecessary canopy, dying at its base on to a temporary roof ten feet from the ground. It was building which took its forms from the whims of the moment. There could not be two houses alike. Such a change from finding it difficult to find two houses different. Inside of nothing, looking out on nothing more than the yard it rested in, would be a sumptuous verandah. Fretwork in wood, lattice windows, arches, alcoves, trees leaning on walls, crannies for cronies, exterior balustrades, windows of ten thousand shapes, flowers, cobbles, a wide area that helped no one, a cramped area which would make a bottleneck for traffic, a grand lazy elegance in buildings which always crowded on to one another, a wrought-iron lamp fixed to an old oak, suddenly twenty plane trees which generations had built round rather than disturb . . . artists, authors, poets could emerge out of any corner any minute: can there really ever be a Dickens, Tolstoy, Ibsen, Rembrandt, Beethoven, emerging from a modern housing estate?

I found myself at the funicular and took it to the top of the 2,400-feet David's Mount. From that height the view was bird's-eye. The city lay in flashing jewellery below: the river as a bar of silver winding in and out of avenues of diamonds with rarer rubies and emeralds. To the south there were a million golden dots, a haze of carmine and all else jet black. The view at first took the breath away, then encrusted the beholder with wonder. Fairy-tales speak such views.

On the terrace of the restaurant at the cliff's edge I sat by two women preparing to part. I heard them tell the waiter they were not Russian.

'But you speak Russian?' I asked the younger.

'I do, but my friend doesn't. We are from Tallinn.'

'Don't you have to learn Russian at school?'

'We hate it and hate Russia.' There were tears in her eyes! She paused and when she was able to get words out she said, 'We only love the old. The Russians only love the new. We have been visiting all the old places in the south. But we want to see London, Paris, Rome.'

She looked about twenty-four, her friend about thirty.

Was she acting or did she really feel things so deeply? She bravely kept more tears at bay.

'I understand your feelings,' I said, 'but you've had very little independence in your history, haven't you? Twenty years all told, that's all isn't it? Do you get to Finland at all? There are two ships daily, aren't there, to Helsinki, without passports, visas, anything? I met Estonians in Helsinki on a day's visit.'

'That's all we're allowed, a day's visit. Yes, I have been often.' She brushed a tear away. 'I love Leningrad best of all. But my mother and father were often in London and Paris. Tell me, why can't I go?' Another tear, flicked off like a fly. She fought to continue, saying I must excuse her. 'My father's always telling me to watch my tongue, but I can't. I have vowed to him that I will never write anything. And he has said I can always deny my tongue but not what I have written. You should come to Tallinn. You would like Tallinn.'

They stayed half an hour and talked Estonian between themselves. The younger's name was Linda. She was attractive. The emotions persisted. Every time she thought of a place she might never see she broke down and struggled to get out: 'Excuse me, I can hardly speak.'

The waiter never came near. The next table called to us and asked if we were having waiter trouble also? They invited me to join them and the Estonians left.

One of the three I joined was an Estonian also. The other two were a brother and sister, each about thirty years old from near Moscow.

While I was changing seats and still standing, anothe table, a group of seven, got mixed in with our conversation Just as I sat down one of the seven came over, put his hand on both my shoulders, whispered in my ear: 'We in Georgi hate the Russians.' Two characters appeared from nowher and demanded to know what had been whispered to me. said: 'He told me that Armenian brandy from Erivan wa the best in the world and that I should try it.'

We did eventually see our waiter. Kolya, the Moscow brother, went and asked the head waiter to point him out, and there he was opposite us arranging some things on a table by the wall. He only had one table to serve—ours—and this other table was where he could rest the dishes while serving us, so the head waiter explained, there'd be no trouble, we'd get immediate attention. The immediate attention we got was to tell us that he still had to arrange his other table better. The waiter was very young and disarming; I felt I could forgive him anything. He was 99 per cent in a dream and 1 per cent with us. He might be a poet or composer or merely just in love, but he smiled to himself and to us the whole time. An hour later when he was giving us serious attention and he brought five bottles of wine instead of three, he smiled his distant smile through that and thought it remarkable: one goulash instead of three, yes, that really brought a smile out, life really was remarkable. No soups were ordered? He had brought four. Remarkable. A quantity of wrong dishes followed. Astonishing. We kept the wine, it seemed such a pity to give the man extra work. Two hours later we discovered he couldn't understand Russian and since none of us could speak Georgian that really brought the smiles out, remarkable the things that happened. He kept on re-arranging things on the table opposite, but it must be admitted he was mostly absent. 'One of those people,' said Kolya, 'who does nothing so nicely it becomes something.' He left us with the feeling that he had given us remarkable service. I'm still curious to know what dream world was swimming in his head: I've never enjoyed bad service so much and and, as I write this, that far-away contentment in his smile is creeping over my own face: we all felt bound to hope through an interpreter that we had not been too much of a nuisance to him, and if he was ever in our parts and if he would allow us to repay his kindness . . .

The bill was £7.10.0 and Kolya paid and wouldn't listen to anyone else contributing.

The three of them were travelling together. They were in a camp five kilometres out where eight more Estonians were staying. They stayed three or four to a room.

They had made all their plans together before leaving Moscow. They had paid all their money into Moscow too. They also loved Tbilisi and had enquired about staying longer, but the upheaval it would cause would be too much.

Both brother and sister were very tall. The sister looked gangling, ungainly, unfeminine, but nevertheless took time away from us to have a passionate flirtation in the larger restaurant behind our verandah, which grew ugly with the emergence of a third person but, just as a fight was imminent, it split up.

Suddenly there were fireworks! Someone said it was an Artillery holiday. Kolya said it was God trying to catch the eye of our waiter. Up the sky the fireworks slipped milken rays of silvern bamboo, bursting in an effort to thread ten thousand needles, groping further out as oriental fingers then a sigh, a throb farewell, a scattering of the treasury about, out, dark.

The young Estonian man talked of the Beatles non-stop only breaking off once to explain why he didn't like the Rolling Stones. He had Beatlemania.

The sister from Moscow wanted to know where, outside the U.S.S.R. was the best food, men, climate, joy and jazz and love.

We wanted to say goodnight to our waiter but he was busy arranging things on his wall table and it did not seem right to intrude.

82

t was all mist down the Georgian Military Highway.

The day started with a visitation: the sky fell solid to arth to visit us and remained as a white wall of upright iano wires for ten minutes. Yesterday's heat had gone, the louds shut out David's Mount: but hoping it was all to eturn to as-it-was we left, a driver, an Intourist guide and nyself.

We could see the Kura River running fiercely a little elow us but could see nothing above us except hope: the louds were playing ghouls and ifrits and the sun, repreenting hope, was attempting a break through.

The guide and I talked of Stalin and Jews. I had seen a elief above a porch showing Stalin 'Leading the children o Light', a plaque elsewhere saying where he had been to chool . . . which was more than any of the rest of the ountry had to show. I had stopped in the street and gazed p at the relief. 'That is Stalin?' I asked. And some bytanders had stopped to talk about him. 'I saw him twice,' told them. 'You are a lucky man who has seen him,' they aid. 'He always sent your Mr Churchill Armenian brandy nd the best cigars,' they added. 'We hold reverence for im.'

'Did Stalin visit here often?' I asked the guide.

'Once I think. Nearly never.'

'I have heard there are many Jews in Georgia?'

'There is a large community of them outside Tbilisi. They

clan together, help one another and are very rich and very mean. They just hoard.'

'Is it true Israel has been asking your government's permission for some to go to Israel?'

'Why should they go to Israel? They are happy here.'

'But has your government passed on the message?'

'No. Why? If they had wanted to go they would have gone long before the Revolution.'

'Israel is a new country,' I said. 'They had no ancestral home to go to before.'

'Israel isn't new. I never heard it was. The Jews are happy here. They don't want to go anywhere.'

This had started because of the story she had told me. 'A Jew in the second century went far away and brought back a present for his daughter. It was a robe of Christ's She was offended, hoping for something rich from her ricl father. When she touched it, she died and no power coulc remove it from her clasp. She was buried with it. Abov her grew a beautiful cedar tree. In the fourth century princess received a command in a vision that she shoulc recover the robe. But although the branches of the tre were cut with great difficulty, nothing could even inden the trunk. So the princess ordered a church to be buil around the tree. In the eleventh century orders were t build a church around the church. And all of this you wi be seeing soon.'

We saw the remains of a monastery.

'It was where the Christian religion began in Georgi Before a church was built, believers gathered round a cros to worship.'

The monastery was perched high on a hill that looke down upon the confluence of two rivers, one was the Kur which ran past Gori, Stalin's birthplace, and on to th Caspian Sea, and the other was the Aragvi which ran u the same valley as the Military Highway up which we wer proceeding.

Where the Kura joined the Aragvi lay Mtskhet th

piritual centre of Georgia and the capital until the fifth entury. It had already celebrated its 2,500th anniversary. The view below us was memorable but above us was all till shuttered off by backdrops of rain clouds.

We drove down to Mtskhet to see the tree within the hurch within the church.

In 323 B.C. Alexander the Great died. Twenty-one years ater the Georgians threw off the yoke Alexander had imposed on them. In A.D. 323 Christianity became the state eligion. With a population varying between 2 and 4 million only, the Georgians have fought off invader after invader, etained their religion, and enjoyed independence for more han 2,000 of their years.

Oak, beech, yew, chestnut, pine and boxwood are Georgia's trees. Tbilisi was avenued with gracious spacious planes. Oranges, lemons, tea, liquorice, and grapes abound —the country has always flowed with wine. In the year 1900 two-thirds of Georgia's exports and imports were with England. Bison, bear, boar, reindeer and antelope abound in the forests. We crossed the Kura and drove into what seemed a very large village, Mtskhet. Well-being was there, more alive in its today than in its yesterday. We went to the eleventh-century church and saw inside of that the fifth-century church, but inside of that was no tree. The place was to undergo an absolute renovation and, as I saw it, it was all dust and ladders and awnings. After restoration it might be a masterpiece, all the background is there in old graves, ikons, frescoes (that have been whitewashed over for centuries), brass and iron ornaments: and when the Soviet Government set their hearts on a restoration a jewel is often the result. We met two priests who told us that still to this day patriarchs were crowned in that church.

Though small, Mtskhet, perfectly placed where the two rivers joined, exhaled nobility.

The Georgian Military Highway is 213 kilometres long. It starts at its far end at Ordzhonikidze and in its first half from there is one of the world's great scenic spectaculars through mountain territory. For the second half it runs with the valley of the Aragvi River to the Kura and then to Tbilisi, and the broad-treed easy grandeur of this second part, making such a contrast to the first, makes the whole add up to a glory journey.

We, beginning in reverse, did the second half and stopped at the village of Pasanauri for lunch. Rains and mists hung around and to have risen to the mountains would have been to traverse a glory of the mountain world and to see no more than steam from a kettle. It would have been masochism and we would not proceed.

The lunch was in a garden restaurant where tables were isolated in alcoves of wood fretwork, in bowers of shrubs, rhododendrons, roses, in nooks on little hillocks staring at scenery that crowded sheer in, but all with its head cut off by rain-cloud. My guide shivered. All was a summer scene in a winter setting.

But if I was writing a guide-book for world tourists all Georgia would have five stars.

83

The low clouds stayed with us almost into Sochi.

A few miles out they cleared; the Black Sea, crinkled like an elephant's skin, was below us and down we came.

'What do you want to see in Sochi?' Intourist asked.

'Scenery,' I said.

But an enemy turned up. A stomach companion. In heory I was to have had three days in Sochi. In fact I had ess than one, the rest being spent on a throne from which ny abdication proved unacceptable.

Sochi is the pride seaside resort of the Soviet Union. There's 145 kilometres of it. It has no centre and if it has a High Street it's the promenade which is 10 kilometres long. The town, if it can be called that, straggles all over the place, very affluent, very elegant.

I was overweighted with books and wanted to despatch ome to England. But neither in Sochi nor Irkutsk where had wanted to do the same, could I purchase paper or tring. When it is remembered that this country might be he first to land on another planet it is an odd comparison hat there is nowhere else where it is so difficult to purchase he most elementary daily articles. As in Irkutsk I had to ake my parcel to the post office, as everyone else was loing, and they prepared the packet and secured it. This necessitated a long slow queue for stamps, another long queue for parcelling, another for weighing, and another for posting. One hour and a quarter. Neither parcel arrived in England intact, so feeble was the quality of he wrapping paper. One man turned up with his parcel already done up, and was told to take it home, iron the creases out of the paper, it was shameful to make it look as if Sochi couldn't afford proper paper. But can they? And where is it? Where are the very first necessities? And what percentage of the necessities work? Chairs can break within a week, stamps can have no gum, envelopes, if obtainable, might not seal, matches not strike. Moscow and Leningrad —especially Moscow——are in a world apart, a world ahead, yet even in Moscow . . . there's one place only—in the capital—for repairing spectacles. There also a tourist broke his suitcase and set forth in search of a new one with a Muscovite, a taxi driver and myself. After two hours we found one in the outskirts of half size and poor plastic at £9.

'I could buy it for less than £1 at home,' he said, 'I'll settle for rope.' No rope, 'I'll settle for string.' No string. 'I'll settle for a letter to Kosygin asking what would be his reactions in similar circumstances.' Instead he settled for cord given gratis by a porter.

And now, neither in Irkutsk nor Sochi, two supposedly wealthy towns, neither paper nor string that an inhabitant could direct me towards.

For fifty years the Soviet government haven't stopped telling its people how wonderful they are. The countryside is littered with placards which infer nothing else. The Swedish government, which deserves top marks for what it has done for its people, hasn't any placards in the countryside and, as far as I know, makes no outrageous efforts to drum it into anyone's ears. I met a Negro correspondent in the war in Moscow who was a communist and had little to say while there. Outside in London he told me he was appalled how little a nation with all the power in its hands had done for its people. What would he say now after twenty-five years of peace? The Revolution was for the people. It might just be true that the government had a very very backward nation and has had to put priorities first. But if so, when oh when are they going to start to give their people some fruits? We outside will know. It will be when they stop boasting that they are doing so.

The Intourist shop had a notice up saying it would open at 10.0. At 10.45 I went to the manager of Intourist's office and asked why the shop had not opened yet. 'Why should they? It's Monday morning. Naturally, they won't hurry in on a Monday.'

A pair of black eyes smiled at me. I went to their owner, said I had to pay a debt in a shop, would they wait for me? Their owner, Larisa, said they'd meet me in one hour outside my hotel.

Larisa turned up with three women and two men. Larisa wanted a cigarette. I hadn't any but thought I had some in my luggage. I hadn't, so she suggested the hotel shop for foreigners. I went and bought a packet but she, suddenly at my side, made it three.

Then I dallied buying a record for myself and she piqued, playing an impatient tantrum. We rejoined her gang and a restaurant was suggested. I was wondering if I had enough money without changing a cheque; there were six of us; but decided, to hell, the other men would have to help. Larisa took my arm. She was eighteen. We went out of sight behind some houses where the two men and two women made cuddly-come and started snogging. The other three of us hung carefree round, I wondering if my barricades shouldn't topple. Larisa, whose eyes were waxy, mucous, soft as the inside of cherries, was being wildly warm and I was not prepared for it. (A person shouldn't have to be prepared for it: but I have a background of Baptists' blood to fight against.)

Then the men left and I was alone with all the women. We went to a place which looked like an apartment block but it had a sumptuous coffee house inside. Larisa said she'd get the coffees, would I give her some money. She returned with two coffees only and put the change before me. 'But what about your friends?'

'Oh, they're not staying.' And they rose. Larisa said they were her sisters, but in the short time I was to know Larisa she introduced me to twelve sisters. They all three kissed me and said: 'Why don't you take Larisa to England?'

From there Larisa and I went to a beautiful restaurant on a beautiful terrace. She schooled me in the lies I'd have to tell to get us accepted there but the fibbing proved unnecessary. Our candles flickered on our table, the Black Sea was all before us and the moon came out, the wine was in the glasses and the stars jumped into the wine and played winking: the Hollywood cameras could have been called in except that I am not of the age that Hollywood usually casts with romantic eighteen-year-olds. I told Larisa about my stomach companion, so if I suddenly flew off at Olympic speed she'd understand. I told her I once queued up for a Kuibyshev cinema with another Larisa and had left to buy her some chocolate. While gone I had a terrible accident which laid me low for three months. That Larisa never believed me! Which hurt me after all I had been through to get her some chocolate.

Larisa was tall, had a lazy walk, looked sultry, and her eyes were such jet farthings I could not distinguish where iris began and pupil finished.

Her coat, cream gaberdine, was German, her dress, blue wool, was Dutch, her shoes Czechoslovakian and her bag Swedish. Where had she got them all?

'From the Dollar shop.' The Dollar shop, called Berioska, is the Intourist shop for foreigners.

'But you can only buy with dollars there?'

'Yes, that's right.'

'But it's against the law for a Russian to have dollars?'

'Yes, that's right.'

'Then how do you get them?'

'We buy them off foreigners.'

'And then go in the Dollar shop and spend them?'

'Yes, that's right.'

'Yet everyone in the shop knows it's against the law for you to have them? You could go to prison for having them?'

'Yes, that's right. How else can I dress? They are the only nice places it's possible to buy things in those shops.'

Why did the authorities flaunt these shops in front of their own people who could be put into prison for having the wherewithal to spend there?

She was here from Orel on a three-week holiday. She lived—with a sister—in a room in the town. All the proper places to stay in had been full.

Larisa loved Tom Jones, Frank Sinatra, the Beatles and Laurence Olivier.

I told her I wanted to go inland, and had booked for a

tour to Ritza, noted for its scenery, on the morrow, if my stomach could hold its own. Would she come?

'Not on a bus with foreigners,' she said. 'And not on an Intourist bus.'

So I agreed to cancel my excursion and we'd go on a public bus.

I said to her 'If you like foreign things why don't you get work with Intourist?'

'You have to be acceptable,' she said. 'I am most unacceptable.'

'Couldn't you take your holidays in Poland or Rumania? Many Russians go to Iron Curtain countries.'

'Only if they are trusted citizens. I am not a trusted citizen. I have no interest in politics: and if a person has no interest in politics she is not a trusted citizen.'

'You really couldn't go to any Iron Curtain country?'

'I'll never be given papers.'

Far far away across the Black Sea was a storm. It was so far away only the lightning reached us and we heard nothing. The silence of it made it unreal. There was sheet lightning as well as forked lightning but, something I had not seen before, flashes within the sheets. Once the whole sky above the water filled with a sheet of sheer white, then, once more, within that came a fork; it was a fiery fork against a wall of white flame. Something else, lightning went up instead of down: but surely my eyes were deceiving me?

A hydrofoil, nose in the air, hurried by.

A helicopter, egg-beater in the sky, lit up stark when the wall of light was switched on behind it.

The candles burnt low.

84

We arranged to meet next morning at nine.

Larisa was not there.

At 9.20 I decided she had 'been got at'. I'd give her til 9.30. I decided that to meet a Russian, best get all valu out of the first meeting as there'd be no second. Unde Stalin there would not have been the first—except clan destinely. I know of a very prominent Englishman—a M.P.—who wanted to meet again a very prominen Russian he had been friends with in London and had ha to do it for ten minutes in the darkest alley like the viles of conspirators. Progress: now we get a first meeting. Whic means that now Soviet citizens are not so indoctrinate against the pitfalls of conversing with foreigners: it's onl if they do so that they get a fatherly tip-off.

At 9.28 Larisa was not there.

At 9.29 she came panting up like a cart-horse. 'I . . . I . . . struggling for breath, 'I overslept.'

And the Russians have done it again. Every time I hav reached a positive conclusion about the country somethin has happened to prove it was not so. So Larisa, the self styled unacceptable, had not been got at.

Her great blackcurrant eyes were lined with a tear a she struggled for breath and half cried from laughing.

My stomach and the weather both were doubtful starter for the inland journey so Larisa and I settled for a day i Sochi. 'Can I . . . phew!' still getting her breath, 'do you mind if I start the day with a bathe?'

So we left for the beach. Halfway she asked for a cigarette. hadn't any. I said I'd return to the foreigners' shop to get ome. It had gone up to cartons now, not packets. She'd vait for me on the promenade.

When I met her she was in animated conversation with young man, a Georgian.

He wanted to buy me a present. He bought me a sea-shell vhich I could take home to England and by placing it at ny ear hear the Black Sea. He then asked me if he could uy dollars or pounds off me. I said I had just that moment een to the bank and a person could not take surplus oubles out of Russia. I had enough. He accepted the ituation pleasantly, warmly shook hands and was off.

Larisa, elegant in yellow and sage green taffeta, knew veryone on the beach. She stopped minute after minute, ntroduced me to hundreds, and finally decided to bathe vith a jazz group all of whom were wearing Beatle shirts. n Mongolia they said a dust-storm could penetrate through nything anywhere. The Beatles are like that, and here was group of twelve musicians all wearing the shirts too— Your Lenin!' one laughed to me pointing to Lennon. These were a jazz group who were played every day on Moscow radio. They begged me to go to their concert hat night.

'So sorry,' said I, 'but I must leave for Odessa.'

They told me the wave-length on which I could hear hem from London.

They had met the 'Animals' in Warsaw and deeply evered one of them, I forget which. They had wanted to ear the 'Animals' but the noise the teenagers in the audience ad made had drowned it all. How they loved Belafonte! They hinted that they themselves might be on the conervative side and perhaps err in a too intellectual approach. Then one of them pounced in among us: 'I bet anyone a ottle of vodka he can't thread this cord through these athing trunks.' He had just purchased new trunks and the ord had been given separately. I accepted the bet. I threaded

the cord on to my biro and searched for the entrance t
the waist band for the cord. It had no hole: irrefutably ha
none! It was the third bottle of vodka the young man ha
collected that morning. 'I'll never make a hole. These ar
my treasure trunks!'

A more elderly man asked for news about Georg
Formby: was there some trouble with a wife, a will,
mistress? 'I am so indebted to George Formby. He helpe
save me my sanity during the war.'

Larisa had a lithe willow figure in a bathing costum
Her hair she did in the style of the ancient Egyptian wome
and with a fringe. Her face went from ear to ear in a round
Both her eyes and her bamboo form made a Man of a man
Off she set swimming.

At least twenty of her friends crowded round me an
talked nineteen to the dozen. All Sochi men were he
friends and all Sochi women were her sisters.

Larisa frolicked away in the water then, out, ran up t
me and asked: 'What is this?' and she hummed a tune.
did not know. 'It's my favourite song in the world. Fran
Sinatra sings it.' She hummed it to everyone. '"Stranger
in the Night",' said someone.

'That's it! That's it! That's my very favourite in the whol
wide world!'

I told her of my cycling. Many think I'm a nut-case i
Charlie Chaplin guise to do such things and Larisa, I shoul
have thought, would have preferred me if I had mentione
Rolls-Royces. Not at all! She was elated, cried out to a
others to crowd round quickly and made me tell them abou
my cycle, kissing my cheek with the excitement it gave he
that I could tell such things. I was staggered: I could hav
sworn she would have reacted oppositely.

Whether it was lunch or breakfast I don't know, bu
Larisa and I returned to our restaurant of yesternight an
ate there at the same table on the same terrace. And th
waitresses, instead of questioning our presence as w
expected, bade us gladly welcome.

The Black Sea was the garden before us.

I said I wished to see the Dendrarium. She said she had ever heard of it—though it was as famous as anything in ochi and this was her third visit.

On the street she stopped a car, hitched us a lift and soon ve were there.

1,400 different species of trees to stare at. Had I been lone I would have stared; as it was, so much talking was ;ot through we might as well have been anywhere. Larisa vorked in an architectural office. She was of Tartar origin he said. When she walked she projected herself forward n a fetching gangle. She noticed a wasp eating a long-since lead beetle. It upset her, turned her over inside, and many imes she drove the wasp away. She loved the furriness of ome palm trees and ran her hands over them. She wanted o talk of make-up. She used little, some kohl effectively bout the eyes and otherwise none. She said it was because f her tan but in the winter she used more. I told her, her riends she had met me with the night before had all over-ainted, she must not make their mistake. I gave her dvice attributed to Oscar Wilde: '"Spend two hours in ront of a mirror, then go out and forget all about it."'

We sat on a seat high above the garden among a concourse f wild shoulder-high sunflowers.

And talked.

Of this and that.

She hitched us a lift back to 'our' restaurant where at our able on our balcony we had what might have been tea or night have been dinner. And more cigarettes. She sang me song 'How Blue is the Black Sea'. Then said she had never een it white as it was today. And added that it was called Black because there had been so many shipwrecks and loss f life in storms on it.

We were together until five minutes before my parting.

We talked slower. And slower. And slower. So that the alk would go on after we had gone.

85

All were delayed half an hour boarding the plane at Sochi. A Russian father was carrying a child in his arms and not holding the hand of an eleven-year-old boy because beside the words 'age of child' he had put 'eleven': 'I couldn't put "one",' he said, 'he is not one. I couldn't put "nought" that looks silly, so I put "eleven" because he's eleven months.'

We were turned back when in sight of Odessa. There was a flash-bang-wallop storm in front of us and our pilot funked it. The passengers were violent in their criticism. 'You can get to the moon and you can't face a little storm!'

We landed at Simferopol. We stayed twelve hours. I could see no Krim Tartars. We were so near Bakchisarai the setting for the famous ballet. I could have got to Bakchisarai except we never knew when we might leave. I was told I would see no Krim Tartars there either. There were sinister rumours of their wholesale extradition. We were near Balaclava too. We were shown some television in which an African said his wife had just had a baby in a Moscow hospital 'on the state': where else in the world did such magnanimity exist? A few of my countrymen could have told him. Then we were shown a film of Russian women getting the better of wicked German invaders in the war. The audience thought the Russian women were marvellously clever. When will the hate stop?

Three more planes. I lost all my fellow passengers and my luggage. It's as well I did not know about my luggage:

had all my films and all my diaries in it and was going at n alarming number of miles per hour in many different and nostly opposite directions while I slept sweetly at Simfero- ol. My bag had a busy forty-eight hours, Erivan, Frunze, 'ashkent, Alma Alta and then finally arrived at Odessa six ours before me.

By the time I finally arrived in Odessa I had lost nearly all ny time for that city so I asked the cost of waiting till the ext boat for Istanbul. The Churchill Fellowships had been nost generous to me but they had not made me a millionaire. Vhy must this Workers' State fleece its visitors as no apitalist state would do? Strange . . . I did not want to eave Russia. I was in my last day: the Czechoslovak crisis ould still blow up into a hundred difficulties any minute: t was a country of difficulties . . . yet I wanted more of it. 'es, lots more of it. A month in Odessa at least, six back n Tbilisi, four in Khiva . . . But twelve hours more only vas to be my lot.

Six-thirty in the evening and I put through a call to eningrad. I had promised to phone Nikolai before leaving. At eight o'clock I must go to my ship.

There was a stirring in my belly, I should not waste time vaiting for calls to get through. At 6.40 I decided to leave. But I had promised . . . Five more minutes I would wait. forced myself down on the bed. A storm in my belly and nreason forced me up after two minutes and flung me out nto the street . . .

Otherwise I would not have met Lavrenti.

86

I went to the Odessa Steps, the Potemkin Steps.

Slowly I went down. At the bottom I looked up them

'Eisenstein Steps?'

'Yes, I saw Eisenstein's film,' I said.

A man, looking as if he had been poured into his clothe and someone had forgotten to say 'when', said: 'So! Ha We call them that. *Potemkin*. Film. 1926.' He stood straight then at the top of his spine bent his head out at right angles as if a nail had been squared, so that although he walke straight his eyes surveyed the pavement.

'Do I disturb you?'

What could I say? I had an hour to see all Odessa, al Russia, all the thousand million things I had not seen, I di not want to be lumbered with a hanger-on, yet how coul I offend him?

'It's all right,' I said. A terrier passed knee-deep i puppies. 'I was wanting to get a good picture of the steps, I said.

'Over there,' he said. 'See the new voksal we have buil for the ships? Up there, high on the roof. That's the bes picture. Shall I take you? Do I bother you?'

I wished to hell he'd go. 'I'll take one or two here first.

'Ha! So! The steps are 12½ metres broad at the top an 24½ broad at the bottom so that standing on the top perspective is allowed for and they look the same widt the whole way. So! From the top looking down you se only the platforms between each group of steps and no steps; from the bottom you see only steps and no platforms. Your Intourist guide told you all that?'

'Yes. But our Intourist guide only showed us the top view which is not a quarter so impressive as is the bottom view.'

'So! Ha! They are nits. They show you monuments to leaders and offices of trade unions and expect you to be filled with admiration. Are you at Hotel Odessa?'

'Yes.'

'It was called always "Hotel London". It wouldn't hurt them to tell a Londoner that, eh?'

He was oldish. A mop of grey hair. He wanted to hang on. I wanted him to leave.

I began to cross the road.

'Is it all right if I come? I won't cling like a cobweb. I'll show you where to get the best view.'

I said an O.K. that I did not mean.

'You have *Dr Zhivago* in German?' I said. He carried the book in a box-case in his hand.

'Yes.'

'Can you read German?'

'No. But I must have the book. In any language. You see, I must have the book. Yes.'

'Have you read it in Russian?'

'How can I? It is banned. It's a rouble a page to borrow. And you have to do it . . .' and he went through complicated motions of secrecy. 'Ah! I want to. I want to read it for its nuances. I will buy a German dictionary. I will go through it word by word. I might not. But I feel better for its being by me. Yes.'

'Might I ask how you got it?'

'Out there!' he pointed to the sea. 'Everything comes in from out there! My name's Lavrenti. I am sixty-nine.' He handled his book. 'So! Like trying to smuggle day in past a rooster, getting this in.' And he caressed his book with his free hand.

Someone was watching us. We stopped talking and stoo
still outside the voksal. The shadow went on and Lavren
spat after him after surveying him a long time to find ou
a spot he despised most. 'Always following. Their veins ru
vinegar. Do you have informers for Scotland Yard?'

'Yes. But not nearly so numerous or so obvious. And
don't think they are ever paid employees. Nor do I thin
they are paid, except a nominal amount.'

'They are here. I spit at them always. I can't stand them
We were afraid under Stalin. So! We are not afraid now
He is watching us, can you see him? Sound travelled faste
than light under Old Whiskers.* Let's go up. There's a lift
Do you find Russia dear?'

'It's not so much the dearness that I mind,' I said, 'bu
the fact that we can't make friends makes it dearer. Americ
is dear, but I could make a friend who could board me o
advise me on cheap places and cheap restaurants. I coul
buy my own food and cook it. Here I must pay for a Firs
Class hotel whether or not I want it and pay for expensiv
food whether or not I eat it.'

'I could not be your friend. I can meet you in the ope
street. Which is more than I could do before. But I dar
not take you home. They know me. I play the rule to th
razor's edge. I correspond with twenty countries. They
know old Lavrenti! I go to the edge but never over. They
know me. I am old. Sometimes a little white lie turns into
a double feature in technicolor! Ha! So.' His grin could have
been used as a foot rule and he slapped me on the back
'Ten years ago I stopped fear. You said you saw Eisenstein's
Potemkin?'

'Yes. I used to work in films.'

He stopped. Faced me squarely. Suddenly jumped to life
'Do you know Korda?'

'Yes. Vincent Korda I know well.'

'I kiss your feet.' And he nearly did! He bowed. And
reached my knees. He was elated.

* Stalin.

'Alexander, Vincent, Zoltan! I know all about them,' he shouted. He wanted to jump as on hot bricks and only just held himself back.

'How?'

'I'm a Jew! Eisenstein was a Jew. Korda. I follow up all that Jews do. So! Ha! The Kordas are worshipped by us all over the world. I saw *The Jungle* forty times. And Sabu. I love Sabu. And *Lady Hamilton* twenty times. And *The Thief of Bagdad* twenty times. With Sabu. And Conrad Veidt! Tell me, can you tell me, please can you tell me, what happened to Conrad Veidt?'

'He died twenty years ago.'

'Oh. Ah. My name's Lavrenti.' He shook my hand this time. Wrung it. Poured out name after name. If there was one I had even so much as glimpsed in a film studio he wanted to kiss my feet.

'The funicular has been taken away,' he said. 'It used to go up the steps. Now there'll be an escalator. It's a very good idea, yes, a good idea. This is the best view.'

We had begun by walking up; but had waited for the lift as he lost his breath quickly. 'I'm as worn out as an old woodpecker in a petrified forest.' He panted as I stared at the famous landmark. But he still disgorged names. 'Carol Reed. David Lean. Hitchcock. Noël Coward . . .' I understood many things but one thing I did not understand, yet found refreshing as if sparkling water had been given, that was to find a devoted admirer of Noël Coward: the 'Soviet Union—Noël Coward', it didn't fit. More than James Joyce, Spike Milligan, Bertrand Russell, surely Noël Coward was the absolute antithesis of the Russian-state-image mind: yet here was a man who gloried in him like a starved man.

87

'There are our Steps. So! The lights are going on up in ou city.' Lavrenti had his hands on the balustrade and talke straight ahead of him. 'Ever studied physics? Funny thin I read: the scientists know what the mass will do, yet neve the individual photon. Funny thing, we need so man engine drivers, so many postmen, so many builders: no even our great government with all their powers can dictat who shall be which. They try. And they can make labourer out of geniuses, but they can't make geniuses out o labourers. Funny. They can't stop me wanting to see th outside world. They can only stop me seeing it. I under stand them a little. Stalin tried to mould men to his will and millions died who would not be his type of peasant It's glory be that men bounce back like rubber balls t become themselves and cannot mould to fit a theory. If mar could mould man, mankind would become a horrifi mechanical thing. But, you see, I do understand them quit a lot. I do understand them, I do. So! It was right tha America and England fought alongside our motherland ir the war, because although they did not know it, they ar tied closer to each other than to Nazism. They each want in the souls of them, they do, they really do, they want th most good for the most people. Yes. The Germans wantec good for the Germans and for the rest it was slavery. Bu for thousands of years man has struggled to get out o forms of Nazism like that, up to what we, you and I anc ours, want. Yes, the best for the most. It's instinctive in us, you and me and ours, if not in our authorities, that the best for the most is right. Perhaps we will always be against each other in peace and always fight with each other in war. Eh? But I do understand our leaders, and the way we went.

'You see, I will tell you how it was. It was like the birds, like the animals. In times of stress they herd. They survive as a herd. The herd is the one, is the individual. But after a danger or a migration is over a herd becomes smaller individuals: geese mate with geese, deer with deer; they fight for their mates, they ferret and fend for themselves. Yes. This land in 1919 had to become one single unit to survive. Yes. The herd feeling is very great, perhaps greater than the chopped-up non-herd feeling. A country united fighting for survival is much happier than an affluent land of millions of egos. But nature is undeniable: after the survival we continue to develop only by each finding his or her individual trait. A herd can offer no development, only survival and a sharing of a common exploit. A land in affluence in our age becomes technical. Yes. Technical men are not herd men. No. It is the problem of our leaders: they have to let us go our ways in order to help them go theirs. Mmmmm. Wait here.' Lavrenti moved off ten paces then came back. 'See that boy with the ball by the balustrade on the steps?' He was beginning to rock-hop from one leg to another getting excited.

'No.'

'Come here.'

From ten paces away he showed me the boy. Lavrenti continued his rock-hop.

'The balustrade was hiding him!'

He wanted me to ask something but I wasn't sure what.

'You see! So! You thought you were looking at the same steps as me? But from here I have a different perspective. Those steps are my steps! Over there they were your steps! Mmmmm! Look!' He closed his eyes firmly. 'No steps,' he murmured before opening his eyes. Then he added: 'If there was a moon over the Black Sea the moon would lay a reflection across the sea to me. If you stood a mile away, see! so! it would send down a reflection just to you! Two different reflections. See! We both close eyes! So! Both reflections gone! So!' He turned to me, dire seriously: 'We think we see the same things! That's the mistake the leaders make. We can only see from our point of view!' He was drilling it into me. 'That boy with the ball!—Life is Good Morning for him. It's Good Evening and nearly Goodnight for old Lavrenti! Have you seen much in Odessa?'

I told him of a feeble tour I had had with Intourist.

He banged his books angrily on the balustrade: 'Lenin Squares, Marx Boulevards, Faculties for Foundry Workers! Did they show you the inside of the Opera House?'

'No.'

'No one will believe that you've seen Odessa if you have not seen the inside of the Opera House! How long have you got?'

'Less than one hour.'

'Less than one hour! Quick!'

We hurried away. On the road he tried to hitch us a lift. 'The Opera House is sold out. Been sold out a month. It's Moseyiev's new ballet company. Don't know how we'll get you in. Mmmmm. Why didn't they take you in this afternoon when there was no performance? And that dreary Arcadia! Why go all that way to show you that. Nothing.'

Arcadia had been a beach about half as good as Eastbourne, Southend or any English resort: not worth so much precious time.

A car stopped. Said it was to go the opposite way, but would be back for us in five minutes. We sat on the steps. But Lavrenti jumped up. He was as restless as a rumour and even waited in a hurry. He looked down at me with a brow barnacled with thought:

'We have lived in the dark so long that, in emerging, we have to live through the dark, use it all up, so that there will be no returning. I used to draw morbid pleasure from suffering: yet this held me back and kept me from greatest attainment. It left me grey and introvert. Over years I burst for brief spells into an Avenue of Light, kept myself there by strong vows, yet always the Road of Dark pulled me back into its sensuous caverns. There came here a wise counsellor in the form of an old schoolfriend. He was a professor and taught here for a year. "The road of excess leads to the palace of wisdom," he said quoting your poet, Blake. So! He took me down the entire Road of Dark and that I knew it all, and that the wise counsellor, the Professor, he journeyed with me too and left no dark cavern unexplored to finality, until we came through together to the Opening of Light, and all was used up and there was nothing to return to, and I have lived in the Avenue of Light ever since. Don't lick at a vice, he said, wallow in it till you're sickened with it, use it up. Russia must live out its dark, he said, use it up, he said, till it is sickened sick and comes to the light refreshed. Always remember, he said, seeds are nourished in darkness. Zenkovsky was his name. So! My friend returned to Kuibyshev. Professor. The car, quick! Lenin praised him. Zenkovsky.'

88

We swept up the hills to the centre. There were seven in an overcrowded car. I kept silent. I did not know whether I would be endangering Lavrenti if it was discovered I was English. My accent is probably fearful, my grammar non-existent. I have no idea how good or bad my Russian is, it might be appalling. I understand most, and I'm understood mostly, and cannot seem to get interested further: I have never learnt and Violetta said my Russian was so funny she would never dream of correcting it.

No one wanted the Opera House except us, yet we went: all who have cars in Russia are very generous in helping others: quick farewells and Lavrenti planned how to storm the bastion.

Lavrenti became a Uriah Heep, a Micawber, an 007, a dozen roles as he wormed his whining way past official after official. 'As busy as a flea trying to get through to a dog to retire on! So! Ha!' he chuckled. The ballet performance was in its middle. Now we came to the final ticket-collecting woman. I was told to hide myself. Yet I watched. Would charm and sex appeal and emotion work on the austere middle-aged custodian of the tickets? She was wilting! We were in. We swept past, made for the stairs for the gods, and Lavrenti became Lavrenti again. 'All Odessa would give its soul to have got in here tonight!' he laughed proudly. And his laughter was shared by all of him.

We even got in at the extreme rear of the gallery. What a theatre! How it had been restored! The white and the gilt of it! The cleanliness and the candelabras of it! The plush affluence and the grand manner of it! We watched six elegant young men and women doing the stereotyped leaps pirouettes, glorified sparrow-hops . . . it was a ballet concert and ballet concerts are to be avoided: they are collections of versatility from repertoires and are dull show-offs. Any ballet itself however, is another thing, and should never be missed. The constant surprise is the beauty of the performers: these three young men and young women were heart-stoppers all. Yet out in the streets the Russians are not a beautiful people: it's only that when the rare one comes along he or she is excelling: and the stage frequently fills with them. A director of the Bolshoi told me I had stolen the most beautiful girl in their country. Yes, that wa my luck. I had. Russia, alas, is not full of Violettas.

Lavrenti was annoyed; we had no good view. He pulle

me out. He said he had arranged to get me into the stalls during the interval; let's have a drink.

The cafeteria women said they were not serving during the dancing. Neither coaxing nor whining nor straight talking succeeded. Lavrenti put on a face as pathetic as a line of linen hung out by a man, his hands spilled dismay, then suddenly for all his near seventy years, he leapt over the bar and disappeared. After three mysterious minutes he appeared with a rotund castle of a woman. 'This is the manageress. The most marvellous person in all Odessa. I was in the Pioneers with her father.' I found he was neither ever in the Pioneers nor had he any idea who her father was. He fawned; but as a majestic beau and in no sickly manner. 'She says we can have anything we like. Would a beer, a sandwich and a cake do?'

And we enjoyed our little meal.

He took me out from the bar to a balcony. 'Look,' he said, winking—all of him seemed to wink; he could never show emotion with his face alone. 'I've been coming to here for thirty years. See the dressing rooms! From this side corner you can see all the undressing.' And he chuckled; all of him did. Peeping Tom Lavrenti.

He wanted to tell me a secret joke. He looked very carefully everywhere, stood as still as an image in a niche. 'Why,' he asked, 'is Israel luckier than Czechoslovakia?' I gave up. He looked each way. He whispered. 'Because Israel is only surrounded by its enemies!' He had cushioned his words between chuckles. Now he went away, raised his eyebrows, put his top lip over his bottom lip, chewing it to stop his outburst of laughter and danced about like a frog on heat jumping up and down with glee. He came back. Looked each way. Whispered: 'Why did the Russians need to take 56,000 men and 10,000 armed vehicles into Czechoslovakia?' I gave up. He looked each way. Whispered. 'Because they had to find the man who had invited them in!' He did not move away this time. He whispered, agitated, 'Go on! Ask me if they found him?' I asked him. He split it out between his teeth. 'No. The son of a pig had used a telephone kiosk!' Then he went away. Danced up and down, one foot to the other, beside himself with glee. From when he set out on a first chuckle you knew he'd started on a voyage to a good time for the all of him. Half dying with bubbly joy like a boy, he took my hand and led me to another part of the balcony balustrade: 'But we did right?' he said. 'To nip this act of Germany in the bud?'

'Of Germany?'

'Don't you think we have to be frightened of Germany?'

'Germany!?' I asked. 'No,' I said.

'Are you serious? Don't tell me that Germany are not the enemy?'

'Why Germany? They are not going to attack you.'

He flung down his book and all he carried. He beat the balustrade. Nearly in tears he said: 'Tell me, come on tell me! But don't tell me they have deceived us again! We all think we must tremble before Germany. Oh dearest God, how, how can we know what is right? They soft-soap us till we can't see for the suds. But I've always believed that. Surely we have a right to be frightened and wary of Germany? Tell me, now tell me quietly, I will try to hold on to myself. Tell me, who are our enemies?'

'Not China?' I asked.

'China? Why China? We are not afraid of China.'

'It is not feasible for you to regard Germany as your biggest enemy,' I said. 'Given present circumstances not even Hitler, in all his madness, would attack you now.'

'Tell me. I am listening. I want to know what you think.'

'Whatever the Germans' private feelings are towards you, they cannot be a danger to you on their own. If they could drag in half the world with them that might be another thing, but thinking has changed. Kruschev knew it. Kruschev was asked at a private London dinner party by the Burmese Ambassador: "Mr Kruschev, are you going to start the third world war?" And Kruschev answered: "If I started the third world war my wife and children would be dead in two weeks. I wouldn't like that." And if Hitler ruled Germany now and began a war against you, chances would be high that he himself would be dead in two weeks. And not even Hitler would have liked that. Russia might get embroiled in a war somewhere, in Czechoslovakia, in anywhere; any country might get embroiled: but if you are thinking in terms of someone making a direct assault on the Soviet Union I should have thought China was the only possibility. But let us, Lavrenti, be slow to abuse China. The whole world has selected her as the new enemy, everyone's going to abuse her for some years to come. We'll hear no truth about her. Best to realize that. Even so, I would have thought that was the only direction from which you might get a direct assault.'

'The Germans were here,' Lavrenti said. 'Here in this Opera House. They stole the library of 150 most rare volumes, all first copies of operas, ballets, symphonies, works by Tchaikovsky, Rimsky-Korsakov; unique, beyond price. Tchaikovsky conducted the world première of *The Queen of Spades* here. The first two acts of *Eugene Onegin* were written in Odessa. Pushkin began his *Fountain of Bakchisarai* here. Did your guide tell you of the wicked Tzar banishing Pushkin, Gogol, Gorki here: of poor Pushkin . . . you know his banishment for writing against the Tzar? A year in sunny Odessa, with a house to live in and an office to write in, at the nation's expense. Not bad compared with what Daniel and Sinyuvsky have got for writing nothing against anybody, is it? Gogol wrote much of *Dead Souls* in Odessa. We turn out world musicians like sausages from a machine here. Men like Oistrakh. Let me give you this medallion.' He gave me a three-inch medallion of the *Aurora*, the ship that fired the gun that was the signal for the Revolution. I had a Kennedy Silver Dollar on me and gave it to him. Now he really did jump about! That funny hopping movement from one foot to another. He was overcome. 'My hero! John Kennedy! I only have two heroes. John Kennedy and our astronaut Komorov. What Russia lost with

Komorov. He had a brain beyond them all. And Kennedy! I'll wear it for ever and ever. In my lapel! I'll have something made!'

The interval still hadn't begun. It would begin any moment. We had spoken of Zenkovsky.

'But he's in with the authorities,' he said. 'You would have to be careful.'

'I am an unreasonable man,' I said. 'There was one blot on our friendship and although I certainly knew Zenkovsky could not help himself, I who have lived always in democracies and cannot grasp utterly the full darkness of living under a dictatorship although I really should be able to, I never could quite forgive that on the Kuibyshev beach once he questioned me about Violetta. I denied all knowledge of her, couldn't think who he was speaking of, though I was chasing her at the time; I felt friendship should be above being made use of for the politicians, and I could never get it out of myself, that he questioned me, suggested I must have noticed her, must have tried to meet her . . . it lowered him.'

'He'd have to. Have to. Violetta . . . Violetta . . .' He chewed the name over. 'He wouldn't be meeting you at all in those days if there wasn't reason to it. Easy for you people to know our spies: they would be the only people allowed to behave as a normal human being to you. Strange: if a Russian behaves to you as any man might anywhere else, and with no fear, then he must be a spy. Yet you know . . . Violetta, Violetta, I've heard that name . . . Russia is not bad for the Russians. For the first time in history we eat well, we are educated, we have pensions: for a majority of the people here it is paradise compared with the past. And the government have their priorities. First, is defence. Second, outer space. Third, well-filled bellies. Fourth, reading and writing for all and stadiums to run about in. Fifth, houses. But there the priorities come to a sudden end. Oh no, one more: watches. We all have watches. The country became ill, pathological, for watches. Our watches are very fine and very cheap and we all have them. Not a thing else. The whole land is a desert otherwise. And freedom is too slow in coming. When the belly is full the mind becomes hungry. We have stepped forward since Stalin but only one step, and we need a hundred. It's all slow. Will I ever see London, my friend? Trapped here like a rat in a cat. Tears are in me with the thought. Better too soon than too late, I have told them. I want to come and knock on your door and say "Lavrenti has come. Show me your London." I know London. Every corner of it. But will I ever see it? I don't want to live in a golden palace if somebody else keeps the key. Let Lavrenti out! But tell me, how can you bite the dentist? Violetta? Violetta Prokhorova!'

'You knew her?' Now I jumped; though the audience were beginning to stream out to the bars.

'Violetta Prokhorova! Danced under your name in England, didn't she? Pudovkin! Zenkovsky told me too! But I saw her dance!'

'Where?'

'In Moscow! One of the six brides in *Swan Lake*. One of the fairies, the Lilac Fairy in *The Sleeping Beauty*. The fire! Yes, the fire in her! Oh, we all knew her! and Kapustin—remember Kapustin?—he told me: "Our best prospect is going for export!" '

'She was to have made the Pudovkin film in Odessa,' I said.

'Of course. *Admiral Nakhimov*. Russia's answer to Korda's *Lady Hamilton*.'

'Pudovkin,' I said, 'went to a party and told our diplomats how excited he was with the young lady he had discovered for the film. I again had to pretend I had no idea who they were talking about, though I had just come from Violetta who had told me it might mean going to Odessa for six months, what should she do? It worried us. And then the Embassy diplomats began naming her, and talking openly of her in front of me.'

'But . . .'

'Yes, but,' I smiled. 'You know, I'm sure, the authorities decided against the love interest in the film, it was to be *Lady Hamilton* without Lady Hamilton, so the storm proved a storm in a tea-cup.'

He banged me on the shoulders. It was meant kindly but it sent me half sprawling. 'Let's go in.'

89

'That should do your English pride some good!' he said.

All the ceiling frescoes were of scenes from Shakespeare. Two were from *Hamlet*, one from the *Midsummer Night's Dream* and one from *The Merry Wives of Windsor*.

For one and a half years the theatre had worked at its renovation and it was only recently completed. It was brilliant rococo: delicate lines of gold streaking tastefully through fields of white. The boxes receded tier behind tier the whole way to the ceiling. The candelabra were tremendous. Copies of paintings by Lefevre were on walls and in foyers, executed brilliantly by contemporary Russian copyists. There were no pictures of Lenin anywhere nor of any leader. The seating was elegant unpatterned plum colour. The curtain was of the same unadorned plum velvet.

We were approaching the top of the Steps along the high boulevard.

Lavrenti said: 'You have made a long journey in my land, and I have lived here sixty-nine years. Let us leave each other with a sentence which identifies your thinking with your journey and my thinking with my living.'

I said: 'I love your country yet somehow I can only leave you with a quotation from Churchill: "Russia is a question-mark inside an enigma." ' I could not think of the Russian for 'enigma' and wanted him to have only the exact word so said I would write it down for him. 'Only the word,' he said. 'Not the whole sentence. So! Just the word. You understand? I'll look it up.'

'Yes. I understand.'

He turned to face me to give me his sentence. He pawed the ground with his foot. He put his hands on my shoulders. He stared at the ground and only as he finished his sentence did he stare me in the eyes:

'When a cloud hides the sun the earth is shadowed.'

There followed the most un-English of embraces.

Just as we reached the top of the steps I said: 'I heard that Zenkovsky has at last been giving some attention to his wife?'

He stopped and faced me again.

'Zenkovsky's wife is dead. He is affected as he never was in her life. You know the circumstances of their marriage?'

ꕥ 91 ꕥ

'It was here in Odessa,' Lavrenti said. 'We were all nineteen or thereabouts. There was this beguiling man Nikita Alexandrovitch Zenkovsky. He had hair that had never been seen before . . . Perhaps you saw him grey. If there was a colour, it was rust. But it was like rust with a sun buried a living light inside. Then there was this Tonia. She was blonde, rather slight, but it was her eyes. Eyes that had never been seen before. They were everything that was ugly and everything that was beautiful. They were beguiling. They had all the ill of the snake in them, all the violent flame of the tiger. They were liquid, even watery, yet strong in spite of their liquidity. They were cesspools, only cesspools filled with orchids if you understand me. I was never her lover, I swear to you, yet I could only fall as all could only fall, before those eyes. And as I stand before you now, I swear to you, I can see those eyes, vivid before me still. They were a freak, as his hair was a freak: but both beguiled. Then there was Shura. Now Shura had no accomplishment, no call, she could pass you now and you would not even turn. But when she spoke her voice bound you. It was a voice which had never been heard before. I remember once she took Zenkovsky to the beach and sang to him and he told me laughing, "I know what Odysseus went through." But it was no laughing, for he went back and back just to hear that voice. Both loved Zenkovsky, yet truth is, Zenkovsky only had true love for Tonia. Tonia went to

Sochi for a visit and in a cave stumbled across a fortune in jewels. Alarmed, she told the world. One of the old princes sent for her. She did not want to go and begged Zenkovsky to forbid her. But he thought little of it somehow, the prince sent his coach and off Tonia set. The prince had a son, Boris, who detained Tonia and would not let her return. At some point Zenkovsky moved into a hut, a sort of cabin, with Shura. Terrible times came. The princes all fled or were murdered. Tonia tried through all the maze of internal strife to return. She had resisted to the last the approaches of the young Boris. She was virgin. She arrived outside Odessa, met a friend, Georgi, who did not recognize her so awful was her condition, but then informed her that Zenkovsky had taken an oath of loyalty to her and although living in a sort of hiding hut with Shura had never consummated any union. Tonia cried out loud with a great ecstasy and ran through the darkening evening to the place where the pair were living. You must know, they were terrible times. Zenkovsky heard noises in the brushwood, took his gun to the balcony, heard little, only the distant breaking of twigs, fired one shot into the dark as warning. A cry went up. Shura heard it too. That same Shura who was to become his wife. Zenkovsky dashed like a madman into the shrubbery. He stumbled on the torn and bleeding Tonia. She was dead in his arms.'

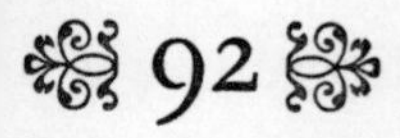

The single town of Constanza in Rumania had more arts and crafts shops than the entire Soviet Union put together.

The single city of Istanbul had more worthy things to buy than the entire Soviet Union put together.

No food on the Express from the Turkish border to Venice took some of the joys away from the delightful scenery. A pleasant Suffolk priest, the Reverend Farmer, told of Englishmen in Prague at the time of the Czech crisis who had given reports to British journalists only to find them twisted out of recognition in the British papers next day. They were in danger of losing their jobs as the result. 'How could you say such things?' they were asked. 'We didn't,' they retorted.

In Italy nine men in our carriage got worried when a tenth took out a noose, tied it round the luggage rack, put his head through it and started to nod. Then he opened his eyes and said: 'The railways ought to supply these things free. Everyone knows that when you go off to sleep your head falls to one side.' Then he dozed off.

Paris to Euston was a roundabout journey. The last time I had been on the Le Havre section had been unintentional. I had been cycling and grown thirsty. I had downed a bottle of wine like lemonade, zig-zagged to the nearest station, figure-eighted down a platform and woken up in Le Havre with my arm around my bicycle.

93

No furniture had arrived in my new flat in Euston.

I phoned up the contractor.

'Blimey is that you 'arold? The bloke what took your

stuff rings from gawd knows where, says he met a copper what told him the road was up and he couldn't get from St Pancras to Euston. "Nonsense" says our bloke. And we ain't seen 'ind nor 'air of 'im since.'

Index

INDEX

The Incredible Mile

Siberia – Mongolia – Uzbekistan

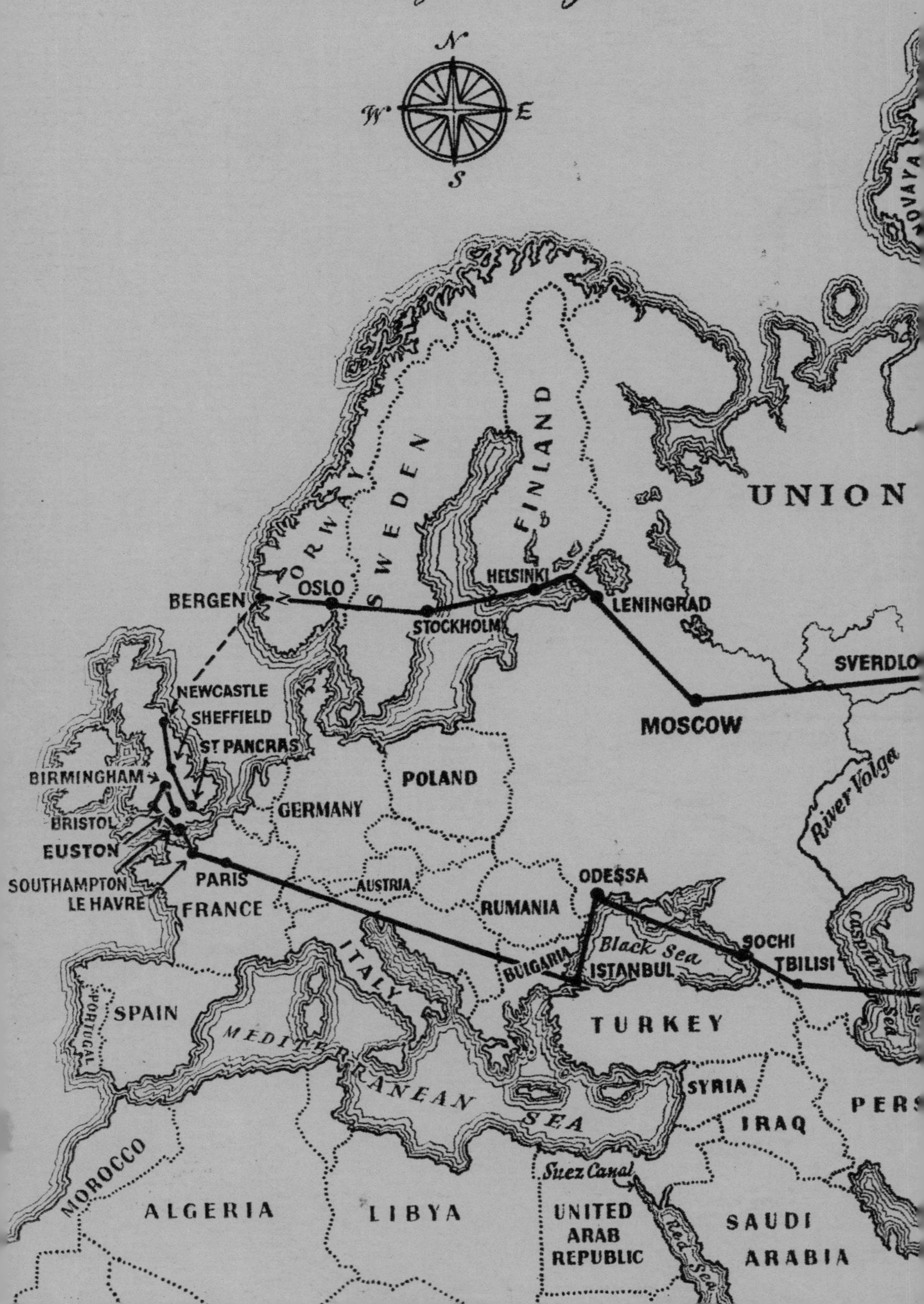